Well, I forget the rest

THE AUTOBIOGRAPHY OF AN OPTIMIST

QUENTIN
CREWE

Well, I forget
the rest

HUTCHINSON
London Sydney Auckland Johannesburg

© Quentin Crewe 1991

The right of Quentin Crewe to be identified as Author
of this work has been asserted by Quentin Crewe in
accordance with the Copyright, Designs and Patents Act, 1988

This edition first published in 1991 by
Hutchinson

Random Century Group Ltd
20 Vauxhall Bridge Road, London SW1V 2SA

Random Century Australia (Pty) Ltd
20 Alfred Street, Milsons Point, Sydney, NSW 2061, Australia

Random Century New Zealand Ltd
PO Box 40–086, Glenfield, Auckland 10, New Zealand

Random Century South Africa (Pty) Ltd
PO Box 337, Bergvlei, 2012, South Africa

British Library Cataloguing in Publication Data
Crewe, Quentin
Well, I forget the rest
I. Title
920

ISBN 0–09–174835–6

Set in 11 on 13pt Plantin by
Speedset Ltd, Ellesmere Port, South Wirral.
Printed and bound in Great Britain by
Clays Ltd, St Ives PLC

Ah, did you once see Shelley plain,
   And did he stop and speak to you?
And did you speak to him again?
   How strange it seems, and new!

But you were living before that,
   And also you are living after;
And the memory I started at –
   My starting moves your laughter.

I crossed a moor, with a name of its own
   And a certain use in the world no doubt,
Yet a hand's-breadth of it shines alone
   'Mid the blank miles round about –

For there I picked up on the heather
   And there I put inside my breast
A moulted feather, an eagle-feather –
   Well, I forget the rest.

                        Robert Browning

CONTENTS

ACKNOWLEDGEMENTS

Strictly speaking, one has only oneself to thank or to blame for an autobiography. Against that, I would never have written this book had it not been for the charming insistence and encouragement of Angie Howard-Johnston. If any readers enjoy it, then I am immensely grateful to her. I would say to those friends who have been left out that the depth of my affection had no bearing on who was put in. I thank Jackie Ford and Amanda le Fleming for their help. I would also like to thank Roland Philipps for permission to reproduce the letter of Rosamond Lehmann, Lord Stockton for permission to use letters by members of his family, and Lady Boothby for permission to reproduce letters by Lord Boothby.

Quentin Crewe
May 1991

LIST OF ILLUSTRATIONS

LIST OF ILLUSTRATIONS

Section 2

Wedding to Angie
Angie's grandmother
Edgy and her pekingese
Angie and myself with Peter Sellers
Princess Margaret and Tony Snowdon
Ken and Kathleen Tynan with their daughter
Myself in the 60s
Wilfred Thesiger
In Jeddah
Huamel showering me in the desert
Guides bringing Abdullah back
On safari with Jock and Betty Leslie Melville
With the Butler family of Gipsies
Sue
Going round the farm on my golf buggy
Princess Margaret with Charity
Planning our ideal village
Nat feeding a Rothschild giraffe
A family group

CHAPTER ONE

A SICILIAN CHILDHOOD

Once I met a man who claimed to remember the trauma of his birth, the long labour of his mother, the shock of bright light. I was born in 1926 in London, but I remember nothing of the first year of my life, spent mostly in Tripoli. Then we moved. I could not say which of many early Sicilian memories came first. This makes me wonder which sense is most important to a child. The smells of Palermo were an intense experience – fennel cooking, the open drains, and that now lost smell that I loved of 1920s cars with their spark too far retarded.

The sounds I have no memory for, except again the er-ur-er of car horns and the scrape of carriage wheels on the cobbles. The visual came far later. I must have been at least six when we went for a picnic to Segesta, in the hope of seeing a blue roller. For the first time I understood what people meant when they said something was beautiful. The near-perfect Greek temple stood quite alone in the rock-strewn, grey-green hills, as natural to the landscape as the ancient ilex – at least I suppose it did, for that is how I remember it, and I have never been back.

Touch was important. The rough feel of the long, engraved door-handles, as opposed to the round china handles of my half-sister's house in Essex that were hard to turn with childish fingers, and the claws of my pet goldfinches (bought in the market to save them from some cruel Sicilian fate, only to drown on my balcony) clutching my thumb – those sensations come back.

But taste was supreme, not just what Caterina, a half-Italian, half-Austrian woman of unsurpassed ugliness, cooked as she sang 'Ach, Du Lieber Augustin', but everything. My wooden Italian soldiers I disliked, not so much for their drab appearance, but because the taste of them was completely uninteresting compared with the bright and delicious lead soldiers that my coeval niece and nephew played with. Rubber bands had a very special taste, not pleasant, but somehow irresistible. Best of all was the rim of the pond in the garden of our second house, Villa Sofia. I lay on my stomach gazing at the languid carp, while I licked the algaed stone. It was supposed that it was this habit that gave me typhoid.

In our first house, I had the comfort of my brother Colin, who was four years older than myself. We had a governess, Miss Bush. As it seemed to me, she was a brisk woman who walked with long strides and who stood no nonsense. She must really have been twenty-three and full of romantic fantasies. She dressed only in green and smoked always with a green cigarette-holder. We lived very separate lives in our schoolroom. Miss Bush was a good teacher. By the time I was four, I read happily to myself.

As British Consul, my father spent his mornings in his office. My mother spent an hour every day after breakfast in the kitchen, discussing the day's food with Caterina. Otherwise she wrote letters. In the afternoons, my father drove us to the beach, while he went to play golf on a course which he had created. My mother might or might not go with him. At weekends we sometimes went on expeditions with our parents, but usually the only time we spent with them was at about six in the evening. If there were visitors, I would go down to the drawing room alone. I had flaxen curls and a cherub's face. I used to invent stories and recite them. The Sicilians were dazzled by this and would pat me on the head, exclaiming. Colin had a cleft palate and a scarred lip. He spoke indistinctly. My mother was ashamed, so he was kept in the schoolroom.

Colin's generosity of spirit was already such that he bore me no grudge. But almost as soon as we moved to the Villa Sofia, he went to school in England and I was left alone with Miss Bush. She did not last long. My mother told me later that Miss Bush fell in love with my father and was forever to be found mooning on the stairs or in the corridors, in the hope of an apparently chance meeting.

Mademoiselle Buricot was also inclined to wear green, but it was a very different kind of green, like sharp emeralds, chosen to complement her sweep of rich red hair. There was, I could recognize, a whiff of the exotic about her, so removed from Miss Bush. She, too, taught well, grounding me in French. I spent three months in bed with typhoid and she taught me also to be unbeatable at nine-men's-morris, which she, being Swiss, called *charret briguet*. My mother would play cards with me and read to me, but one day when she left the room I changed a few cards around to my advantage. My wooden soldiers were taken away and my mother did not visit me for a week. Mademoiselle Buricot, who had a conspiratorial nature, managed to convey some sympathy without saying anything.

She conspired with my mother, on the other hand, about some things. 'Keep your hands above the sheets,' my mother would always order when she said goodnight. I didn't. Mademoiselle Buricot showed me an illustration in a book. It was a line-drawing of a Victorian family in their kitchen. The father, on the left, held a broken chair above his head. He had already struck his wife with it and was about to do so again. She crouched, her hands raised to protect her head. Their children cowered under the table.

'*Voilà tu vois, il est fou. Il veut tuer sa femme, et pourquoi est-il fou? Parce qu'il joue toujours avec sa quiquette, comme toi.*'

In view of what happened later, this was grotesquely unfair.

Because we lived such detached lives, I formed no impressions of my parents' relationship. There must have been tensions. My mother's first husband, Arthur O'Neill, had been killed in the First World War. They had had five children. My mother's father, the Marquess of Crewe, was a not very inspired statesman from an ancient Whig family, although he had the distinction of being the first Secretary of State for India to think it worthwhile going to that country. He and particularly my mother's stepmother together with her O'Neill in-laws, who claimed descent from the oldest recorded family in Europe, regarded my father, Hugh Dodds, who came from a line of Scottish Covenanters, sons of the manse, as irredeemably middle-class. They had done everything to dissuade her from marrying him. Her children too had discouraged her. But he was handsome, a brilliant horseman, the most elegant fencer in Britain, and she was in love. So, in 1922, when he was forty-two and she was one year younger, they married. At their wedding they chose for one of the hymns 'Lead Kindly Light Amid the Encircling Gloom', which her children affected to believe was a reference to them.

I suspect now that my father, having been so long a bachelor, was by habit certainly flirtatious, if not actually unfaithful. Thirty years later, I met John Mosley, the brother of Sir Oswald. He cut me dead. Evidently he believed that his first wife had had an affair with my father in Sicily. Her photograph appeared quite frequently in my father's photograph books – usually taken on his small yacht, which might have been why my mother suggested that he keep a note of everything he spent on the boat, in the hope of frightening him into selling it. It was a suggestion that was to plague all our lives, as he was to become obsessed by accounts.

Sicilian society was grand. My friends were the children of the aristocracy of Sicily, whose lives cannot have been so very different from the days of *The Leopard*. I used to go to teas in resounding palaces, where major-domos in knee-breeches led the way up solemn stairways, and pairs of footmen in white gloves brought sandwiches and little animals of marzipan. They were stiff, those teas, but the albums show freer occasions on the beach. And I like to imagine that the children had more fun when they came to me, as I had a small house in the garden, where Anna, the maid, brought cakes and we could pick tangerines from its own orchard within the main garden, which was more exciting than any number of footmen.

One or two of the children had American mothers, an exchange, no doubt, of money and titles. How grim Sicily must have seemed to those princesses from the New World. Of my companions I only remember two very clearly, Caline and Bunny. They are fixed in my memory because they both died. Children that I knew in England simply didn't die. The American ladies must have pondered their bargains. Sicily was fierce and in its way glamorous. The Duca di Verdura e Bagheria gave a ball. To pay for it, he sold Bagheria.

It was glamorous, too, in the medieval sense – full of spells and witchcraft. My father, although well accustomed to African super-stition, believed that it had no place in Europe. He was shocked by the story of Count Maurigi. When he was twenty, this rather sensitive young man had an unhappy romance. He attempted suicide by jumping from a high window in his palace in Palermo. Instead of killing himself, he landed on someone else and killed him.

Naturally, he was judged to have the *malocchio*, the evil eye. His social life ended. No one asked him to any parties. He did not marry. I do not know how my father met him; presumably he required some service at the Consulate. Maurigi was now in his forties, a charming man, according to my father.

My parents were giving a dance. Father decided to invite Maurigi. The Count hesitated, but concluded that the British Consul's residence

4

was somehow different. He put on his tail-coat, now tight and tinged with green from disuse.

He came alone, a little late perhaps, so as not to appear too eager. When his name was announced, a strange silence spread in the ballroom. The guests stared. They clutched their medals, touching metal to ward off the evil eye, and pushed their thumbs between the first two fingers of their hands.

As Maurigi stretched out his arm to take my mother's hand and kiss it, the chandelier fell shimmering to the floor. No one broke the silence left by the crash. Count Maurigi bowed to my mother, turned, and walked out of the house.

Unlike Caline and Bunny, I got better and could go out again. Mademoiselle liked walking in the mountains. So my father used to drop us on many afternoons at the foot of Monte Pellegrino and we would climb. It was steep, yet possible for a child of five, but I was glad always when we reached a particular cluster of rocks.

Here Mademoiselle picked me up and set me on the top of a high, round boulder.

'Sit here. Don't move, and don't get down until I come back. If you disobey me, the snakes will get you.'

This was not an empty threat. I sat often for nearly an hour, dozing sometimes in the warm sun. Everything was quiet, except for the occasional tinkling of the sheep bells. Quite often a stumpy black snake would slide across the path. Far below, by the sea, I could see the green circles of the golf course where my father was playing. When Mademoiselle came back, we scrambled down the mountain, her red hair flowing free in the wind.

She never said that I was not to talk about those lonely vigils on the rock, but I knew it. One of my older O'Neill half-brothers, Brian I think, came to stay and was puzzled by these outings. Somehow he managed to follow us. When Mademoiselle Buricot left me on the boulder, she climbed on up to a small stone shelter. There she met a young shepherd and made love.

Soon after the abrupt departure of Mademoiselle, I left Sicily for the last time. We had always gone to Britain for the summer; and every time it was an elaborate performance. My mother would start packing at least a week before we were to leave. New dress preservers had to be stitched into the armpits of all her dresses. Shoes, all with shoe trees, went in the bottom of the huge leather Pukka trunks; they were wrapped in newspaper and sealed over with more newspaper. Heavy tweed clothes followed. The secret of packing, she would explain, was to keep everything flat, in even layers. Between the layers went tissue paper. Blouses (which she pronounced bloozes) were folded with tissue paper inside. There were hatboxes, boxes filled with bottles of Florida water, eau de cologne, jars of creams, powder puffs and all manner of flannels, sponges, loofahs and cotton wool. But she was not a vain woman. It was merely that her list of essentials was long.

If we were all going, we might have as many as fifty pieces of luggage. At last, they would all be piled in the hall, the Pukka trunks bound with broad leather straps, each piece with a label printed with my father's or my mother's name. They were counted and had to be counted again at each stage of the journey. It was not too bad if we were going the whole way by ship, but sometimes we took a boat to Naples and then went by train. At any change, we needed four or five porters, and the counting of baggage was feverish. Travelling through Italy, my mother liked me to sit in the van with the luggage. Thieves, she said, would steal the straps from the trunks, even cut panels from the lids, so short of leather were they in Italy.

We stopped once for a night or two in Florence and, even at the age of six, I noticed how many leather objects filled the shops.

'They seem to have a lot of leather.'

'All stolen from trains,' said my mother with finality.

At Victoria, a small bus would meet us and take us across London to Euston or King's Cross, depending on whether we were going to Scotland or Ireland. Endless counting.

Those summers fuse into one another in my memory, for they continued until the war. One early summer, we got out of the train at Blairgowrie in Perthshire. Our forty-seven pieces were loaded on to a horse-drawn cart and we drove to Drumore, the house my parents had taken for the holidays. It was a white pebble-dash house, set on the top of a bank. The interior was dark and, for eyes used to Mediterranean light, forbidding. The place affected several of us strangely.

My father became irascible. When he teased Colin, whom he found dancing by himself in the library, it was a teasing coloured by cruelty. He was afraid, I believe, that we might grow up to be homosexual.

I was terrified of the dark, a terror not helped by there being no electricity at Drumore, nor by my half-brother Terence, who used to jump out of dark corners. My father despised this weakness and would taunt me.

'You must really be a little girl. We'll call you Rosie.'

A large capercailzie fell wounded into a thicket. No one could see it. Father told me to crawl in to find the bird. He gave me his penknife. I hesitated.

'Go on, Rosie.'

I wriggled through the brambles and the brush.

'Can you see it?'

'No.'

'You can't come out till you've found it.'

Then it was there, on an open patch of earth. It looked bigger than me. It stood glaring, its large beak a little open.

'What do I do? It's so big.'

'Take it by the neck and push the knife into its eye, hard.'

I wanted, with a desperate longing, to impress my father. The Scottish afternoon was darkening. The bird's eye glinted.

'I can't.'

'Rosie.'

I grabbed the bird. It fought. Its wing beat on my face. I held on, squeezing the neck. For a moment it was still. I pushed the knife into its swelling eye. Crying, I managed to drag the huge capercailzie cock out of the thicket. Donald, the ghillie, took it from me. He held me to him for an instant. I decided that he was my real friend. That night I ran away to Donald's cottage and told him that I wanted to live with him for ever.

It was at Drumore that I first became aware of an unusual facet of my mother's perception. At its simplest, it was a very highly developed gift of telepathy; at its more complicated, it wandered into realms of the paranormal where I could not follow it and about which, in any case, she would never talk.

One day I heard by mother describing what had happened to her in the night.

'My candle went out, so I lit it again and almost at once it went out again. I couldn't understand it, because there wasn't a breath of wind. I tried once more, but the same thing happened. Then something pulled at my eiderdown and twitched it off the bed.'

'Whatever did you do?' they asked.

'There was no point in lighting the candle again, it would only have gone out, so I picked up the eiderdown. Whatever it was started pulling it off again. We had quite a tug-of-war. It wouldn't let go, so I did.'

My mother had a very agreeable laugh, like a pigeon's cooing.

'What did you do then?' they asked, amazed at her sang-froid.

'I turned over and went to sleep. There wasn't anything else to do.' So matter-of-fact was her tone that, despite my fear of the dark, I was not frightened.

My mother's generation believed in ghosts. Her sisters, Celia and Cynthia, both used to recount stories, in special, would-be authentic voices, of the curse on this or that family; of the monster at Glamis Castle; of Lord Halifax's stepping back out of a lift when he remembered the liftman's face from a dream. The lift fell to the basement, killing all.

My mother on the other hand would, as it were, acquiesce in listening to them but, while doing so, wore the wry smile of someone who knows more than the speaker. On this occasion, she decided that what had troubled her night was a poltergeist. Terence, who was eighteen, had a friend, David Gladstone, staying. I imagine there must have been other happenings, for she insisted that some pretext be found for David to leave, as she was sure that he was unconsciously responsible.

The next year, perhaps, we had a house in Hertfordshire. This was in order to be near my father's mother and sisters, who lived at Berkhamsted. I have no idea what sort of discussion had preceded this decision, but it was the only time that it happened. My mother was a woman of fine principles. She was fascinated by other people's lives and would enjoy listening to the most tedious accounts of anyone's everyday doings. She was deeply conscious of every person's dignity. Her most extreme reproaches were kept for occasions when any of us was rude to a servant, or a shopkeeper, or a railway porter.

The odd thing was that these admirable and genuine traits withered when her children or her husband's family were concerned. It was not so peculiar with her children, for she disliked nothing so much as responsibility. She was undemonstrative as a mother but, provided no demands were made upon her, she was an entertaining and informative companion.

With my father's relations she must have been driven by a snobbery which never surfaced in a pejorative form with anyone else. She loved titles and could weave a gossamer-thin pattern of cousinship over half the peerage but, apart from an occasional ruminative speculation, she never evinced any contempt on the grounds of class. Middle-class taste and customs, she did condemn.

'I had never seen fish-knives until I got married,' she once remarked, the ancient lineage of the O'Neills being no protection against such a solecism. She had certainly schooled me in every word of the U and non-U nonsense later propounded by Nancy Mitford. To this day, I stumble to say mirror, mantelpiece or phone and could never encompass serviette or lounge.

My mother lectured us one morning about Lizzie, the chirpy young housemaid.

'You may hear Lizzie going about her duties, singing in an odd way. It is called crooning. You are not on any account to copy it. It is extremely vulgar.'

It was typical of my mother to add: 'But you are not to mock her for this. She is a cheerful young person and cannot be expected to know better.'

I am not sure how she managed at that time to convey to me her feelings about my grandmother and my father's sisters, as her unfailing courtesy would never have allowed them to show and she would never have spoken overtly of them to a child, but I was always aware of them. I can remember the glass cases filled with mementoes of Japan, in my grandmother's house. I loved them, but soon learned to think of them as 'common', together with certain kinds of furniture – anything bamboo, coloured glasses, dumb-waiters (presumably one had to have the speaking kind). The very names of my father's sisters, Beryl and Ruby, were inadmissible. Ruby, in fact a half-sister, was a strong character and was somehow set a little apart from the general disapproval. Beryl, extremely large and sometimes a little deranged, was easy to demolish.

'Poor Aunt Beryl, you must never mention how dreadfully fat she is, nor that you know she had to be shut up for a while when she was a girl.'

I was rather fond of Aunt Beryl, who was the first person to expound to me the theory, which I later found in Samuel Butler, that one should always eat the biggest and best grape on a bunch first. By doing that, one promotes the second grape – so that one is always eating the biggest and the best.

I am not sure whether my father's family were aware of my mother's view of them, but my father was. These tensions were unsettling, but the whole of that summer was unhappy. The only pleasure I remember was my father's making Colin and myself each learn a poem. Colin had Gray's 'Elegy'. I had 'The Burial of Sir John Moore'. I was pleased with mine, preferring, as I still do, the sharp words of Wolfe to the monotonous sentiment of Gray – the one forward-looking, the other steeped in nostalgia.

Colin opened the car door as we were going through a gate, pulling it off. There was a distressing scene. My disgrace was graver. I was left alone in the house one afternoon. Father used to smoke Kensitas cigarettes, which he bought in boxes of one hundred. I was mooning about. I found a sheet of stamps and pulled off a part of the white surrounding strip. With this I sealed up the box of cigarettes that sat on the chimneypiece in the drawing room.

When Father came back, he went to get a cigarette. I got ready to laugh.

'Who's been at my cigarettes?'

His voice stilled all laughter. He thinks I have been smoking.

'Quentin?'

'No, Father.'

The battle went on for three days, my father waging it with weird ferocity. In the morning, he called in all the servants. They stood in a line by the door. One by one, he asked them whether they had sealed up his cigarette box. They all denied it. Father paid no attention to Lizzie's comment: 'I can't see what all this fuss is about. Everyone knows it was Master Quentin.'

'It wasn't,' I said.

Father then said that there was only one way to get at the truth. He would call the police. They would test the box for fingerprints. This, I realized, would be fairly conclusive, as I could see on the white stamp-paper a dirty, perfect print, a forensic scientist's dream.

I still held out. I was given only bread and water. Colin tried to explain that I would, in the end, have to give in. I wouldn't. Then Miss Bush arrived for a visit. She came, with her familiar no-nonsense look, to talk to me in my bath. The atmosphere in the whole house was unbearable, she said. I must end it for everyone's sake. I confessed to her.

In the morning, Father spun it out, while I hid in vain behind the sofa. I knew that he would beat me; he waited until midday to do so. It hurt, but I knew that at least I would get some lunch. It certainly did not stop me from telling lies.

Instead of going back to Sicily, I went to live with my eldest O'Neill half-sister, Timmy. My parents may have thought that it was better for me to be in England than in Sicily, which was regarded as fairly primitive. It was a decision that might today be thought of as peculiar, but in those days before air travel, when so many people served overseas, it was not so unusual for children to be separated from their parents for long periods.

Timmy was married to a brewer. Edwy Buxton was a kindly, bluff man, of whom I was both fond and frightened. As a child, one never questions the motives of adults. I never wondered why Timmy, who was quiet and fastidious, had married this heavy, noisy man, who talked in a roaring voice, thickened by the cigarette which hung from his mouth, the smoke rising and yellowing his moustache, the ash falling and greying his clothes. It never occurred to me that she might be unhappy. I now believe she married him to have a home. Her father had been killed when she was twelve. Our mother had never been kind to her, because she was a girl and was fat. Timmy was dumped on aunts and neglected.

The house was in the middle of Epping Forest, not far from the place where Boadicea took poison and died rather than surrender. I enjoyed the forest, the soft feel of fallen beech leaves under our ponies' hooves, the flat quality of sound among the deadening trees, the glimpses of black fallow deer, the tense wait for badgers to emerge in the moonlight. But it was not enough. I did not suffer from homesickness, but from some other lack I could not understand.

Round about, in various country houses stretching away towards East Anglia, lived Edwy's cousins, all noisy and shaggy and talking of shooting and stalking and fishing and hunting – even comically losing their g's and quoting from Surtees. Timmy submerged herself in all this, her own identity lost. I found it impossible to do the same.

I was happy to be living in a family, for Timmy's children were the same age as myself, yet I somehow never felt part of it. In a way, it was my home for about six years, and a refuge for many more, but it could never really be home. There is a profound sadness when there is an ambivalence between love and belonging, because it undermines one's faith in love.

11

It was Timmy who first noticed that there might be something wrong with me. My walking was odd and I could not run as fast as my niece and nephew. I fell over a lot. Eventually, when I was six, she persuaded my mother to take me to a doctor. My mother had a view about doctors. One went always to the best, usually to the one who attended the King. For some reason, this did not include dentists. She went to one called Molony, an Australian, whose first patient she was and who later appeared in Ian Fleming's books as James Bond's dentist. The King had no neurological complaint, so my mother must have used some other method to find Dr Gordon-Holmes of Harley Street, said to be the most distinguished neurologist of the time.

I loathed him. He was tall and powerful looking, but his voice was pitched high. He wore a black coat and pin-striped trousers. His eyes were hard to see behind extraordinarily small but thick round lenses, set in steel rims. The other shiny point, as he bent over me, was his gold watch-chain. His hands, feeling my body, were soft like a woman's. When he took my hand in his and told me to squeeze hard, I did – as hard as I could, in the hope of hurting him.

He told my mother that I had muscular dystrophy and, I learned later, that I would die when I was about sixteen. He told me that I would be all right when I was sixteen.

Can he really have said that? I am sure that he did. Because when we emerged into Harley Street, my mother said: 'Well, that's done. Now let's go and have tea with Cousin Nellie.'

She did not refer to my muscular dystrophy again for twelve years. I did not see another doctor about it until my father insisted, when I was eighteen. But I clung to my memory of what Dr Gordon-Holmes had said. In an idiotic way, although common sense told me otherwise, as my sixteenth birthday approached I used to wonder whether some sort of miracle might not happen.

It is impossible to judge with any certainty my mother's motives in her approach to the subject. It may have been that she thought it was pointless to fuss about something when there is nothing one can do to change it. This is a view that I share. Her ignoring the problem made no difference to the physical progress of the disease. Other mothers might have dragged me from one consulting room to another. I was spared that.

Alternatively, it may have been a shrinking from responsibility. When, so much later, we did speak of it, my mother blamed my father. It was suggested to her that muscular dystrophy came, like haemophilia, through the female line to boy children. This was unacceptable. Without troubling to look it up, my mother could name her mother's mother's mother back through five generations to Mrs Sheridan, wife of the playwright. There was no history of any kind in her family. She had had five perfect children with her first husband. It was plain that Colin's cleft palate and my dystrophy must come from our father.

For my part, I am glad now that, for whatever reason, I was not treated in any way differently from Colin. My nature is indolent and I would surely have taken advantage of any indulgence. More important, because I was given a normal upbringing, I never thought of myself as abnormal. Because no one around me appeared to think about it, I did not think about it.

There is, of course, a great advantage in having a disease which progresses slowly. To be robbed suddenly of the ability to walk must be a savage loss. For it to happen gradually is not so bad, as one can adjust almost unconsciously. Human beings have the capacity to put up with anything, but it is kinder if it comes upon them slowly.

Such thoughts came later. It was galling at first to lose every race, but once it was accepted, it was funny. If no one else minded, why should I? In any case, I always won at pelmanism.

The front part of the school was a low, white building where the headmaster's son-in-law, Mr Green, lived with Mr Crawshaw's bulging daughter. It had a friendly look, like a Regency rectory. It was at the back that the grim classrooms and dormitories had been added. I was seven. The mixture of terror and pride that I felt on going to school for the first time was soon turned to terror alone. For some reason, I was taken to school in the middle of a term. There was no question of being lost in a jumble of new boys. Everyone stared. I had counted on Colin's support. He merely looked horrified. A believer in savouring things without haste, he had not read my mother's letter telling him that she was bringing me. Older brothers, anyhow, by convention, had little to do with younger ones. I felt alone and puzzled by the general air of coarse brutality and what often seemed to be deliberate philistinism that were common to both the masters and the boys.

Broadstairs, in 1934, was full of boarding preparatory schools for boys. Selwyn House was probably neither better nor worse than the others, although there was a horrifying snobbery in our attitude towards them. I cannot imagine how this was propagated, but it was quite clear in our minds that St Peter's Court, just over a wall and with which we shared a French mistress, was our only social equal. Wellesley House, Hildersham, Hawtreys were graded in that order. Bottom, without any doubt, was Stone House. I had a first cousin there, on my father's side of course. To lose a match against Stone House was a matter of shame. Against St Peter's Court, it was hard luck.

Such attitudes and many others to go with them can only have been attributable to the teachers. I remember their ghastliness clearly. Mr Crawshaw, the headmaster, was old; I do not think he taught any longer. Each night, however, he toured the dormitories and administered any punishments that were due to the juniors. He had two kinds of slipper with which to beat the smaller boys. A flat black pair for lesser offences, a red pair with sharp heels for graver sins. The quality of a misdeed, I noticed, varied with whichever pair he happened to be wearing.

'I don't much care for boys who eat in bed,' he would say when sporting his black ones.

'Eating in bed is the most disgusting thing a boy can do,' was his opinion in red slippers. Justice had very little to do with anything.

Mr Steemson was the classics master, a short, humourless man with a shiny pink complexion, a little like an uncooked sausage. In his class one's interest lay not in learning Latin, but in avoiding his giving one his 'trademark'. On any slender pretext, he would roll up a boy's shorts and slap him hard, high up on the inside of the thigh, leaving his open handprint stinging red.

A great bear of a man called Meade-King taught mathematics and boxing. Good marks in the first seemed to be associated with courage in the second.

History was the responsibility of Mr Harbord, who instilled in us a respect for kingship which made Metternich look like a republican. The subject took on an *Alice in Wonderland* quality, without its charm. Battles were the thing. The English kings didn't like the French kings, so they went to war. The battles were Crécy, Poitiers, Agincourt. Draw maps.

Poor, demented Griffith-Evans, egged on by the other boys, stood on a chair by the door with *Chum's Annual* uplifted. As Mr Harbord came in, George felled him, crying politely: 'Take that, sir.'

Mr Harbord's replacement was a tall, nervous man with sharp

14

features, the skin of his face taut and pale. Mr Hall, who was thinking of taking holy orders, astonished us all. In the first class he took, he explained the system for the selection of a Pope. The cardinals were sealed up at the time, choosing Pius XII. He gave us a brief introduction to the history of the papacy. History was suddenly interesting and relevant to the present.

Mr Hall was, of course, too good to last. He had not the least idea of keeping order, for he treated us like human beings, which we had long since ceased to be. Even so, he had a temper that would flare up once in a while, under the provocation of paper darts and ink bombs. One morning, he hit a particularly odious boy. In this there was nothing surprising. But, in the afternoon, Mr Hall's good nature had returned. He apologized in public to the boy. Sweet sanity was too much. He left soon after, universally derided by boys and masters.

The unpleasantness of the masters was matched by that of the pupils. There were gangs of older boys who stole things from the younger ones. It was unthinkable to report them. The bullying was merciless, grounded in the worst human instincts.

Harold Jones, it was decided, came from an inferior social class. Four held him, naked in the changing room, while two others brushed his genitals with stinging nettles.

No one explained to us that George Griffith-Evans was mentally retarded. His nature was in truth gentle, but he could be goaded into rage, when he would perform acts of surprising strength. He could, with a little ingenuity, be persuaded to drag some unpopular boy by the hair for the full length of the triple classroom, with its splintery wooden floor.

For the most part, I was lucky, despite my inability to run. My calf muscles were, in the way of muscular dystrophy, enlarged in their uselessness. 'Hammy-legs,' they shouted. I had long since learned to laugh with the mockers, and found out that this not only defused their malice but, in some strange way, really made me see the comic nature of my movements.

I was by no means invulnerable, however. When the war came, the school moved to a large country house in Wales. It was beautiful. Walks were no longer along tarmac paths, running between fields of cabbage. At Broadstairs, the few reasonable pleasures that the district offered were denied us. One might have thought that many half-holiday afternoons might have been spent on the beach. In five years, I remember only two or three. We went once to Rochester Castle with

15

Mr Hall. We rode on the last tram to go through Ramsgate. I did go to Dreamland at Margate, but I think that was with my mother. Otherwise we were confined to the gloomy school buildings and the two playing fields across the road.

The roaming space of Wales was intoxicating. But I was not happy; my two special friends had left. There was a lonely boy called Mansergh, whom nobody liked much. His divergence from the norm and consequent unpopularity lay in being a Christian Scientist. I thought this intriguing. He lent me the works of Mary Baker Eddy and we became friends. The principle of guilt by association worked faultlessly.

At tea one evening, their tormenting of me reached a peak. 'Hammy-legs likes Mansergh. We hate Hammy-legs. We hate Mansergh.' They threw tea over me, smeared Marmite on my face and jam in my hair. They punched and mauled till I fled from the dining room.

Weak, sobbing and, in schoolboy eyes, despicable, I stumbled to the headmaster's quarters. The slippered Mr Crawshaw had long since retired. Now his son-in-law, Mr Green, was in charge. It was hard to judge what he thought. He lacked that imperial streak of off-hand brutality which dictated the other masters' behaviour. Perhaps that is why discipline was so hopeless under his regime. But he knew his duty now. He disentangled my story from my whimpers.

Then: 'You can't come snivelling to me. Only you can sort this out. You must just go back and face the music. You're old enough to know that. Go. Face the music, like a man.'

He was right, of course. Had he done anything to protect me, they would have found subtler ways to punish a breach of the code.

We were being trained to be tough. We were being taught to conform. I don't know how many times I had to listen to the story of the little Spartan boy who let the fox gnaw his vitals, rather than reveal that he had it concealed under his robe. He was our model. We were British, the new Spartans. There were some who could see that it was all over, that a new world was coming, but comfortable notions die hard. My mother once told me that, when she was a girl in the 1890s, she and her sisters would wander listless by the lake at Crewe Hall and wish that something would happen in the world. In their sheltered youth, no hint of revolution ruffled their confidence in the eternal nature of the British Empire.

So it was with our schoolmasters. The Boer War, the First World

War, the Russian Revolution, the first Labour Prime Minister, the schisms of the Liberal Party – enough had happened. But they could still teach us with globes that were three-quarters pink. We had not long ago celebrated King George V's silver jubilee, and watched the troops of four dominions and countless colonies and protectorates parade through the streets of London.

The world may have moved on, but we were still being trained for Empire, to rule those nations from which the troops had come.

CHAPTER TWO

THE FRENCH RIVIERA

Holidays, apart from the summer, I spent with Timmy. The ambivalent feelings of love and alienation persisted, but a dismal experience early on in my time at Selwyn House taught me to be grateful. One Easter, she could not have me and I went instead to something called a holiday home. I suppose that there must have been many of these, catering, in the days before air travel and child psychology, for the children of diplomatic, naval and military families, for whom education other than in Britain was unthinkable.

The name of the Berkshire village comes back easily in its appropriate association – Cold Ash. But I can remember nothing of the women who took in these luckless children. Probably they were kind enough, but I was not interested in their kindness. The other children were all younger than myself, some of them barely more than babies. I resented the early hour at which I was made to go to bed. The food would have met Cardinal Newman's suggestion for a Friday – 'little and that unpleasant'. I was made to play endless games that I thought beneath me. I was bored in a way that I was never bored before or since.

I do not think I have ever again set out with determination to be as unpleasant as possible. I did everything I could to annoy. My greatest triumph was to set the whole hillside of gorse below the house on fire. There were no punishments, as this was a holiday home. Instead, I was pronounced to be ill and was put to bed for several days.

Both my half-brother Shane and his castle in Northern Ireland, which bore the same name, were for different reasons impressive. He had once taken a house at Sandwich and sent his car to pick me up from school for the day. Life with my parents was sedate; with Timmy it might be noisy, but there was nothing farouche about it. Here was another world. Goddesses of girls, with lips and nails of scarlet, smoked black cigarettes with gold tips, or coloured ones in matching holders. There were cocktail shakers, pouring drinks as varied in hue as the cigarettes. The radiogram crooned. The guests rattled dice in endless games of backgammon, talking of sums of money which I decided must be some kind of private joke. Everyone called everyone else darling. I thought it wonderfully glamorous.

Shane, as the eldest son, was distanced from the rest of the family by the system of primogeniture. The O'Neill estates were large and belonged entirely to him. He was due, one day, to inherit the Crewe estates, which had been even larger. To his brothers, Brian and Terence, he gave an allowance of £200 a year each, at a time when his income from the estates was about £10,000. To Colin and myself he showed an uninterested friendliness. He was, I feel, a sad man lacking overt *joie de vivre* and warmth – qualities which were ever thinly spread in the O'Neills – although Colin, who was older and better able to judge, remembers much laughter. But Shane's life was to be a sad one.

Shanes Castle was a place of unusual beauty and, for me, magic. The ruins of the old castle, remodelled by Nash and burned in a fire, stood by the shore of Lough Neagh. On the battlemented terrace, eight cannon pointed out over the lake. It had been a tall house and the ruins had a proud look. The only part remaining intact was a conservatory, filled to a towering height with scores of specimen camellias. More exciting, behind the castle, was a tunnel wide enough to take a cart. In the eighteenth century, this was the servants' entrance and all deliveries were made through it, so that nothing unaesthetic, like a servant or a cartload of provisions, should be seen near the house. We, as children, saw the tunnel very differently. We conjured stories of smugglers and daring escapes and chained prisoners walled up in dark dungeons.

When the old castle burned, the family built a new house, set five hundred yards back from the lake, attached to the old stables. This in turn was replaced by a larger house which was also a ruin. We did not in those days approve of late Victorian Gothic, so it did not stir our imaginations in the same way. Moreover, it was dangerous. But even this second-class ruin had a story, gripping in its way, from recent days, so that we had first-hand accounts of its destruction.

One afternoon in 1922, unusual boats were seen on the lake, but no one paid much attention. Late that evening, men burst into the house, drove everyone into one room, poured petrol on the roof and set fire to it. They were Sinn Feiners, intending to kill Shane's uncle, who was Speaker of the Northern Ireland House of Commons.

Shane's grandmother, a formidable Scotswoman, had always refused to take any notice of sectarian problems. She employed Protestants and Catholics indifferently. The man whose job it was to ring the fire bell was a Catholic. He had none of the free and easy views of his employer. He refused to ring his bell. The carpenter was a Protestant. He managed to prevent the fire spreading to the old stable block.

It was in the part that he had saved that we now lived. The children's rooms were in a long corridor, running the whole length of one side of the courtyard, under the clock tower. The doors to the rooms were recessed a little. It was certain, when I went to bed, that Terence would be in one recess or another, waiting to jump out shrieking.

My fear of the dark had increased one summer when I came to Shanes in quarantine. There were several other children in the house, so I was put in a cottage in the park with an old woman, the widow of one of the estate workers.

She was an enveloping, motherly woman, who talked all the time in a rich Ulster lilt, telling stories of the little people, although I am not sure that she called them that. 'They' was all that was needed for me to know whom she was talking about.

She told me about the Banshee.

'The poor wee thing, there was no harm to her, you know. It was her father was cruel, a powerfully cruel man. And she had her lover, she had. But her father would have none of it. So they went to elope. He was for coming to below her window. He was to throw a rope up to her. She was to slide down and they were away on their own, to be happy.'

The old woman's face was round with the thought of it. Suddenly, she would sharpen.

'But the wicked man knew. He set a fearful great mantrap with jaws like the wildest beast you ever heard of. And the jaws they snapped on the waist of the bold young lover. Deep, oh so deep, they dug in him. But he took his time to die and the hurt was greater for her.

'She couldn't live without her lover. So they came for her.

They took her away to the bottom of the lough. And that's where she lives.'

It was the Banshee, the old woman told me, who burned down the old castle.

'The O'Neill gave a party, a big, big party. The lake shone with the lights of the party, glittering on the water. There was one guest too many. They gave him her room, the Banshee's room. No one had ever slept there, not since the night she vanished, the night that her lover died. Ooh, she was angry. The lights on the lake disturbed her below. And they used her room. As they slept, she burned the castle.'

The Banshee used to wail in time of disaster, usually a death.

'I've heard her twice. There's no mistaking her. It's not a sound you'll hear on earth, unless it be the Banshee. I heard her before Captain Arthur was killed. And I heard her again before his lordship died. You'll hear her, if there's bad news to come.'

I half longed for bad news. But what if the bad news was me? I so often infringed rules that I had no knowledge of, but which the old woman knew all about.

'Did I see you hitting the hawthorn tree with a stick, I did? You must not do it. They love that tree with a real love and you'll anger them. And they could come in the night.'

The nights in the cottage were terrifying. The old woman blew out my candle when she put me to bed. I lit it again as soon as she had gone, but it guttered and threw shadows. The little house creaked as the night cooled. Would they come?

Nothing, not even terror, could spoil the pleasures of Shanes. It was not simply a house, it was more like a village. A village that had hardly moved into the new century. On the far side of the courtyard, there were coach houses, and all the coaches and carriages were still there. The big closed coach, with its soft upholstery of yellow cloth, was a good place to hide. It was best to keep very still, otherwise clouds of dust would come out of the cushions and sneezes would give one away.

In the next courtyard were the stables and the forge. The blacksmith taught us how to make S-hooks, bashing the glowing metal rod round the sharp end of the anvil. I loved the sparks and the way that the hot metal flaked in red-black patterns as it curled, as easily as warm sticks of liquorice. It gave a sense of power to play so pliably with what one knew was hard. When we were more proficient, he let us make other things and eventually, with a lot of unobtrusive help, an actual horseshoe. We watched him shoe the carthorses. The pungent sizzle of smoke, the long nails to hold the shoe on, and yet the calm acceptance of the horse, I found fascinating.

Round the corner was the carpenter and wheelwright. There the smells were subtler – wood scorched by the circular saw, the fluffy scent of new sawdust, the repellent odour of the glue. The wheelwright never measured. He made a few marks with his flat oval pencil and I would wait to see how the four quarters of the wheel would fit. They always did, in a perfect circle.

Shanes was practically self-sufficient. There were so many activities to watch – the laundrymaids pushing the sheets up and down on their washboards, the dairymaids turning the churns to make butter, the paddles slapping the thickening cream with a wet, woody splat. The electrician, among his huge glass accumulators that almost punctured the nose with the smell of acid, might be mending the engine which charged them, to provide the whole place with electricity.

The keepers, the grooms, the chauffeur, their work was entertainment for children. Many of them lived in the furthest courtyard, their wives and families comfortable friends.

Another kind of magic lay in the park. This was enormous – two thousand acres enclosed by a wall – but made even more so by the variety of landscape. To come in by one drive and leave by the other was a journey of five miles and, in the course of it, the changes of scenery were extraordinary for so short a distance. Open parkland, green in the way that only Ireland is green; shoreline beside the inland sea of the lough, with sand in which to bury potatoes under a picnic bonfire; swamp where the duck would fly in in the evening; woodland where the deer ran shy and fleeting; farm fields where we would build small Irish haystacks like igloos or, as the holidays wore on, pile the scythed sheaves of corn into nodding stooks; above all the river Maine, rocky and wild, salmon jumping in the peat-stained waters, which flowed down from the North Antrim hills, across the park and into the lough.

It was a paradise, and there was never any reason to venture beyond the park wall; nor did we, except to go to church. There, no doubt, we sang 'All Things Bright and Beautiful', quite satisfied that the Lord God had ordered our estate.

It is hard to judge how much of one's memory of oneself as a child is hearsay, how much self-deception, how much hindsight, how much truth. I remember myself at the age of ten as a sly child. But I cannot be sure whether this is not an overlay from late adolescence and early manhood, when I believed firmly that there was, in me certainly and in others probably, no such thing as an unselfish act. Altruism was desirable, but unattainable. Earlier, it had not even been desirable. That other people saw me differently was merely proof of my belief. I went to great lengths to beguile people. If they liked me, the sly child, it just showed that goodness was a myth.

It cannot really have been as conscious as that. Another part of me believes that I just drifted with little purpose.

Even before Mussolini actually invaded Abyssinia in 1935, it was impossible for my father to stay in Sicily. Haile Selassie had become a friend during the thirteen years Father spent in Abyssinia. He had, improperly perhaps for a diplomat, encouraged Ras Tafari, as he then was, in his revolution against his libertine, syphilitic cousin, Lij Yassu, the regent. Colin had been born in Abyssinia and the Emperor was his godfather.

The Foreign Office proposed various postings – Galveston in Texas, Antofagasta in Chile. These were vetoed by my mother. Her notion of America was peculiar, not least in believing that every American started every sentence with the words 'Say, Bo . . .' In Antofagasta, she told me, one had to change one's clothes four times a day. Her father still had influence. Father became Consul-General on the French Riviera. Two more unsuitable people than my parents to send to the South of France would have been hard to find.

They were both, in different ways, country people. My paternal grandfather had broken away from the manse and become a Far East merchant. When Father was seventeen, his father pushed him into a job in the Hongkong and Shanghai Bank. He hated the City and joined up to fight in the Boer War.

On the way to South Africa, there was a parade on deck. 'Fix bayonets.' The ship rolled. The man behind drove his bayonet into my father's back. By the time he had recovered, the fighting was over. However, he remained in Africa – at first in the South African police, later as a District Commissioner in British Somaliland, and finally in the consular service in Abyssinia. It was a life lived mostly out of doors, on horseback or on foot, in wild country.

My mother had the quiet upbringing of a landowner's daughter. Her mother had died when she was five. She might have expected, as his eldest daughter, to have become my grandfather's hostess, but at her 'coming-out' dance he announced his engagement to someone only a year older than she was. He was a man of few feelings, certainly as far as children were concerned, having, for example, gone abroad on a long journey when he knew that his only son, aged eight and motherless, was dying. It may have been this complete lack of outward affection that inhibited maternal feeling in my mother.

Neither of my parents had any knowledge of, or any desire to mix with, the kind of smart society that had villas on the Riviera before the war. Nor did they seem inclined to make French friends. They must have felt lost. For Colin and myself the difference was that, for the first time for several years, we spent all our holidays with our parents.

Our lives, considering that we were living in what was thought to be a glamorous place, were very simple. Father, deprived of his yacht by the revelations of his new-found interest in accounts, spent every afternoon on one of the four neighbouring golf courses. His partners were usually old fogeys who had retired to the sun. I found them boring, but I have a clear memory of one who made me laugh. He was George Cornwallis-West, the stepfather of Winston Churchill. On the next fairway the huge figure of the Aga Khan was heaving his lugubrious way around the course. I gazed at him in awe, fascinated by the idea of his being weighed in gold by his devout followers and given the bullion by way of tribute. Then Sir George said: 'I wonder if he ever says to himself, "Let begums be bygones"?'

My mother's routine was precisely the same as it had been in Sicily. The first hour after breakfast she spent with Caterina in the kitchen, planning the day's menus. (Caterina and Anna had both come with us without question.) Then she read the papers and wrote letters. In the afternoons, she might or might not go to the golf course. Otherwise, she went for long walks, birdwatching.

My father had his duties, though generally these cannot have been very arduous. We went to the unveiling of a statue of Queen Victoria on the front at Menton. The Germans threw it into the sea four years later, but it is back now. We went to watch a boat race between Oxford and Cambridge rowing across the harbour at Cannes. The French, even then aware of the riotous nature of British sportsmen, had locked the two crews into separate coaches of the Blue Train. When the train arrived, they were all in the same coach, having climbed along the roof. We went to occasional operas and film premieres. And Father read the lessons on Sundays in the Anglican church in Nice.

24

One afternoon, I went to the Consulate to meet my father. It was nearly four o'clock and time for golf. A thin man with a stick sat waiting. I said hello to the secretaries and sat near the man.

'I must see the Consul,' said the man. He was talking to me. Then I saw that he was blind. His eyes had no reflection to them. They might have been made of cloth.

'I don't think it will be possible today,' said Miss Parser, 'it is almost closing time.'

Even with his matt eyes, the man looked desperate. I had never seen such an expression. 'Why?' I asked him.

He told me that he was Jewish and German. German to a schoolboy meant an enemy, but this man was not an enemy. He described his flight and his capture. He told me that he had been stood in front of a searchlight to make him talk. It had burned out his eyes. Somehow he had escaped. Now, he must get to England. I went in and begged my father to see him. We got to golf a little late for once.

At the coronation of George VI, Colin was to be a page to my grandfather and had to stay in England during the Easter holidays for rehearsals. I had to travel out alone at the age of ten, but I had made the journey at least twice before, so was expected to manage. At that age, I felt sick in any means of transport. The crossing was rough. I was so ill, that when I found a quiet corner in a passage, I curled up on the floor, crying. I had chosen to lie outside a first-class cabin. The couple whose cabin it was found me, took me in and looked after me.

When we reached Calais, I was separated from my benefactors; they went first and I went second class on the train. Second class had the added disadvantage that, on arriving in Paris, one had to change stations. I took a taxi, rather than the groaning train that went round the *Ceinture* – a special concession this, not easily granted by my father's account books. The tip I gave the driver was evidently not enough. I had my first French row, during which I learned the phrase *procès verbal*, which still makes me jump when I hear it. Having been rescued by the crowd that gathered, I felt elated and well enough to go to eat in that beautiful restaurant in the Gare de Lyon. I judged my stomach and my remaining money with care and ate an omelette, with a very little wine.

I was always excited for some reason by the rich, red colour of the earth in Provence. As the train slowed down through the Cézanne landscape after Avignon, I had a sensation of coming home and of achievement in having done so on my own. Father was less impressed. Somehow, I had mislaid fifty francs, perhaps when I finally gave the taxi-driver an extra five francs, or when I paid for dinner, or somewhere. My report from school did nothing to improve matters. It was a silent holiday.

But out of it came unexpected results. There arrived an invitation from Sir Pomeroy and Lady Burton, my benefactors from the ferryboat, for luncheon. It was addressed only to me, not to my parents. They were puzzled by this, but sent me nonetheless. The luncheon was formal – about twenty people and what seemed to me to be an equal number of courses. I was the only child. From that luncheon sprang others. I found myself in the odd position of being the only child on several similar occasions. It still seems to me improbable.

It was perhaps less so when the hostess was Baroness Orczy, a great, swirling, pink figure, extravagant of speech and gesture, married to a bumbling, donnish man with the almost too English name of Barstow, who was nonetheless a modern painter, whose work my parents regarded with suspicion. I could recite, and she was not averse to my doing so, page after page of *The Scarlet Pimpernel*. But I do not like the memory of it all. Too much of the sly child.

My bedroom looked over Villefranche harbour. In 1939, HMS *Warspite*, with nine fifteen-inch guns, looked superb as she lay at anchor in that curiously deep inlet. I wanted to join the Navy. My mother opined, in a rare reference to my disability, that I would be unable to climb the rigging. I argued that there was no rigging. Sir Dudley Pound, Admiral of the Fleet, came to lunch. He responded with kindness to my enthusiasm for his flagship and invited me for a journey on board.

On the night that we sailed, Italy invaded Albania. The *Warspite* was ordered to sail to the Adriatic. I have often wondered whether frantic messages went to the Admiralty, asking what should be done with the small boy on board. In the event, we put in at San Remo and I was bundled ashore. My father arrived to pick me up and we lunched at the Royal Hotel. In the middle of lunch, all the guests at the other tables stood up.

'Keep your seat, no matter what happens,' said my father. A large man in a white uniform came in and sat at a table not far from ours. He bent greedily over his soup. It was Goering.

CHAPTER THREE

SCHOOL

For lunch at home Caterina made the same dishes that she had made in Sicily – *riso giallo*, a rich saffron rice; *gnocchi alla romana*; red mullet or tarragon chicken; and superb puddings. Her *Mont Blanc*, the chestnuts feathery and light, the cream rich but not sweet, I have never seen equalled, nor her *pain perdu* with a special rum mousseline sauce. The recipes (or receipts, as she always called them) were my mother's.

My mother could cook nothing, but she could teach anyone. Her receipt book, written in her curious beetle script, was a treasure house, enlivened by bizarre or arcane asides: 'Take a common French cafetière,' or, 'This is an old Dutch secret, taken by the Dutch to the Cape and thence to Jamaica by Miss Knollys.' There was no explanation as to who Miss Knollys was, nor as to how the secret came back from Jamaica.

My father sat at one end of the table with the pekingese on a chair beside him and *The Times* crossword puzzle by his plate. He would read out the clues, occasionally passing the paper rather grudgingly to my mother at the other end of the table. She was better at it than he was, but less interested.

But there was always conversation. To a child it seemed endless, this talk of politics, and so contradictory. There seemed no doubt in my parents' view that there would be war, but people came to lunch who knew quite definitely that the German tanks that went into Prague were made of cardboard. It was all a bluff, they said.

I seemed to live in a mist of understanding. For example, anti-Semitism of a mild kind was quite normal in everyday talk. 'Of course, she's Jewish you know' explained something untoward. But, when a fascist book entitled *Our Jewish Aristocracy* was published, it was a matter for pride that my mother's family was included. 'Certainly, we have Jewish blood – Sephardic, through the Villareal, the royal house of David,' said my mother, adding, 'As had Jesus Christ.' Yet another cousin?

Whatever the political situation, our lives continued evenly. We skied or swam in the sea, once both on the same day. In the evenings, we read Shakespeare with the manager of Barclays bank in Nice and his family, each of us taking several parts.

When the war finally came, it still made little difference. Colin and I spent two more holidays in France, amazed to find the lights still bright at night, when England was shrouded in the blackout. We even moved to a new house.

My father called me to him. He wore a grave face. 'Some American friends have written with a kind offer. They say that, if we like, you can go to stay with them in America for the duration of the war. Then you would be safe from bombing, safe in case England is invaded. Now, do you want to go or not? You are old enough to decide.'

I was thirteen. I knew all about America. In the summer, we had stayed in Scotland with a cousin of my mother's, who had turned one of his castles into an hotel. A childless American woman befriended me. Every evening, I used to go to her room before dinner and she would tell me in her entrancing drawl (which I soon learned to imitate) about her ranch. While I was there, she would always telephone to her husband in Texas. She would put me on the line so that I could tell him about the day's doings – the fishing, the riding, the rabbit shooting at night. She would take back the telephone and ask him if I wasn't just the cutest kid. I made sure she was going to leave me all her money. (I still wonder. She must be about eighty-five.) She, it must be, who had written.

'Oh, yes, Father, I'll go. I'll go.'

'What? Have you no patriotism, boy? You'd run away from your country in its hour of need? You're a little coward, that's what you are.'

It had been a test. There was no question of my going to America.

Colin and I went back to England in April 1940. Only two months before the fall of France, the war made little difference to our journey, except that we had to wear life jackets on the ferry. My mother followed in May. Just before France fell, my father, rather sensibly I

28

would have thought, drove the Duke of Windsor to Lisbon to make sure that he was not captured by the Germans. Father was reproved for deserting his post. When the French surrendered, he moved to Marseille, where he was attached to the American Consulate.

Colin joined the Army. My mother had, therefore, only one responsibility left – myself. She was tempted to shed it. She announced that she would go to live with a bachelor cousin in Cambridge. Various members of her extended family told her that she could not do this. So, for a while, we went to live with one of her sisters in Yorkshire.

Eton I found as confusing as life at home. It now seems to me as if I sailed through those years which are supposed to form one's character in lazy refusal to be shaped. There was no active rebellion, but I used to make solemn vows to myself not to regret the missed opportunities that everyone assured me I would regret.

I had had an odd desire to go to Gordonstoun. I can't remember why. Perhaps it was to do with my journey in the *Warspite* and an earlier wish to go to Dartmouth. It would have been marvellously unsuitable, but then so was Eton for different reasons.

Nearly everything about the school seemed absurd and unnatural, largely because so much of the day-to-day organization had been devised over the years, even the centuries, by the boys themselves, at their *Lord of the Flies* age.

Discipline within each house was maintained by an autonomous clique of senior boys, who had the right of corporal punishment. There was no appeal from their decisions. Once they beat Colin for making too much noise falling downstairs. It was not the tedium of running messages, lighting fires, and cooking tea for my seniors that depressed me, not even the beatings if I did it badly – letting the fire go out, burning the toast or whatever – 'incompetent' was their favourite word. It was that people so little older than myself could enjoy creating barriers to friendship and could wish for me to do tasks badly so that they could punish me.

The rules which governed behaviour outside the house were even sillier than those inside. We were only allowed to walk on one side of the High Street. There were many useful shops on the other side. To get from one to another of these, we had to cross the road, walk, say, thirty yards and cross back again. Whatever the weather, we had to turn up the collars of our overcoats. We were forbidden to roll our umbrellas neatly, but must carry them unfurled, flapping like wounded rooks.

These rules were made by a self-elected society of older boys, usually good at games, who wielded extraordinary powers over the whole school, which they enforced with a special knobbed cane. Their imagination was thin. The privileges they arrogated to themselves amounted, together with a few extravagances of dress and the right to sit on a particular wall, to little more than those things that they denied to us.

The masters were hardly more inspiring than the boys. It may be that those younger teachers, who might have brought some freshness to their work, had gone to fight in the war. Those that remained were stale and dull, either staying beyond their time or disinterred from retirement.

I was the only new boy in a house taken over that term, or 'half', by a new housemaster, Mr Jaques. Our common strangeness drew us together at first.

'Eton masters have a way of becoming peculiar after a time,' he said. 'Will you tell me if ever you think I am getting odd?'

It was not hard to see what he meant. In the house opposite was Mr Marsden, a monstrous shambling man, with the slouch and grime of a hobo. He had a reputation for beating the boys in his house with an oar, contrary to all custom. Beating was the prerogative of youth, apart from the Headmaster and his deputy, the Lower Master.

In the house next to Marsden was Mr Beasley-Robinson, an eager-faced man who owned a black and yellow Bentley and who had a measure of religious mania. He raised his hands in geometry class and pronounced: 'Chaps, chaps, God is in this room.'

Mr Upcott had a vendetta against Mr Babington-Smith, who held his classes in the next-door room. 'Scuffle your feet and stamp. Louder. Ruin his class. He shan't teach them.'

Apropos of nothing, Mr Rowlatt, who had been gassed in the First World War, would cover his mouth with a vast, expensive handkerchief and announce thickly: 'I am a passionate man.' He would then sit silent, shivering with rage, for half an hour. We sat, trembling too, with nothing to do.

The only man who stirred my imagination was Mr Hope-Jones, who strode about barefoot and in wild disarray. He made us construct icosahedrons out of paper and explained much about circles by cutting up a cake, that he had baked himself, using his own rations for the purpose. Thanks to him, I can still recite π to its thirty-sixth decimal place, as engraved on the tomb of Ludolf van Ceulen in Leiden.

The day was bound to come with Mr Jaques. One morning he was lecturing us about sex, about 'boys putting their penises up other boys' bottoms'. He always got everything wrong. We may have done many things but, so far as I know, none of us ever quite did that, so we were ready to giggle. 'Self-control, that is the cardinal rule in life,' said Mr Jaques. He stood in front of the study fire wearing his Corps uniform, with thick leather leggings. The heat from the fire seeped through the leather. It must have been extremely painful, but the sight of his furious, unavailing struggles to get the things off made us laugh.

He was still enraged when he came on his rounds to our rooms that night.

'But can't you see it is funny if a man gives you a long lecture on self-control and then can't get his leggings off for lack of it? You asked me to tell you. I think you have lost your sense of humour, and that's what makes all the others so peculiar.'

He had me beaten, once for impertinence and again for saying that that proved my point.

I like to imagine that other and better teachers would somehow have fired me with enthusiasm for all those things that I now enjoy, but I wonder whether that is not self-deception. Perhaps I was a late developer. Again, the boy I remember was still sly and was now indolent as well, thoroughly tiresome and unlikeable. Yet at the beginning of each half, Mr Jaques would provide me with letters to be shown to any masters by whom I had not been taught before. I had to bring them back to him initialled.

The letters read something like this: 'Do not be deceived by this boy's charm. If you allow it, he will do no work at all.' It was confusing; but it was true that I did little work.

I was neither happy nor unhappy. I was just drifting. My father used to write to Colin telling him to tell me to keep my pecker up. After the America incident, he decided that I must be terrified of the bombing – echoes of Rosie.

The Provost of Eton's wife, Lady Hugh Cecil, had been deaf for years. When the bombs fell on Eton, she said: 'What a comfortable sound bombs make.' I did not think that, but it was exciting and the incendiaries were pretty. In the mornings after a raid, one could occasionally find an incendiary bomb that had failed to go off. The penalties for keeping these were extreme, but we all had the metal tails and the magnesium noses of those which had fallen in soft fields, burning out on the earth.

I put a nose on to my coal fire one night. It burned with surreal brilliance. I had half an hour of agony as to whether it would set the house on fire, whether to call for help. At last it was spent. The grate had melted and the firebricks were a ghostly white.

'What happened here?' asked Mr Jaques.

'I can't imagine, sir, it must be this wartime coal.'

'You're lying.'

'Oh no, sir. We have a coal mine on our land and this sort of trouble is reported all the time.'

'I see,' he said in tones of doubt, but it ended the matter.

He was a snob and curiously naive.

At Eton, I could still walk quite well, but I could no longer even pretend to play football or cricket. Few concessions were made to my disability. Although I could not play, I was obliged to watch others do so, on cold winter days. In the summer, I had to row a boat for a certain distance every day. Later, I used to go on two afternoons a week to work in the Hawker aircraft factory near Slough. I drove a Lister trolley or sprayed camouflage on the Hurricanes. It cannot have helped the war effort.

The great difference from my first school was that I was not teased or tormented. This was not due to any gentleness among the boys, but rather to a subtler choice of victim. A lame boy was too easy.

The scholars, for whom the school was originally founded, were much despised. Intelligence was not admired, unless accompanied by athletic talent, but coupled with poverty or social inferiority it was unforgivable. To be Jewish was even worse.

The snow was thick one February afternoon. Football was impossible. There was little to do. Somebody started to chase the Rossiter twins. Others joined in. Soon fifty, then a hundred. In the end, a baying crowd, crushing the snow into hard, ice-sharp balls to throw at the Rossiters, shouting 'Jews'. Luckily they could both run fast, faster than their pursuers. It was a hideous sight – the beginning, though, of unlearning. Unlearning about Jews; seeing the pain in Baker's eyes, unlearning about his mother in her cherry-bedecked hat being common; finding a lonely woman working in the factory, unlearning that money is important. Only a beginning.

Against that, not much academic learning. So that when, at the end of 1941, my father came back to England, he made me sign a document in duplicate, with a blob of black sealing-wax on the back of each copy.

I, Quentin Hugh Dodds, do hereby undertake to work to the very best of my ability for as long as I remain at Eton. I fully understand that if I slack, as I have done in the past, my parents reserve the right to remove me from Eton and send me to some local school. Given under my hand at Madeley this fourteenth day of January 1942.

What was it about school that made everyone behave so strangely? Anyhow, the pseudo-solemnity made no difference. Whether from bravado or boredom – I cannot recapture – I went for the day to London and was found out. I was not sacked, but it was suggested that I should leave. I went to be taught by an impoverished vicar near Henley. He did well and so did I.

CHAPTER FOUR

A COUNTRY BOYHOOD

The house had stood empty for twenty years or more. The original Madeley Manor had been left to fall down in the seventeenth century, when the owner married the Crewe heiress and moved to Crewe Hall. This new one, some nine miles from Crewe, just over the Staffordshire border, was built in 1805, for a great-great-aunt of my mother's, or rather a white stucco wing was added on to an Elizabethan timber-framed farmhouse. The farmhouse collapsed at the turn of the century and a plain, practical block replaced it.

My mother's father, who was both extravagant and poorly advised, money and business being unmentionable topics, had sold Crewe Hall as well as his house in Yorkshire. Madeley and some four thousand acres, and two thousand or so in Wiltshire, was all that was left of the thirty thousand he had inherited. He lived in a house in Surrey. Madeley was to belong to my mother.

She hated it, because it represented responsibility. For my father it was a challenge. For me, it was my first real home. I had never really lived with my parents; there had been no sense of continuity, only that endless time of childhood stretching with no real belief in ultimate freedom. It was too late for the blind love that I saw in others for their parents, and too soon for understanding, but at least now I could get to know them.

For my mother I grew to feel sad. She once told me that she would have liked to have been an opera singer. Whether it would have been musically possible did not matter; it was socially unthinkable. With no mother and a distant father, she had married and had five children, but had no capacity for loving them. Her husband was killed in the

First World War. She had been in love with my father, but that only brought two more children and a life of exile. Her friends were few, because she had not the least idea of how to foster a friendship. Now, in her sixties, she, who had never really had to do anything, was landed with a large house, tenant farmers, local obligations. It was wartime. Already she had lost one son, Brian, his troopship bombed on the way back from Norway. In ordinary terms her life might not seem hard. We still had a cook, sometimes a butler, and a distressed old woman who had been my half-brothers' nanny and who had married a Belgian. Widowed, Nanny was without language. She had learned little French and had forgotten English. In addition to them, a number of girls came from the village to clean.

My mother's day followed its regular pattern of an hour with the cook after breakfast, the newspapers, letter writing. To this was added the shopping. She would trust no one else to buy the rations. She walked across the park to catch the bus to Newcastle-under-Lyme. She came back with her heavy patent-leather bag filled. The walk back from the bus stop was steep, a quarter of a mile. The Ayrshire bull which had pinned my father up a tree for two hours, eyed her. She was careful never to wear red.

Behind the house she kept chickens, Rhode Island Reds. Each day she cleaned their pen, picking up each dropping with a special small hoe. She followed the most complicated instruction book with minute observance that we all mocked. However, the hens laid prodigiously.

Our rations were scrupulously measured. We each had a screw-top Bakelite pot for our two ounces of butter, and our own monthly pot of jam. Our sweet ration came by post in gold boxes from Ailsa, of Connaught Street in London. Designed to hold a pound of chocolates, one quarter of the box was filled with paper. Mine lasted a couple of days, my mother's exactly a month. When the new ones arrived, she transferred from the empty box a card which sat on the top of the sweets saying 'Stop thief'.

Once, I came triumphant from the Post Office shop with a tin of golden syrup, given to me by Mrs Rayner, the postmistress. I was told to take it back.

Father was less punctilious. It was quite late in the war when Mr Hanning, the Anglo-Indian who kept the garage, was had up for making indecent advances to a young soldier. He had also exposed himself to the barber. My father was indignant about such things:

'I remember when I was young, a fellow in London made some

suggestion to me. I knocked him off his bicycle, and when I told them at the Travellers' about it they all said "Jolly well done".'

When Mr Hanning came out of prison, Father said he was never going back to that disgusting man. My mother protested: 'You have accepted black market petrol from him for two years, you cannot abandon him now. He has paid his debt to society in prison for six months. The matter is over. The only thing is that, when we stop for petrol, Quentin shall not get out of the car.'

My mother was at heart a liberal in the Whig tradition of her family, while my father was a conservative and, indeed, after my mother's death joined the Conservative Party.

She was absorbed by other people's lives, and her only real enjoyment at Madeley was in the hours she spent visiting families in the village. When I went back to live in Madeley thirty years later, my wife was irritated by the number of old people who would say to her, almost, she felt, accusingly: 'Everybody loved Lady Annabel, she was a real lady, always had time for everyone.'

The credulities of one generation must always astonish the next one. Between my parents and myself there was really a gap of two generations.

God was never a subject for discussion. Belief was assumed, healthy Protestant belief. Roman Catholicism was a matter for suspicion, but allowable in the case of the Dukes of Norfolk and, naturally, for 'dear Gerrie', my mother's cousin in Cambridge. It was perhaps in medical matters that my parents' views were strangest. My muscular dystrophy was still never mentioned, but every other possible complaint was seized on with enthusiasm. If I had a cough, my father would cup me. He brought a tumbler, fixed a piece of cotton wool to the inside, lit it and clapped the glass on to my chest. As the cotton wool burned, the flesh on my chest rose in a hideous lump inside the vacuum.

My mother's beliefs were unusual. She had, for instance, arranged that Colin and I should both be boys. It was simple. After making love, if one lay on one's right side the child would be a boy, on one's left a girl. She had not wanted girls, because at their coming-out dances she would have been at least sixty.

I, too, never brought up the question of my disability. My sixteenth birthday came and went without any miracle change, as common sense had told me it would, but for a while I resented it the more.

The challenge that my father found at Madeley was trying to bring order to the neglect. Where my mother was infinitely lazy, he was obsessively industrious. For me, his enthusiasm opened up two aspects of life.

The house stood on a rise, looking south over the oak-studded park, grazed by Ayrshire cows. To the east, the land fell steeply to a lake. The great-great-aunt, bedridden upstairs, had cut a deep V in the park so that she could see the water, the huge spikes of reed mace at the far end and, if her sight was sharp, the great crested grebes dipping their beaks in the shallows. Beyond the lake and the stream, where Izaak Walton used to fish, the land rose again, wooded now, until, at the top, a grey heap of slag and the whirring wheel of a coal mine broke the skyline.

Behind the house, on higher ground, was a wood, known as the Bryn – the great-great-aunt's husband had been Welsh. Immediately in front of the terrace which ran round the Georgian wing were lawns, with three low rings of oaks, their roots pruned to stunt them, and a monkey puzzle. The lawns were goitred tufts of yellowing grass, the bonsai oaks sprouted high, even the monkey puzzle looked bedraggled.

In the Bryn, there were traces of a track, once wide enough for a pony cart to drive. From different points on this track one could see, a short mile away, the red sandstone ruins of Heighley Castle, the medieval home of Lord Audley, the first man to be charged with helping another man to rape his wife, Lady Audley; further round, past Crewe and across the Cheshire plain, the sudden hump of Beeston Castle; and forty miles to the west the blue-grey knuckles of the Welsh hills.

The whole wood was tangled and twisted. Rabbits burrowed in the red-brown earth below the path. Jays and magpies swerved with raucous protest through the undergrowth. It was a jungle.

The balcony of the boathouse by the lake had half fallen down. The roof was doubtful, and the path along the shore had in some places slipped and was in others blocked by trees.

My father visualized green lawns, the trimmed oak rings filled with rosebeds, the rusting rails shutting off the park painted and gleaming. The woods should be tidy, free from vermin and filled with pheasants forever clearing their throats. The lake should leap with fish, to be caught either from the sturdy boat or from the neat banksides.

There were difficulties. No materials for repairs, no paint for inessential purposes. Worse, there were no men to do the work. They were either down the pit or away in the Forces. We did get a gamekeeper, but he did not cut down undergrowth, scythe bracken, shore up footpaths or repair bridges. There was Father and there was myself, some of the time.

I learned a lot, but our enthusiasms did not agree very well. After three hours of hacking or sawing or burning or digging, I began to think it would be more amusing to wander off on my bicycle, perhaps to visit the Furnival family. The rent rolls showed that Furnivals had been tenants on the estate for four hundred years or so. On their farm were the last stone fragments of the original Madeley Manor. They were a remarkable family – humorous, skilled and generous. What weighed with me more after hours of scything or paving or planting was the enormous tea that I knew Mrs Furnival would be getting ready. Ham, scones thick with butter, several cakes – so many things we never saw, but that farmers could fiddle from their own produce.

'I'm off now, Father.'

He threw a rake at me.

I never much liked the shooting. Carrying a gun made walking even harder. Through the dense woods of Hey Sprink after woodcock, over marshy ground at Hungerford Farm after snipe, across heavy plough on Bar Hill after partridges. I fell down so often. I was afraid the barrels would get filled with earth and I would blow myself up. Father never appeared to notice. 'Come on, it'll be dark soon.' I preferred the rifle and shooting rabbits or rooks for rook pie. I was better at it, with time to raise the gun and take aim.

It was the lore that appealed to me. The gamekeeper did not last long, but I learned from him how to trap a magpie, how to set a snare. Poachers' tricks, cruel but somehow an exercise of knowledge, not something learned at a shooting school but on the soil. I came to know the way that animals lived, their paths, their ruses. I loved the smell of ferrets.

The gamekeeper taught me, too, about pubs – until my mother heard. 'You must know that it is bedrock to go to a pub in one's own village.'

A parallel chaos inside the house affronted my father's sense of order. When Crewe Hall was sold, much of the furniture had been dumped at Madeley. The books sat in packing cases in the damp stables. The paintings were piled up in the house. Other furniture and paintings had been sent from the south for safekeeping in case of air raids. Our own furniture had mysteriously arrived from Nice in the midst of war.

Briefly, at the beginning, my grandfather and his second wife, another of my mother's sisters and her husband had all come to Madeley. Carpets were flung down, beds put up, odd pictures hung, some books stuffed in shelves.

My step-grandmother, an easy victim of ennui, soon removed my grandfather back to London. She would rather be bombed than bored.

Father fretted to sort out the haphazard arrangement of the house. It started for him as an exercise in orderliness. It finished for both of us as an education.

The history of art was not a subject that had appeared in any curriculum I had followed. Now, from piles like an antique shop, I sorted with Father what might have been the inspiration for the line in Noël Coward's song about 'the Gainsboroughs and the Lawrences and some sporting prints of Aunt Florence's some of which were rather rude'.

As neither of us was informed about painting, we made some curious arrangements at first. My mother would protest at our banishing two rather dreary Canalettos to a back room, and ask us to remove a bare-breasted, sub-Lely from the morning room. Occasionally, we became over-enthusiastic about, say, Dutch painting. We robbed the dining room of its Reynoldses and brought Cuyp and Ruysdael, Van de Velde and Neefs. There might be too few good ones, so we added dreadful still lifes of dead animals and lifeless flowers, and hideous red-cheeked women, which ruined lunch, until we were overcome by a new craze for sombre Jacobean and Elizabethan panels. By the time it all settled down and we were exhausted and the gilt frames were rather chipped, we had both acquired some knowledge.

With furniture and china, we went through the same sort of practical education, but it was the books that fired my imagination most. They came from two sources – the ordinary country-house library at Crewe Hall (though it was a little above average), and the library of my great-grandfather Richard Monckton Milnes.

While there were no rude prints, I had high hopes of the Monckton Milnes books, because he was known in the nineteenth century to have had the largest and best library of pornography in Britain, if not in Europe. It was a spur that prevented me from groaning when

Father said: 'We'll do six packing cases of books this afternoon.'

On some days, we might just find four hundred books of sermons, which we put away in the backest of back passages. On others, astounding treasures emerged. To start with it was the books with associations that I most liked. King Charles I's copy of Spenser's *Faerie Queene*, for instance. Or Sir Philip Sidney's copy of Jean Bouchet's *Les Annales d'Aquitaine*; and in the back of it he had written a poem, the only one to survive in his own hand:

> Sleep, baby mine, desire; nurse beauty singeth;
> Thy cries, O baby, set mine head on aching:
> The babe cries: 'Way, thy love doth keep me waking'
>
> Lully, lully, my babe; hope cradle bringeth,
> Unto my children alway good rest taking:
> The babe cries: 'Way, thy love doth keep me waking'
>
> Since, baby mine, from me thy watching springeth;
> Sleep then a little, pap content is making:
> The babe cries: 'Nay, for that abide I waking'

(The book is now in the Biblioteca Bodmeriana, Cologny, Geneva.)

I used to imagine the owners and wonder what they would make of my sitting, centuries later, with their books on the terrace of a house, the look of which they could not have imagined.

What did Oliver Cromwell want with a book on furnaces, by someone called Glauber? Or had he just snatched it up when he had no paper, the night before what battle, and drawn his plan with unaffected simplicity? 'Me', it said on the flyleaf, 'Fairfax' to the left and the 'Enemie' opposite.

The only two 'rude' books we ever found were an odd catalogue of prostitutes, illustrated by Hollar; the most expensive of the women, if I remember right, cost two guineas, the cheapest sixpence. The other was a first edition of Rochester's *Poems*. Both, oddly enough, came from the Crewe library. My grandfather, with Victorian prudery, had somehow managed to get rid of the whole of Monckton Milnes's pornographic collection. It would have been illegal to sell it and he would never have committed a crime. Against that, I find it hard to believe that he could ever have brought himself to destroy a book.

As I grew older, other aspects of the library took my interest. It was somehow wonderful to handle the *Lyf of Catherine of Siena*, started by Caxton and finished by Wynkyn de Worde. On the desk where Father made me, at fifteen, write in a child's copybook, 'Procrastination is the

40

thief of time,' sat a copy of 'Kubla Khan' in Coleridge's hand. At the bottom he had written: 'This fragment and a great deal more not recoverable was written during a reverie induced by a grain of opium, taken to check a dysentery.' There was much food here for procrastination. Why had he changed it later? – for the text that we now know is slightly different from this version. I could see that 'with walls and towers were girdled round' was better than 'compass'd round', but was 'twice five miles of fertile ground' an improvement on 'twice six miles'? Ah, of course.

There was a brocade slip-case which covered the 'Kubla Khan' manuscript. My father came into the room when I was writing a letter to a girl. He liked to read my letters. I pushed it quickly into the slipcase. Father wanted me to go to dig a trench or to hang some pictures. When, a day or so later, I thought of the unfinished letter and its mildly erotic tone, I could not remember where I had hidden it.

When I had been back at school for some weeks, I received a blast from Father. He had shown some visitor the Coleridge. My letter fell from the case.

'What sort of filth is this?'

Somehow, nothing went right in our relationship. He wanted to teach me things, but his temperament and my ineptitude were illmatched.

He thought that I should learn fencing as he had done. He told me to borrow masks and foils from school. I was wary because, one pre-war summer, he had decided to teach me to ride. Usually he didn't bother to teach me anything physical. Colin was agile and a more suitable subject. Colin, however, disliked horses, while I thought I quite liked them. Apart from anything else, riding was easier than walking.

My father could do anything with a horse. Even the most obstinate, lumbering creature became a dancing circus horse as soon as he mounted it. He hardly needed a bridle, let alone a saddle.

On our first ride across Ashdown Forest, his horse pranced prettily. Suddenly, it rushed in a wild circle thundering up behind me. My terrified horse leapt forward at full speed and did not stop for two miles.

'You've got to be ready for anything,' said Father, ambling up at a light, elegant canter.

After two more lessons, I gave up.

Now we faced each other on the terrace. Father pushed the point of his foil down on the stone until it was bent in a semi-circle. He let it go and the sword sprang up, twisting over so that the hilt fell neatly into his hand.

'*En garde*,' he cried, as if he were d'Artagnan.

Snick-snick. My foil flew down the garden. I fetched it. The same thing happened again and again.

I stuck fencing for four lessons.

The drive was long. At the steepest point, banks rose on either side topped with thick clumps of rhododendrons, now reverted to ponticum. I had to push my bicycle, slowly, daydreaming. At the top stood my father.

'Well, then?' he asked.

'How do you mean?'

'What did you see?'

'Nothing particular, Father. I just went down to the village.'

'You spotted nothing?'

'I don't think so. What sort of thing?'

'You wouldn't last long in the bush.'

'I don't suppose I would, Father.'

'How can you be so unobservant?'

He had taken down from the walls a number of his heads – a nyala, an impala, Speke's Gazelle – and propped them up in the bushes. He had brought even his black Ethiopian leopard rug, that over the years had faded and now had spots like an ordinary leopard, and draped it over a branch.

Another failed test.

It is a paradox in failed relationships that it is in many ways easier to live with someone when the failure is in the realm of fundamentals than when it lies in the trivia of everyday life.

I can remember only two or three occasions when my mother and I came anywhere near discussing anything that actually mattered between us. She was hard to provoke.

After a long time:

'You are irresponsible about money because you are sub-normal.'

'But you have had this argument with every one of your children.'

'Yes.'

'Then all your children are sub-normal and you dislike them?'

'Exactly,' the broken veins in her cheeks dark and sharp with anger.

A raw, shaking silence, as we both knew she meant it. The next day she said nothing to deny it. Merely, with her special honesty: 'You are never to trick me into saying something like that again.'

Our first cousins thought my mother wonderful. She laughed so easily and was so interested. Their mothers, her sisters, had their oddities, but they were loving – it never occurred to their children that my mother was not the same. She in turn thought them wonderful. David Colville, the first Gentile director of Rothschild's, Philip, a mathematical prodigy, and Jock, best of all, secretary to the Prime Minister; Bob Coates, so brave a soldier, Anthony, so good looking. Why couldn't we be like them?

Yet, as we both wished to avoid the frontiers of intimacy – she perhaps from guilt or, more likely, reluctance to confront an inadequacy, and I from guilt too, perhaps, or from a reluctance to confront a pain – much of our relationship was conducted on the enjoyable level that my cousins found so attractive.

My mother was in her way a good teacher. I learned with pleasure from her enthusiasm about wild flowers, about birds, about the gentler aspects of nature. Her views might be peculiar, but she had a store of knowledge on an unexpected number of subjects.

Father said he had never seen my mother cry. I cannot remember their ever kissing one another. Was it that emotions should never show, or did she have none, or were they different from other people's? Her unquestionable gift of prescience possibly detracted from feelings, certainly from surprise.

The butler from her father's house telephoned in the morning to say that there was a telegram for her.

'That will be about Brian's being killed,' said my mother. She went on with her plans for the day and did not go to fetch the telegram until late in the afternoon. 'I know what it says.'

She had had the same kind of foreknowledge when her first husband had been killed.

Three years later, 'Shane writes to say that he has had all his teeth out. That was a painful waste of time.'

'Why?'

'You will see.'

Soon, another telegram – Shane killed in action.

Later a third telegram – menacing, with 'Priority' on the orange envelope.

'What on earth can that be about?'

Colin was missing. And we had heard that so many had been killed at Anzio.

43

'Your mother didn't know. He must be all right,' said my father. Nine days later we heard that Colin was safe, a prisoner of war.

Terence's wound at Arnhem produced beforehand nothing more than a slightly puzzled 'I hope Terence is all right.'

It took no prescience to know that Timmy was dying. Two sons and a daughter in seven years. But no one ever saw my mother cry. Yet tears rolled down her cheeks with laughter when she listened to Tommy Handley in *ITMA*.

With my father the situation was quite otherwise. Naturally, as a good Victorian, nothing was mentioned which might prove embarrassing. Any real expression of affection must be suppressed. He had quixotic views on the other hand. His father had told him that children must be brought up to be afraid of their fathers. While he believed this, it conflicted with his actual nature, which was, in its way, affectionate.

Other considerations clouded the issue.

'Do you love your mother?'

'Of course, Father.'

'And so you should after all that she has spent on you.'

Money and economy had now become an obsession. He kept account books into which everything he bought was entered twice. Matches – 1½d appeared under the day on which he bought them and again under smoking, so that he could see what he spent each month or year on anything.

'Good God, do you know we spent £29 13s 6d more on laundry this year than last. Why do you think that is?' No one had much of an opinion. 'Well, at least we've saved on dogs. Poor old Don dying, I suppose.'

At the end of each month, he would have a major reckoning. Late in the night, when I got back from firewatching in the village, he would be hunched over his books.

'I cannot find where two shillings has gone.'

'It's late, Father, nearly three in the morning. Go to bed.'

'I must find it.'

'I'll give you two shillings and you can forget it.'

'But I would have to enter it under receipts and nothing would be solved.'

Father's economies were elaborate. He managed to find fifteen-watt light bulbs which he put into all the bedrooms. He crossed his letters, writing first across the page and then, on the top of that, at right angles down the length of the page. This practice was apparently common in the eighteenth century.

Petrol was very worrying. When the war was over and new cars appeared, we went to a showroom.

'I'll take one of those,' said my mother pointing to a Humber Super Snipe, in the tones of someone buying a toothbrush. She complained later that the back seat was too high. 'We will ask your Aunt Beryl to stay. She will sit it down to a more comfortable level.'

The Humber used a lot of petrol and Father developed many ways of conserving fuel. He backed out of the garage, went forward in first gear for a hundred yards and then changed into top gear where he would stay for the rest of the journey, unless stopped by traffic lights. On any downhill stretch, he would switch off the engine, until the car slowed to about five miles an hour, when Father would slip into top gear again. Someone told him that a fearful amount of petrol was lost by evaporation. From then on, Father insisted that the tank be absolutely full when the car was put away at night. On long journeys, the thought of petrol sloshing about in a half-empty tank bothered him. We would make frequent stops to fill up, so that the area exposed to possible evaporation should be as small as possible.

When, in 1944, the time came for me to go to Cambridge, Father consulted my tutor at Trinity as to what allowance an undergraduate would need. Mr Burnaby said that a generous amount would be £400 a year and that the minimum would be about £250.

'You will have to manage on two hundred,' said Father.

CHAPTER FIVE

CAMBRIDGE

How I came to study law is something of a puzzle to me now. The girl to whom I had written the torrid letter that my father found so shocking was training to be an actress. The idea of the theatre appealed to me.

'How on earth do you imagine you could walk on to a stage?' my mother asked.

The thought of performing instead in court may have been the spur. I worked for some months in a solicitor's office in Newcastle-under-Lyme. That was interesting for what it taught me about the daily life of people in the Potteries. But when it came to studying case law and, worse still, the rules governing the manumission of slaves in ancient Rome, I found the subject very dreary.

After a year, I switched to economics. While the law had pretended to a flexibility which in reality it did not have, economics laid claim to a precision which it certainly did not possess. I would like to think that such were my reasons for losing interest in both. Once again, the truth lay more in laziness or, at best, distraction.

When I set off for Cambridge, I was, I think, very immature for my age. The restrictions of wartime had confined me more tightly than might otherwise have been the case. Travel was difficult, people entertained very little, so that I did not go to visit friends or relations much. I was, on the other hand, somehow aware that other and, I suspected, better worlds existed. I remember going to see Donald Wolfit in *Hamlet* in Stoke-on-Trent with a wounded soldier I had met by chance on a bus. I had hardly ever been to the theatre before and was completely overwhelmed by the experience and fascinated by the soldier, who, although an officer, was disapproved of by my parents. His conversation about plays and books was far removed from anything I had ever heard.

This blinkered vision covered nearly every aspect of my life. At Cambridge, everything burst open. So much else was happening that my supposed purpose in going to university was forgotten. The influences rained like a shower of meteors. Although my parents saw my behaviour as being entirely frivolous and irresponsible, it was in those two academically hopeless years that I grew up.

Cambridge, like Eton, took on a very different aspect during the war. Most of those who would normally have been there had gone into the Forces. There was little or none of the *Vile Bodies* atmosphere that had pervaded Oxford and Cambridge before the war.

A policeman, discussing whether to arrest me for being drunk, said: 'I see you are not one of them who give trouble. All these scientists. They aren't like proper gentlemen, I mean they don't fight fair. They even kick.' What he did not realize was that the change was more fundamental than a temporary lack of humanists.

For the most part, I have no idea what has become of those friends of the time who opened so much of the world to me. They were a disparate lot, for my taste in friends has always been eclectic; I find very few people boring. Four or five I see occasionally, or hear of – Peregrine Worsthorne, who shone with *savoir-faire*; Colin Welch, who sliced through humbug; Claus von Bülow, who conjured up a whole new exoticism; Humphry Berkeley, who revealed to me real liberal thinking; a Peter who introduced me to jazz and swing; a Robert who taught me what unselfishness means. But what of all the others? Another Peter, another Humphrey and a Christopher who questioned everything; and Stephen who knew about tolerance. And many more. It is odd to think how much one owes to people who are unaware of the debt.

One figure, not an undergraduate, had a far greater influence than any other. John Hayward was, I suppose, a refugee from London and the Blitz. He lived in Lord Rothschild's medieval house in North-ampton Street. John had muscular dystrophy and was in a wheelchair. I had never met anyone else with the same complaint as myself, so this held a certain interest for me, although we neither of us ever referred to it at that time.

The only person I could ever bring myself to talk to about my lameness was Robert. I had met him by chance when having coffee in someone else's rooms after lunch. I mentioned, in a general way, that I was moving out of College and was looking for lodgings on the ground or the first floor. Some days later, Robert got in touch with me. There were some rooms going in the house where he stayed. I went to look. The rooms were perfect and I took them. When I had been there for about ten days, it struck me as odd that Robert should live in less pleasant rooms on the floor above. I asked the landlady why he had not moved down when mine had become vacant.

'Didn't you know? These were his rooms, he moved upstairs so you could have them.'

Robert was a year or two older than I and, having been in the Army, had a far broader experience. He saw that I was refusing to admit even to myself any possibility that I would get or was getting worse. As we walked together down King's Parade, I heard someone say of my walking: 'Looks like a drunken cat on hot bricks.' I was angry and hurt. Robert told me I must get a walking stick. I refused on the grounds that I would become dependent on it. He worked on my obstinacy, explaining that in reality I would be less conspicuous, that people would recognize more easily that I was disabled rather than odd. He forced me to accept that my condition was bound to deteriorate and that I must prepare myself for it.

Eventually, I gave in. I bought a stick. It made many things easier and I fell down much less, but I was still embarrassed by my disability and hated the stares that I felt were always fixed on me. I would wait for ages at the foot of a staircase until no one was in sight before I attempted to climb it. John was an example to me in opposing ways. He was rather timid and allowed his disability to prevent him from doing things that he could perfectly well have done with a little more courage. That made me more determined to do everything that it was possible for me to do. But at the same time he, too, taught me that embarrassment was stupid, although it was to be many years before I could really overcome it.

As I was wheeling John home through the evening fog, a WAAF getting off a bus fell across his chair and lay gazing into his face.

'Oh, my God,' she said.

'No, John Hayward, Merton Hall, Cambridge.'

John was ugly. The disease affected the muscles of his face, so that his lips hung heavily and his tongue seemed too big for his mouth. His voice, however, had an attractive timbre and his strange delivery made what he had to say even more arresting than it already was. The words came rather slowly, but with great clarity. His sentences often ended with an odd, choking laugh.

His humour was coarse and sometimes cruel. This to me was exciting. I had never met an adult who said 'Fuck', nor one who discussed sex in so prurient a way. I was not used to sharp repartee.

John had edited the Nonesuch editions of Donne, Swift and Rochester. He encouraged me to read, more by example than exhortation. And he set me a task. He knew about the library at home and asked me to look at every book of poetry and to copy out the title page. Once again I went through the yards of shelves, and took a long list to John.

I remember wincing at the choke of laughter when he came to Gent, J. G. I had not realized that Gent. meant gentleman and had treated it as a surname, putting it first in cataloguer's manner. But the discoveries were great, making up for the mockery. A first edition of Lovelace's *Lucasta*, a first edition of Herbert's *The Temple*, and again that first edition of Rochester's *Poems*, printed in Amsterdam in 1635. This last was a singular triumph. John owned every edition of Rochester, except the first. He coveted it beyond anything and nagged me for it for many years.

It was when I was at Cambridge that we changed our name from Dodds to Crewe. Lord Crewe died in 1945 and my mother inherited what was left of the estates. In order to do so, she had to add the name of Crewe to her husband's. None of us liked the idea of a double-barrelled name. My father did not feel especially attached to his, so we decided to change it completely.

On the morning of the change, I got a postcard from a friend at Trinity:

> There was a young fellow called Q,
> Who said, 'Now what shall I do?
> All the odds and the sods
> That answer to Dodds . . .
> I know. I will call myself Crewe.'

Auberon Waugh was, much later, to improve on this with:

> How odd of Dodds to choose the Crewes.

At the fairground, I could always win a prize from the Guess-Your-Weight man. I was six foot one and looked large enough.

Even when they felt my wasted arms and legs, they could never quite believe that I weighed barely ten stone.

Being so light made it possible for me to take part in a sport. I became a cox. In fact, I was rather heavy for this role, but for some reason I was extremely good at it. I developed a very fine judgement and could take bends on the river far closer than most and, in the bumping races, I was particularly skilled at evasion tactics, once grounding my pursuer in shallow water. I even became the spare cox for the University.

I had my comeuppance at Henley. The course in the middle of the river was marked out by two rows of floating telegraph poles, laid end to end. The custom was to row up outside these booms, leaving the course clear for people rowing practice runs upstream. At one point one had to cross the course and there there were gaps in the booms on each side, so that one went across diagonally.

The usual way to cross, in an eight, was to stop and then to paddle slowly through the gaps with only the front four oarsmen rowing. In my flash way, I discovered that I could guide the long boat through the gaps without stopping, with all eight men rowing. It was a question of inches, but I found it exhilarating.

A week before the Grand, the main international race, the cox of Leander, the British eight, was ill. They asked me to cox them until he recovered. I had visions of glory. We set off downstream. When we reached the crossing place, I decided to impress them with my stupendous manoeuvre. As we sailed with precision through the first gap and they saw what was happening, they panicked. They stopped rowing.

'What the hell are you doing?'

'Just crossing to the other side.'

'You can't. You must stop and let bow four take us through.'

'I can. Forward. Are you ready? Paddle.' The standard command.

They did nothing. We drifted. I shouted. We drifted more. They argued. Scrunch – we had drifted on to the end of the boom on the far side. The skin of the boat, an eighth of an inch thick, split open in a large hole. The boat and the proud British crew sank.

I still think they should have obeyed the cox.

Whilst my two years at Cambridge may have been a total academic disaster they had, in a way, taught me what I wanted to know. The Justinian Code and the laws of supply and demand may have escaped me, but I knew, for instance, that I wanted to work in some field connected with the arts. I knew for certain where my political sympathies lay. There were still some lingering prejudices that would need to be shed, but a basis had been established, and what more can one ask of a university?

CHAPTER SIX

A LONDON YOUTH

The war was over, but somehow it lingered on. At Madeley our butter pots still sat on the breakfast table, and for the first time bread was rationed. The Labour Party ruled. Leycett, the coal mine, was nationalized, and the local gentry spoke of doom and reviled Aneurin Bevan, cheering when this distinguished man was kicked down the steps of White's by an alcoholic aristocrat of no distinction. Few really understood that the Thirties were over too. A 1939 car was still thought of as new. Not many houses had refrigerators, none had a dishwasher. With half the population not realizing that a new age was upon us, and a large proportion unable to shake off the attitudes of war, it was as if two old moons were held in the new moon's arms.

I went to live in London in 1946. I took a room in a flat in South Kensington belonging to an elderly woman who dressed mostly in thick tweeds and spoke with a deep voice. I think she must have been one of those East Anglian cousins of my brother-in-law Edwy. She actually owned two flats, one above the other. The rooms were large and she had three or four lodgers. For our four guineas a week, we could have dinner in the flat, cooked and served by the maid, Lillie. Miss Strutt, however, showed no signs of finding our presence agreeable. She was not rude, but somehow exuded a general regret. I felt that for some reason she disapproved particularly of me. I dreaded those evenings that, for want of money or an invitation, I spent at home.

Work for me took various forms for the next few years. First was a bookshop. Sotheran's in Sackville Street had an air of faded intellectual stature. It was founded originally in York in 1815, by Henry

Sotheran. He prospered and moved to London, where the business expanded until eventually there were five branches. In the 1880s, the family bought from the executors of the naturalist John Gould all the plates and stock of his exquisite illustrations of birds. This established them further as the leading sellers of colour-plate books. The last Sotheran was run over by a tram in the 1930s. During the Second World War, the four dependent shops closed. Recently the remaining shop had been bought by Rothschild's, and it stumbled along, its former glory dwindling.

The floor area was large and a little dark, but it was a peaceful place. There were shelves round most of the room. The better books were spread out on tables, flat, never upright or on top of each other. There were leatherbound sets of Dickens, Thackeray and always of Surtees, in plain, rather pink calf. The huge folders of Gould had a table of their own, as had the very modern books.

The manager, Mr Styche, sat at a desk on the left. In winter, he wore a shawl over his shoulders and a skullcap. He looked like an antiquary in a mid-Victorian painting, perhaps by H. Stacy Marks. He did not move much, only getting up for very special customers. He dealt with the correspondence, dictating to a secretary who never spoke.

Mr Styche left most of the selling to Mr Sluman, a more extrovert, round man with a vivid complexion. Mr Sluman had that fat man's way of leaning backwards when making pronouncements, which seems lately to have gone out of fashion.

Mr Butcher compiled the closely printed catalogues, which were posted regularly to customers whom we never saw. Mr Butcher had dreadful arthritis. First thing each morning he would tell me how the 'screws', as he called his pains, were that day. At various intervals, little yelps reached me from one corner or another of the shop, as Mr Butcher stretched up too high or bent too low to get out a book for cataloguing.

There were few other sounds in the shop, unless Miss Herz happened to have a tantrum. Ida Herz was a German refugee. She had been Thomas Mann's secretary and was still in love with him, but, apart from that, her life was empty.

She lived in a dismal apartment in Notting Hill Gate. One of the youthful memories that still makes me shudder is of an evening when Miss Herz asked me and another man, who had come to work at Sotheran's, for dinner. He and I went to a party first. We drank a lot and were not in the mood for the correctness of Miss Herz. We wondered whether we could ring her and invent some excuse as to why we could not come. Luckily sense prevailed. We arrived a little late, but not too bad. Miss Herz was wearing lipstick, which she never did in the shop. Instead of her usual gym tunic, she had on a floral print. The table was laid with care, new napkins at each place, the knives and forks so shiny that I wondered whether she had bought them for the occasion too. The food was elaborate. Four courses that must have taken hours of preparation. What if we had not gone?

Miss Herz used to try to persuade Mr Styche to brighten up the modern table, with some new novels or something from Gollancz. She made little headway. She was as frustrated in her work as in her private life. And she had no sense of humour. If she were teased, and she was, she flew into a rage and the shop rang with Germanic fury.

Downstairs in the basement, time had penetrated even less. There were endless shelves filled with books of topography, heraldry, county histories – the dry stuff of country-house libraries, which we bought complete from the executors of small estates. In one dark corner was a musty old person who arrived and left each day with no word to anyone, except possibly Mr Styche. This was Mr Zeitlinger, who ran a department concerned only with ancient books of science. I am sure he was immensely erudite, but he was shut away like a hermit and dealt only with his assistant, a dumpy Czech, once Eisenschimmel then Elliott, who spoke of him as he spoke of everyone in the place, as a peasant.

It was only when I was allowed to go to sales that I came even to meet Mr Zeitlinger. I loved Hodgson's in Chancery Lane, and even better Sotheby's. It was wonderful to get out of the solemnity of the shop, to see a few livelier people. I was briefed carefully by Mr Styche or Mr Zeitlinger as to how much I might spend on the books that they were interested in. On no account was I to exceed the amount they wrote in code beside the number of each lot. The price of books, while absurdly low, was beginning to creep up from what it had been before the war. Mr Styche and Mr Zeitlinger had not noticed this. 'They are just peasants,' said Elliott, 'what can you expect?'

Almost always, I came back from the auction rooms with nothing. It became annoying. At Sotheby's there was a perfect copy of Chandler's *Camellias* – just the sort of book Sotheran's was known for. I bid £20 more than Mr Styche had marked in the catalogue and, surprisingly, got it.

Mr Styche's voice crackled up two octaves. Mr Sluman leaned so far back that I thought he would fall. Mr Butcher's 'screws' took a turn for the worse. Only Miss Herz looked at me with sympathy.

By pestering everyone who came into the shop, I managed to sell the book within a fortnight.

'Quite a quick turnover,' I pointed out to Mr Styche.

'The profit would have been more if you had bought it for less.'

I was not sent to the sales for at least two months.

The changing value of money is perpetually confusing. What things cost in 1947 is quite meaningless now, but some figures stick in the memory. My lunch at Lyons' Corner House was usually ninepence. When Miss Herz was kind, I took her to the Viennese café on the second floor. There the *apfelstrudel* prompted a welter of nostalgic pre-war reminiscence, and lunch was one shilling and twopence.

In another corner of the basement was the accountant, Mr Danter, a tall, angular man. Friday was payday. The custom was for each of the staff, at some time in the morning, to go to the passage outside Mr Danter's office and leaf idly through a book, perhaps *Pilgrimages in Cheshire and Staffordshire* by Fletcher Moss.

As if by chance, Mr Danter would look up from his leather-bound ledgers.

'Ah, Mr Crewe. Do step this way.'

I would go in and Mr Danter would give me an envelope with my name written on it, in a perfect copperplate script.

'Oh, thank you,' I would say with a careful note of surprise.

One morning when my eye was caught and I stepped in, there were Mr Styche and Mr Sluman, as well as Mr Danter, all smiling.

'You have been with us for more than a year,' said Mr Styche. Mr Sluman swayed in agreement.

'It has been decided that you shall have an increase in your salary.' They all shook hands with me in turn. Mr Danter then gave me the envelope. It felt a little heavier. I thanked everybody. It would, of course, have been indelicate to be seen opening it. I rushed to the loo. In addition to the usual four pound-notes, there were two half-crowns. Four pounds five shillings. No one thought, in those days, that this was a 6.25 per cent rise.

I moved houses and changed jobs with no particular aim in view. I joined another Dickensian establishment that organized art exhibitions; I worked as a statistics clerk in a factory that processed Technicolor film; I ended up with the French Line, selling tickets to New York and the Caribbean, until I was promoted to the publicity department.

In the busy season, I soon learned not to be affronted if passengers gave me a tip for getting them a passage. I learned other, less pleasant lessons. When a black person booked a berth, the cabin on the accommodation plan for that sailing would be marked CCC. This meant that one must not put a white person in that cabin, even if there were no other berth free. It did not occur to me for some time to ask what this stood for. When I did, they said cheerfully: 'Coffee-coloured coon.'

I lived for a while with the Bonham-Carters in Gloucester Square. The terms were the same as with Miss Strutt, but the atmosphere was different. Lady Violet was one of the most formidable people I have ever met, in that she expected of one far more than one had to give. In a sense it was flattering that she assumed that one was familiar with every nuance of political thought since Gladstone, on whose knee she had sat, sceptically counting the number of times he chewed each mouthful and finding it woefully fewer than the thirty-two that every nanny told every upper-class child to emulate.

Her husband, Sir Maurice, was as unalarming as she was frightening. He expected nothing of one, except perhaps politeness. When she argued, in her vociferous manner, with some lightly held opinion of mine, foolishly expressed, he would bumble in the background: 'Oh, yes, yes. Never mind. I mean, would you like to lunch at Brooks's tomorrow?' It was comforting in the storm, although I do not believe she had any idea of the ferocity of her attacks.

In her intensity, Lady Violet would lean closer and closer to whoever she was talking to, so that there were stories of a neighbour at dinner popping his fork into her mouth, pretending that he thought it was his own. She had, too, an over developed brand of honesty that prevented her from leaving anything unsaid.

At a party, she said to me: 'There is Tom Driberg, I must go over and tell him how dreadful I thought his article was on Sunday.'

'But why do you have to tell him? It will merely upset him. Couldn't you just say nothing?'

'Certainly not. He might think I had approved of it.'

I learned much later that her judgements were not always as inflexible as she believed them to be. Soon after I joined the *Evening*

Standard, I went to tea with Violet. Everything went well until I mentioned my new job. She stood up. Her teacup shook in her hand. 'That you, who come from a good Liberal family, that you, who have lived in my house, that you, whom I have trusted and been fond of, should do this, should sink to working for that organ of evil, is more than I can bear.'

Sir Maurice bumbled and suggested lunch at Brooks's. I thought that I would never be forgiven, but some time later I got a letter from Violet: 'I must write you a line to say *how* much I enjoyed your account of the Conservative Conference – It was brilliantly amusing – & I am *sure* true. Your description of K. Elliot made me laugh – (But is she an M.F.H.? or a "Bobby"? I am not sure whether I see the top-hat or the helmet on her head?) . . .' Even in an organ of evil, to tease the Conservatives was praiseworthy.

Nevertheless, it was during the time that I lived in her house that the muddled opinions I held on so many subjects were to some extent sorted out. Whereas with Miss Strutt I had dreaded dinners at home, with the Bonham-Carters they were a pleasure. It was after dinner that was exhausting, yet I was in the end grateful for what used to happen. Violet liked to sit up late. If she were alone, after Sir Maurice had gone to bed, she would read. Coming home late, seeing the drawing room light was on, I would tiptoe past the door, which she left ajar. Her hearing was acute. 'Is that you, Quentin?' Violet would be sitting in her chair by the fire. A cigarette would be deep in her mouth, so that the first half-inch of it would just be a damp straggle of tobacco. I could never understand why her mouth was not filled with bits demanding to be spat out. She would be humming with the events of the day and I would not get to bed for an hour. At Cambridge I had decided that my political sympathies were not Conservative, but as a result of my long evening conversations with Violet I formed a definite understanding of what had until then been more of a feeling about social morality, and a measure of certitude about fundamentals took root. This happy development was not necessarily easily discerned by others.

In 1948, Colin and I took a flat in Sloane Street. There were three bedrooms and a double living room, all with parquet floors. It cost £8 a week. A porter, Mr Prince, looked after the block, and an Austrian, Margaret Schaup, came daily to make our breakfast and clean, for five shillings an hour. We were mystified by the problems of cooking, and on desperate occasions Mrs Prince would laugh at us and cook us dinner. We furnished the place with stuff from Madeley – huge library chairs that girls complained of because they either had to sit on the front edge, with no support for their backs, or sit back so that their legs stuck up in the air; a round burr-walnut table with small William IV chairs and two improbable oak and damask chairs like thrones from a repertory company's sets for *King Lear*. Everything was too big and added to what two young men today would think of as absurd formality. But we loved it.

Much of our lives was formal. Colin, when he came back from the war, had no idea of what he wanted to do, so he signed on for another year in the Irish Guards. That over, he went to work in the City, with a firm of Lloyds brokers, run by our other brother-in-law, Derick Gascoigne. His friendships, inevitably, were mainly formed in the army or the prisoner-of-war camp.

Twice a week, perhaps, we would go to debutante dances, dressed in dinner jackets or, if Princess Elizabeth or Princess Margaret were to be there, in white tie and tails. There were still a very few people with private London houses large enough for giving a ball – the Northumberlands in Syon House, the Kelmsleys in Chandos House, the Rothermeres in Warwick House, the Bensons in Walpole House. Mostly the dances were held in hotels or in one of two houses belonging to caterers. We waltzed and foxtrotted, polkaed and rumbaed and tangoed, to the bands of Carol Gibbons, Joe Loss or Edmundo Ros. If the hosts were Scottish, their daughters' cheeks chapped by moorland winds, we might even dance reels.

Our suits were made by tailors in Sackville Street – Wealeson and Legate. Mr Wealeson's father, Mr Weale, used to help in the shop occasionally. They addressed Mr Legate and each other always as Mister. The lesser figures such as the cutter, Freese, were all called by their plain surnames. The shop was filled with bolts of cloth, but the choice in reality was very limited – city or country. If city – blue, black, grey (no gentleman wore brown); if country – tweed, worsted, check, herring-bone, dog-tooth. There were other bolts that we were not troubled with, 'for our American customers'. There was no fashion except perhaps in minutiae.

'Do you think an eleven or an eleven-and-a-half-inch cuff, sir?'

'Eleven please, Mr Wealeson.'

'Very wise, sir, I think, these days. And double-breasted, I take it, for the grey flannel?'

'That's right and no turn-ups.'

'My word, sir. Did you hear that, Mr Legate? No turn-ups on the grey flannel.'

'Very dashing, Mr Wealeson, I would say.'

'But, of course, on the tweed, Mr Crewe, you will have them, won't you, sir.'

An instruction this, not a question.

What we cared about was not a new trend or style but about being smart, our clothes well-pressed and clean. I used to fall down a lot when walking in the street, despite my stick. The pavements cut the tops of my ankles, so that they developed proud flesh that bled perpetually, and tore my trousers at the knee. Again and again I would have to have them mended, until both knees had a lumpy agglomeration of darning, like the kneepads of an ostrich. I did not mind about my ankles, but I minded very much about my trousers and would sit with my hands on my knees in the vain hope that no one would notice. Mr Wealeson lined the front of my trousers with satin so that they would slide more easily and perhaps not tear. It helped a bit, but not a lot.

I did fuss a little more at this time about my disability. It may have been, in part, the feeling that I had really started out on life, that I was on my own. I was now twenty-two. My parents were nearly in their seventies. They had told me that, of the little money that they could leave us, two-thirds would go to Colin and one-third to myself, on the grounds that I was irresponsible and that he would look after me. But I do not think that really had much to do with it. The promise of future disaster does not really weigh very heavily on most of us. We think, like Mark Twain, that it will somehow be averted in our case. I may have been driven by a more immediate worry that girls would be put off by my lameness. The medical profession having no suggestions, I explored the realms of what is called now alternative medicine, but was then called quackery.

Acupuncture was a novel idea. I found it very disagreeable, especially when the points of the needles scraped on the bones of my shoulder and kneecap. There were no effects, apart from a small lump that appeared on my shin where a needle had pricked and which I still have today.

I hated to disappoint a charming healer who lived not far away. She was so sure of her gift. Her hands were soothing and her fingers rippled on my joints in a way that I was certain that she could not control. I always left her with a sensation of lissom pleasure, my neck creaked less, but I walked no better.

Another man, himself in a wheelchair, demanded unpleasant specimens in return for which he sent unnamed potions. They might as well have been lemonade for all the use they were.

The most strange was a man from Barnes who helped me up when I had fallen in the street. He was a doctor of sorts. He asked if he might try on me a treatment he had invented. He came to the flat with a bottle of liquid. He made me strip and with a soft brush he painted every square inch of my body. The liquid felt ice cold and it stung my scrotum fiercely. He told me to dress and walk up the stairs. Without my stick, without touching the banister, I walked with ease up the steps which each morning were something of a struggle.

He came two or three times with his liquid, but it never worked again. Nevertheless, it was unsettling. Why had it worked once? Was my disability really just imaginary? Could it be overcome by faith? Was all illness the product of the mind? I gave up thinking and reverted to my ordinary habit of ignoring the problem, pretending that it did not exist.

Lady Sybil Grant was the sister of my grandfather's second wife. They were the daughers of Lord Rosebery, who was reputed to have said that he had three ambitions – to marry the richest woman in England, to win the Derby and to become Prime Minister. He achieved all three.

Sybil, when she was young, so my mother told me, was very attractive, with a slender figure and a face of delicate beauty. She was married young to a soldier and soon had a son. Unfortunately, she never lost the weight she put on when she was pregnant and remained for the rest of her life a short, almost spherical woman. It was, in fact, rather hard to tell what shape she was, for she wore long flowing clothes and some form of headgear that revealed only the oval of her face, with one bright orange sprig of hair peeking out above her eyebrows.

By day her clothes, which reached to the ground, were usually dark blue, with on her head a matching kepi, the cloth back and front hiding her neck. In the evening she wore shapeless dresses, often in the reds and purples of a fuchsia, with slits at the sides for her bare, plump arms. Her headdress was a golden balaclava helmet.

Sybil had three houses – the Durdans, a large Victorian mansion on the edge of Epsom racecourse; Pitchford, an E-shaped Elizabethan manor in Shropshire; and Bearnoch, a small house in Scotland. It was Pitchford that brought Sybil more into our lives. It was her habit to hint that she was planning to leave Pitchford to whoever happened to amuse her at the moment. There was no question of her leaving it to her son although it was a Grant family house, for she never forgave him for being the cause of the loss of her figure.

At one point, she indirectly encouraged Colin to believe that he was to have Pitchford. Every Wednesday, she would send her chauffeur to pick him up and drive him to the Durdans for the night. The chauffeur drove a taxi that Sybil had bought. Sometimes I would go with him.

Staying at the Durdans was in some ways unnerving. There were never any women there, as Sybil did not like them. At the time her husband, Sir Charles, was unwell and we hardly ever saw him.

At night, ozone was puffed into the bedrooms and one might wake to find a rotund, ghostly figure standing at the end of one's bed with a lantern held high. This would be Sybil, checking that one was breathing well.

Ozone and fresh air played a large part in her life. When travelling on a train, she would take a long tube with an ozone pad half-way down it. She clipped one end to the window so that the air rushed into it. The other end she held under her nose. This worked well until she offered it to other passengers; moving the tube let loose a shower of smuts which blackened their faces.

More often than not she went by road, particularly if she was going to visit other people. She disliked sleeping in strange houses, so she bought a bus and slept in that. The problem of fresh air on the journey she solved by removing the windscreen of the bus, which some thought was hard on the chauffeur, but she said it was good for him. Even at Pitchford she did not sleep in the house, preferring a seventeenth-century treehouse in a broad-leafed lime, about a hundred yards from the house.

Sybil was fond of Gipsies and I have a feeling that they had once done something for her. Certainly she achieved something of importance for them. In one of their periodic waves of autocracy, the Jockey Club were hoping to ban the Gipsies from the heath during Derby Week. During one of their meetings, Sybil burst in. In her deep voice, with its measured emphasis, she proclaimed: 'Gentlemen, I have heard of your decision to ban the Gipsies. I applaud it. And I trust you will applaud mine. You shall have no grandstand and no paddock.'

She swept out, leaving those who did not know her quite astonished at what they took to be the ravings of a madwoman. Those who did know her, like her brother, knew who would win, for Sybil owned the land on which the paddock and the grandstand stood.

Sybil's sense of humour was of a very special, teasing kind. I remember being at the Durdans for the 1949 Derby. There had been a lot of nobbling of horses that year, so that when the favourite, Barnes Park, was brought in to stay in Sybil's stables, two detectives came with the horse. When she had established the stableboys, the detectives asked where they should sleep.

'Sleep? Sleep?' asked Sybil in the tones of Lady Bracknell. 'Ah no, you can't fool me. I've read my Peter Cheyney – detectives never sleep.'

She could laugh at herself, although, in the way of all true eccentrics, it never occurred to her that there was anything odd in her behaviour. The downstairs lavatory was papered with hundreds of rejection slips from all kinds of magazines and newspapers to which she had submitted short stories. She never used her title when sending a story. The refusals were always addressed to Mr S. Grant and were often crushing: 'The Editor regrets that your story falls far short of the standard we require of our authors.' For someone who was so painfully vain about her appearance, her lack of pride in other fields was remarkable.

Not only did Sybil write; she painted. For the most part her pictures were of dogs, though she had none of her own. The choice was, I think, purely commercial. She acquired a hawker's licence and every year sat on the pavement selling her paintings outside Cruft's dog show. Perhaps she had calculated that dog lovers are not usually great judges of art.

Her life, I now suppose, must have been sad. She cannot have had much in common with her soldierly husband. She had no contact with her son. There were often rather second-rate young hangers-on, who were not produced on social occasions, but who she affected to believe were in love with her. One part of her was genuinely rebellious, courageously so, and in different circumstances might have flourished interestingly. So much, however, was resentment and bitterness.

The last time I went to the Durdans was for a week. Sir Charles was ill and Sybil had to go to Scotland. Each evening the taxi would collect Colin and myself from London and take us back to work in the morning. For some reason we were forbidden to go to see Sir Charles. Our role was to keep an eye on the doctor whom Sybil had engaged to live in the house. It is not hard to imagine what sort of doctor may be hired by the week. Every night after dinner Sybil would telephone.

'Let me speak to the doctor.'

'He's just gone out for some cigarettes.'

'I don't believe it. I believe he's drunk under the table.'

While not under the table, he was too drunk to put on the line. Luckily, Sir Charles survived the week. When Sybil came back, she dismissed the doctor and we had an easier dinner. That night Sybil gave me some printed cards the size of visiting cards.

'You may find these useful at boring dinner parties. Just get up and leave one on your plate.' They read:

> The meat is tough
> And so am I,
> I've had enough
> And so goodbye.

Conventionality, naturally, included sex. We had not yet reached the middle 1950s when the hundred-year-old Willie Stone, who lived in Albany, said to Alan Brien: 'When I was young, fellows might keep a woman in a love-nest in St John's Wood, but nowadays I hear fellows sleep with other fellows' sisters.' On the whole, the girls we met were virgins. There was one contemporary of mine who used to entice girls out on to the balcony at dances and expose himself. He maintained that although his face was more often slapped than not, the few successes made up for the slaps. I forget his name.

The Bag o' Nails in Beak Street and the Coconut Grove were clubs where one could pick up girls. I remember one called Eileen, who was living proof of my mother's theory that the most beautiful girls in England came from Nottingham; but I could hardly present my mother with this happy confirmation. At the Stork Club, Al Burnett, a deliberately feeble comedian, repeated the same jokes night after night, the audience joining in with undimmed enthusiasm. The girls at the Stork were not so pretty, but were much less commercial. One Irish girl used always to leave by my bed in the morning a small picture of a saint, usually St Peter or St Anne, with a note on the back saying: 'May the Good Lord watch over you. God bless. Clodagh.'

Or there was 'Ma Feather's'. Mrs Featherstonehaugh had a pleasant house in Elvaston Place. If one telephoned her, she would ask what time one would like to call round to see her. When one arrived, there would be a girl waiting, appropriately dressed for whatever one had earlier told Mrs Featherstonehaugh one was planning to do that evening. Her girls were usually pleasant middle-class girls who liked to make a little money, but who would have been horrified if anyone had called them prostitutes.

The Irish Guards being a little different from the rest of the Brigade, some of Colin's friends were somewhat less conventional than the average Guards officer.

There was one called Kenneth Darrel-Rew, the son of a coster-monger. He had as a youth been taken up by some rich man and become accepted by a set which included the Duke of Kent, or so Kenneth said. In any event, he was commissioned in the Irish Guards. Wholly without pretension, he used once a year to take a suite in Claridge's for his old mother, the costermonger's widow, and ask all his friends to a party in her honour.

Another was Peter Grace, who lived with a captivating Russian girl called Dagmar, the only person I then knew who was 'living in sin'. Peter danced in a sensual manner, his feet turned so that all his weight was on the inside of his feet. His shoulders never moved, but his hips writhed to the rhythms of the music. I tried to imitate him, but usually fell over.

Charlie Brand was unquestionably homosexual. These friends of Colin's introduced me to a world that I had never imagined existed. The sophisticated impropriety of their clubs was very different from the commonplace turpitude of the Bag o' Nails. The Music Box and the Jamboree were filled with people whose interests lay in the arts and whose conversation was more enlivening than that of the patrons of the Stork in search of a lay.

It was Peter, however, who took us to the Antilles. West Indians were beginning to arrive in England, and among the first were musicians. The club was in a basement in Soho – a dark, shabby room, thick with smoke and, had I recognized it, the smell of ganja. The music was lively and different – jazz, not like that of Humphrey Lyttelton, who played at the Chelsea Arts Ball and occasional parties, but crossed with Trinidadian calypso. The trumpeter was Cyril Blake, the first black man I had ever come to know. Peter shimmied on the sides of his feet, and I was entranced by a sense of freedom. Even in the

Bag o' Nails everyone wore a jacket and a tie. Impropriety had its limits. The Antilles was dedicated to enjoyment.

Our lives became less circumscribed, the boundaries being set more by the licensing laws than other considerations. The hypocrisy of British legislation made it possible, in London at least, to get a drink at any hour. There were many small drinking clubs that opened as soon as the pubs closed at three in the afternoon – the Woolly Lamb in Shepherd Market was the most amusing, but I went often to the Little Club in Knightsbridge.

The law mysteriously allowed one to drink one's own drink in a nightclub. They all had arrangements with a wine and spirit merchant called Eustace Hoey. The fiction was that in legal hours one had ordered a few bottles of scotch and gin from him. The club sent a boy on a bicycle to collect one of these. It arrived with one's name on. If one didn't finish it, it went back to Hoey and could be summoned to any other club. The economics must have been complicated, but it worked. At the Antilles, we drank whisky from teacups, on the understanding that, if there were a raid, we would gulp it down and dry the cup. When the nightclubs closed at four or five in the morning, the pubs would be open in Covent Garden for some hours and, for the indefatigable, later still at Billingsgate and Smithfield markets.

Ruth Ellis often sat at the bar in the Little Club. Always she said hello, and I said hello to her again. How could someone I had met be hanged? She was not a particularly attractive woman. A little brassy, perhaps, but not offensive, certainly muddled rather than evil. Another of my lingering opinions was violently overturned.

It was a time for me of experimentation and of trying to decide between so many paths. Everyone that I knew belonged, if not to a stereotype, at any rate to a group out of which they did not venture very far. I had friends from Cambridge who talked of rowing and the good times we had had at university. Probably they still do so today. John Hayward came to live in London, sharing a flat with T. S. Eliot. He would never let me meet Mr Eliot, as he called him, as he was almost pathologically jealous of his friendship, guarding him for himself. John would have made nothing of my rowing friends. Nor would my other O'Neill half-sister Midi's friends – Nancy Mitford, James Lees-Milne, Robin Fedden – who were infinitely kind to me, have taken much to those hearty companions who roared me around the country on the back of motor-bicycles, or for that matter to an

65

increasing number of dissonant cliques. None of them would have cared for Doony Moon or Pauline.

Doony Moon was a regular at a pub in Pont Street. She was noisy and blowsy and Irish and claimed to have been married to some decaying baronet and so called herself Lady Moon. She had that confidential Irish way of talking, as if drawing one into some conspiracy. She was utterly persuasive and convinced me once into a curious adventure.

'Will you be wanting to make £10, you will?'

'How, Doony?'

'It's no trouble at all. Just you come to Montagu Square on Tuesday evening for dinner. Wear your dinner jacket. It will be a good dinner, that I can tell you.'

'But what do I have to do?'

'It's nothing to worry you. I'll be there and some other young men.'

I forget the number in Montagu Square, but the owner was Mr Klein. The drawing room was on the first floor, a light room full of evening summer sun. The furniture was mostly in that delicate French style, inlaid with porcelain panels, and might well have come from the Wallace Collection nearby. There were five other young men. I knew none of them, but recognized one from the pub. Doony brought us glasses of sherry, and Mr Klein made agreeable enquiries as to what we did. He was a short man with a rather stumpy gait, but he was a person of cultivation. After a time, he asked us to excuse him for a while.

'What do we have to do, Doony?'

'Well, my dears, it's just a question of not being too polite to the parlourmaid, Ellen she's called. So you tell her off and things. Say how bad she is at her job and that.'

We went down to dinner. The dining room was sombre with dark panelling. The heavy curtains were drawn. Half-way down one wall was a large marble fireplace. The shining mahogany table was laid for eight, with fine silver and cut glass. Doony sat at one end, but Mr Klein's place at the other end was empty.

Ellen, in frilled cap and apron, brought the consommé. One could not mistake her stumpy gait.

'Oh, Ellen, you are a muff. You've spilled some soup.'

'You aren't very good at this, are you, Ellen?'

When Ellen went to get the next course, Doony told us that we had to be far ruder than that. It was a wonderful dinner with a whole young grouse each. By the time the port came with the cheese, the insults to Ellen were as strong as the Stilton. Suddenly Ellen rushed to the fireplace and, with her back to us, lifted up her skirt and stood trembling.

A little later, Mr Klein joined us for coffee and we chatted of topics of the day as if nothing had happened. When we left, Doony gave us each ten pound-notes in an envelope.

Cyril Blake, the trumpeter, moved from the Antilles to the Sunset and from there to the Scheherazade. This was high up in Rupert Street, a most wonderful nightclub in that it had windows so that the ganja fumes wafted away over the rooftops of Leicester Square. And one had plenty of time as the police lumbered up four flights of stairs to swallow one's whisky and dry one's teacup.

I was alone and Cyril played 'St James Infirmary Blues' for me. At the table next to mine was a girl with dark auburn hair and pouty lips. She was not pretty exactly, but she had an aura of energy and sexuality. She was with a man I knew slightly – Nicky. He had once been in a bar in Cannes, chatting amiably with a stranger, a fellow Englishman. Eventually, the stranger asked to borrow a fiver. 'It will be all right,' he said, 'my name's Lord Victor Paget.'

'In that case, you must be my father,' said Nicky, who had never before met his parent. Now Nicky was drunk.

'God, this man's too much,' said Pauline. 'Will you get me a drink?' Nicky seemed not to mind when she moved from his table to mine. Pauline talked. Her manner was extravagant, full of those gestures that actors use but no one in real life employs – a tossing of the head, a flounce, a startled throwing back of the shoulders. There was an arrogance about her, a contempt for decorum. Cyril played 'Brown Skin Girl' and we danced. When I apologized for my awkwardness, she told me not to be so fucking stupid. I thought she was marvellous.

Pauline lived in a flat at the top of a house in South Kensington. When we had been in bed for a little while, there were footsteps on the stairs.

'Oh, how dreary,' said Pauline. 'He said he wouldn't be back tonight. Get into the cupboard, darling, just for a minute.'

I stood naked in the cupboard amid the swirls of chiffon and satin that Pauline used to wear. I listened to the conversation.

'Go and sleep in the other room. I simply don't want you in here tonight.'

'You've got someone else here.'

'Don't be completely idiotic, and do put that gun away. Jealousy's so boring anyway, but at this time of the morning it's unpardonable. I want to go to sleep. Edward, go away.'

He went and I crept out of the cupboard. Pauline said that I should stay, but I dressed and waited until Edward might be asleep. Then I fled.

Pauline was the daughter of a Colonial civil servant, perhaps in the Sudan. She had married at seventeen and had two children by this husband. He had gone to the war and came back safely, but with a moustache which he refused to shave off. On that account, Pauline left him. She then married one of three brothers who owned a fine manor house not far from a factory. The brothers lay about on chaises-longues while one of their wives looked after the house and the other two went off to the factory to earn money. Pauline enjoyed the first three months as lady of the manor. Then it was her turn to go to the factory. She left and next she married Edward.

Pauline became a friend. Briefly and awkwardly, so did Edward. They took a house in Walton-on-Thames and I used to go to stay for weekends. There were only two bedrooms in the house. Pauline's children slept in one; Pauline and Edward in the other. I had to share their bed. On the first weekend, Edward sat upright in the bed for the whole of Friday night. In the morning he was so exhausted that, when he had to go to work, he took a taxi. When he had gone about five hundred yards, he was so overcome by his imagination of what we might be doing that he flung himself out of the taxi, crying: 'I want to die.' It was a grassy corner and the car was moving slowly; Edward was quite unharmed. The taximan brought him home saying that he wanted nothing to do with a suicide. Pauline shrieked abuse at both of them until they got back in the car and drove away, thankful to escape. That night Edward took a large dose of Luminol and slept uncaring.

He never worried again, but their marriage was not destined to last. Pauline moved out and, from time to time, I stayed with her in various houses that she borrowed or rented. She introduced me to the wilder shores of lust and wiped clean any inhibitions or guilts which I may have nursed, multiplying since the days of my first governess. And, strangely, when all that was done, Pauline was to run as a rogue thread through the pattern of my life, not affecting it, but always as a reminder to eschew pomposity.

I remember those years now as a time not just of experimentation and search, but of seamless selfishness. Cruelties, dishonesties, betrayals bay at me out of that file of my memory if I dare to open it. As before, I wonder how anyone could have tolerated the creature of my recollection, yet there were those who did.

It was in 1948 that my mother died. It meant little to me. I was conscious that things that should have moved me, merely intrigued me. I minded that, as she lay dying, the cancer investing her brain made her talk nonsense. She had prided herself on her clarity and I felt her dignity was insulted when she asked me to tell the Italian orchestra playing at the end of her bed to go away. But I was fascinated at the same time by the paraphernalia of death, by the postures my father adopted, by the greed of normally generous people over wills and possessions. I felt no deep grief, though I attribute my dislike of peonies to the mountains of the beastly things piled upon my mother's coffin.

Often I stayed with Willy Mostyn-Owen, a young friend barely down from Cambridge. His mother, a dotty pyramid of a woman who drank copious amounts of sherry and embarrassed her children, had two houses – one medium-sized Georgian country house in Shropshire, the other a small castle in Perthshire. While Willy had no real need to work, he had a boundless curiosity. When I was between jobs, which was often, we would tour Britain looking at churches, houses, museums or just countryside.

On one occasion, we took with us Rosamond Lehmann. She had been living for some years with Cecil Day-Lewis. He had just left her and was planning to marry Jill, the daughter of a film producer, Sir Michael Balcon. Miss Balcon was about nineteen and immensely pretty. I listened enthralled, but uncomprehending, to Rosamond's tirades. It was beautiful to see her shake her leonine head and to hear her spit out her scorned fury against 'that chit of a girl'.

We stayed in Stratford-on-Avon to see the Histories. In the evening the rage of Glendower could not surpass that of Rosamond in the day. To me both were plays, for I could not imagine such passion, let alone in a woman old enough to be my mother. She said Willy and I were a comfort to her, but I remember more her comforting me when I said that I did not think that I had ever performed any act that did not have a selfish motive.

Then I fell in love.

CHAPTER SEVEN

SARAH

It has never taken me longer than a weekend to fall in love, usually less. Perhaps that has been the trouble. But this was the first time and it took me by surprise. I had been fond of girls, I had had enthusiasms for girls; but it had all been a game, pleasant enough, uncompetitive in that it did not matter if one won or lost. There was always another hand or set or match. And Margaret Schaup, the daily, pretended to be shocked by the turnover of girls at breakfast – 'Ach, but who am I who is talking? When I am young I am a bugger for the boys, always they are on top of me.'

Now it was different. Now it mattered to the exclusion of everything else. There was, unfamiliarly, someone more important than myself. Indeed, there was only one person in the world.

Sarah came, one weekend, to stay with Willy. She was not especially pretty. Her eyes were too small and her lips thin, but when she smiled her eyes crinkled in a way that was for years to make my heart turn over. She had a beautiful figure, which she spoilt much of the time by moving, when she was nervous, with a diffident crouch. There was a vulnerability about her that I found touching, but also, even at the very beginning, there was a waywardness that was challenging and an enigmatic quality that gave me no peace. By the end of the weekend we were lovers, pledged to stay together for a long time.

Those uncertain qualities and her apologetic stance stemmed from the confusion of her parenthood. She was brought up the youngest of the four children of Harold and Lady Dorothy Macmillan. When she was just seventeen, she learned what everyone else had always known. Sarah was in a nightclub; she danced with Colin Tennant, the friend of

Princess Margaret. Another girl who had been brought by Tennant
was jealous and drunk. She came over to Sarah.

'What do you think you're doing with Colin? You're only illegitimate anyhow, you're Boothby's daughter.'

Sarah's imagination, which was vivid, may have dramatized this
story, but she certainly was never told about her father by her family.
Harold Macmillan could never, at that time, have brought himself to
do so; Lady Dorothy always postponed anything unpleasant, and she
somehow convinced herself that it did not matter.

We were happy in that light-hearted, skipping-down-the-street way
that young couples in French films are happy, but that British films
can never capture. I used to go every weekend to Gosses, the cottage
into which the family had moved when Birch Grove, the large house
built by Harold's mother, was turned into a school during the war.

Quite apart from being in love, there was for me an unexpected
excitement in, as it were, joining a family. My own family life having
been so confined, I had no idea of the tempestuous nature of
relationships in big families. The Macmillans were, it is true,
somehow larger than life, but they had that self-sufficiency that closely
linked families thrive on. There was no need for outsiders to provide
stimulus, there was quite enough going on among themselves.
Alliances were formed and re-formed, quarrels came and went. Each
weekend there was news of everybody to be gone over.

Sarah's two sisters were married. Carol and her husband, Julian
Faber, lived five miles away at Horsted Keynes, and had then two
children. Catherine had just married Julian Amery, who almost
simultaneously became MP for Preston North; they lived in London.
Maurice, Sarah's only brother, worked in the family publishing firm.
He and his wife, Katie, lived in a small cottage on the Birch Grove
estate with their two sons.

It was Lady Dorothy who dominated the family. The Macmillan
tendency was towards a kind of languor and a laissez-faire approach to
life. In Harold's case this covered an anxious nature, but it was
somehow infectious. Lady Dorothy, however, simmered with energy.
She hardly ever walked; she ran. It was always a surprise to see her
sitting down. She had a highly developed practicality. On a stormy
night, Katie found her in the garden tying up the roses. She had a
torch attached to her forehead, like a miner's lamp, and a hot-water
bottle strapped to each knee. She explained that the roses would all be
destroyed by morning unless she tied them, that she needed both

hands to do the tying and that she didn't see why she should get cold wet knees while she did it.

It was difficult at first to understand the paradox of her strength and her weakness. She was genuinely shy, at any rate of grandeur and officialdom, and would ask me what on earth she should wear to go to Buckingham Palace or to an occasion in Harold's constituency. She would make me write speeches for her for some bazaar opening and suggest topics to raise with visiting foreigners, of whom she was terrified. In one way, it was nonsense, because she had a charm and a warmth which captivated everyone. Her clothes were dowdy and owed nothing to any fashion. Her hands were rough and cracked from gardening, her strong patrician features were marred rather than enhanced by make-up, and jewels sat ill on her. But these things in her were endearing. She set everyone at ease and was the least class-conscious person I ever knew.

At the same time, Lady Dorothy had a will of unusual strength. If she wanted to do something, she did it. After eight years of marriage to Harold, she had wanted his best friend, Bob Boothby, and she took him. Some of the fault may have been Harold's. His social insecurity made him feel that he must work to earn enough to keep a duke's daughter in the style he imagined she needed. He compounded the devotion to work by becoming an MP. What she wanted was to live in the country. Instead, they lived in Chester Street. When they did go to the country, it was to Birch Grove, which she had to share with Harold's domineering mother.

'I thought I had married a publisher, but found I had married a politician,' she once said by way of explaining to me why she had had an affair with Bob. 'I am by nature very faithful, I have always been faithful to Bob.'

Her capacity for self-deception was great. 'I would have got divorced from Harold, but every time we nearly did, there was an election, so we couldn't.'

I came to believe more and more that the real reason was different. She had, with her instinctive judgement of character, always recognized both the shallowness of Boothby and the steadfastness of Harold, and knew that, with her strength, she could have both. By not marrying Bob, she might miss the careless pleasure of a few years, but she would avoid the inevitable pain that his various instabilities would cause her. She might be furious with Harold for not being what she had hoped, a comfortable escape from her own domineering mother, but he would always stand by her.

Lady Dorothy's furies were dramatic, though seldom directed overtly at Harold himself. Carol as a child found her sticking pins into an effigy of old Mrs Macmillan. When the *Evening Standard* announced the sale of the American branch of Macmillan's for a million pounds, Boothby rang Lady Dorothy at Gosses, saying how nice it was to know that he would no longer have to pay off her overdraft, which he had often done when she had not dared to tell Harold about it. She never liked to be teased, though she laughed a lot at herself. In her rage, she ripped the telephone from the wall. It was not the first time. After that, we pinned the cord to the floor with three or four staples. She had the satisfaction of the tearing gesture without cutting us off completely.

In her determination to do what pleased her and do little that displeased her, she allowed her liking and disliking of people too free a rein, especially within her own family. She never really cared for Maurice, which was puzzling because he was affectionate, generous and intelligent. She liked Catherine better, but not much. They were both more like Harold in character and appearance; and appearance was always a matter of enormous importance to Lady Dorothy – good or bad looks, especially in a man, being the first thing she would mention about anyone. Carol was like Lady Dorothy, though lacking the full measure of her warmth and having a capacity for irritable boredom.

Lady Dorothy treated her two sons-in-law with reserve – Julian Amery because they had nothing in common and because he pontificated, talking all the time of politics. She did not like him, but was a little afraid that he might attack her in some way. In Julian Faber she recognized a dignity and quiet independence that she did not care to ruffle, and so approached him with wary affection. Her daughter-in-law, Katie, she loathed.

She contrived, over the years, somehow to create a barrier between Harold and his children, presenting him to them as someone who must be left in peace, as being too busy to be disturbed. He in turn was uncertain how to treat children and, as he did in public life, he assumed a persona which was unnatural and stilted and rather alarming to children.

This barrier became even more marked when the family moved back into Birch Grove. A wide corridor ran the full length of the house. Harold's sitting room was at one end, Lady Dorothy's at the other, separated from each other by a long drawing room which was virtually never used. In the evenings, after dinner, Harold would go off to his room to work or to read. The only members of the family to defy Lady Dorothy's unspoken ban on anyone's going to Harold's room were Maurice, hesitantly, and Julian Amery, who regarded the frivolities of Lady Dorothy's sitting room with condescension. Sometimes Harold would paddle with his shuffling slippered walk down the corridor and look in on the frenzied game of racing-demon at which all Cavendishes excel, a tentative smile on his lips, which meant that he had thought of some joke he was pleased with, in his hand a paper from the Ministry of Housing. The players would pause, impatient at the interruption.

'This poor fellow has a few acres about twenty miles from where he lives. He bicycles over and works the land. Often he is tired at the end of the day, so he has built a shack, where he keeps his tools, and sometimes he beds down there and saves the long ride home in the rain or whatever. Of course, the council have told him to pull it down, as he has no permission to build. No hope of permission either. So he's appealed to the Minister. I can't help him. I've put a note here. "Advise this man to buy a grouse moor. Then he'll be able to put up whatever he wants and no one will interfere."'

The players would raise a listless laugh and Harold would shuffle back down the corridor.

Harold's rather elaborate sense of humour was often a burden to Lady Dorothy, who enjoyed a more bubbling kind of laughter. Certainly when, needing to get in touch with someone, she cabled him in Africa: 'Have you got Mark's address?' she did not think it funny when he replied just, 'Yes.'

It was a wonder that his humour did not get him into more trouble, for he would forget all feeling for the sake of a joke. After one of the regular Commons debates on hanging, when he got home I asked how the vote had gone. He told me the figures and mentioned how various people had voted.

'Julian, of course, voted against – but then he has a vested interest in the question,' he added, with that tentative smile.

Julian Amery's brother had been hanged for treason during the war.

Somehow the shadow of Boothby hung over everything, although it may be that it seemed that way to me because of my involvement with Sarah. He wrote to Lady Dorothy almost every day, and she was always the first down for breakfast to snatch up the letter, lest Harold should see it. The quality of their relationship was still intense without, I imagined, its being passionate. She loved him deeply. When Lady Dorothy was in London, she usually stayed in one of the couriers' rooms in the Dorchester, for which she paid a pound a night. Occasionally, she would stay in Bob's flat in Eaton Square. Sometimes they would meet in Italy at a hotel on Lake Garda. Plainly he was devoted to her but treated her with cruelty. He had married, in an act of gracelessness, briefly, a Cavendish cousin of hers. He had also had another child by another woman.

Bob, who lived so much of his life in a cloud of self-aggrandizement, enjoyed the situation more and more as Harold's political importance grew. His feelings for Sarah were far less parental than he claimed, being prompted rather by a perverse pride in the scandal. At the same time, he was generous and good company if one could withstand the vainglory. He had a flamboyance so far removed from the modesty of my upbringing that I was dazzled. He used to take Sarah and myself to the opera, generally Wagner. He always had a box, so that when we got to those longueurs which bored him we could go out to have a glass of champagne and come back in time for the splendours.

Macmillan family life seemed at times to be like the Mazo de la Roche Whiteoaks sagas that Macmillan's published, or the kind of story that would now make a television soap opera. Maurice contested the 1951 election in Lincoln but his drinking was a disaster. Carol had another baby, Catherine had a miscarriage, Lady Dorothy crashed a car, and there were dramas such as that of Michael's suit.

Michael was Carol's oldest child, aged six. She and Lady Dorothy decided that he needed a dark-blue suit. It was not clear why, unless they thought it would enhance his already beautiful looks. Michael's father said that it was extravagant nonsense and forbade Carol to buy it. But here was something Lady Dorothy wanted. I am not sure who paid for it, but together Lady Dorothy and Carol bought the suit. They hung it in an upstairs cupboard. The children were sworn to secrecy. Inevitably, they told. For two weeks the topic lasted, Julian displaying dignified anger.

It was not all dramas or melodramas; there was a great deal of rural happiness. Lady Dorothy enjoyed point-to-points, and we spent many afternoons drinking cherry brandy in sickly quantities while Sarah lost money on the horses. One of the unexpected pleasures for me lay in the children. I had never known any since the time when I was a child myself. Sarah and her mother taught me to love them. Often there were expeditions and shooting parties and dances in the neighbourhood, but mostly we were happy to spend our weekends in indolent content. Gradually, I became a part of all this, until I felt that Birch Grove was my home. Then Sarah and I said we wanted to get married.

I do not think either of us really had any idea of what this meant, and I would suppose that few of our contemporaries, whose lavish weddings we attended, had any clearer notion of what they were attempting, but marriage was then more of an imperative.

Lady Dorothy wrote to me in late September 1950:

> I am afraid that I was very inarticulate and somewhat incoherent when we were talking the other evening and also left unsaid many things I meant to say. I have been thinking and thinking about you and Sarah, in fact seem to think of nothing else at the moment and feel it is perhaps better to put these things on paper. They may be rough but have got to be faced. I hate making people unhappy especially anyone one is fond of . . . one can't help being worried and rather unhappy because the prospects for you & Sarah don't seem very bright.
>
> In any case I don't think that Sarah is ready to get married to anyone . . . I know she's in love with you & is very *fond* of you & she's never been involved with anyone in quite the same way before . . .

Lady Dorothy continued with the sensible advice any mother would have given about money, and a firm, but particularly sympathetic, discussion of my disability and the burden it would place on any young girl. She asked that we should not be any more publicly engaged than we already were, and that we should wait.

> Don't hate me for saying all this please, and forgive me for seeming to think only of Sarah, but I love her more than anyone else in the world and having chosen to bring her into the world the way we did I feel a much greater responsibility for her than for any of the others . . . Let her have time . . . She's very young. Too young . . . to be tied down . . . Don't write unless you want to – but just let me know somehow if you can manage what I ask and that you understand.
>
> Yours ever
> Dorothy Macmillan
>
> P.S. I wanted to thank you for being so very kind and helpful. There's hardly anyone in the world that I talk to about Bob & Sarah & it was a great relief.

SARAH

Lady Dorothy need not have worried about Sarah's being tied down or her not experiencing enough of life. There were two strands to her complex character that made sure of that. The first was a desperate need to be liked, to be reassured that her illegitimacy, as she thought of it, did not matter. The second, which may have had its origins in the same cause, was a compulsive infidelity, not attributable to any kind of nymphomania, but more to an emotional nomadism, seeking fresh pastures. She would meet a new person and for some weeks be evasive about her movements and, as I later realized, inventive as well. At the time, my love was so blind, or possibly so selfish, that I refused to think that Sarah's feelings for me could be any other than she protested.

In December, Bob Boothby wrote:

When you said last night that Sarah's performance was unlike her, you were quite wrong.

It was entirely characteristic.

And what she did was rough.

She deliberately dined with Oliver Tetley at the Caprice restaurant, knowing that you were waiting for her alone at your flat; and at a certain stage of the evening, smitten either by an unusual pang of conscience or by something else, she got him to ring you up and tell you lies.

Now you do not do this sort of thing to someone you love – quite a lot of people don't do it to anyone. And I am going to tell you quite bluntly what it has been in my mind to say for some time – that she is not even remotely in love with you. Yesterday she thought she was in love with Andrew Heath. Today, for aught I know, she thinks she is in love with Oliver Tetley. And tomorrow . . .?

The truth of the matter is, of course, that at present she is in love only with herself. And if you persist in the delusion that she loves you, you are going to get badly hurt.

I don't want this to happen, because I am very fond of you; and apart from that, I hate seeing people hurt, especially by someone for whom I bear a measure of responsibility.

Do, for God's sake, chuck all this nonsense about being engaged. If you can only bring yourself to face what you know in your heart to be true, you will not only save yourself much agony of mind, but you will be able to be of real use to Sarah when – later on – she needs a true friend, as she will.

It doesn't require the sensitivity or penetration of a Proust to see into the heart of this girl; and I read her character like an open book. Not even the ghastly story unfolded to me this morning by my dentist, and – until lately – hers, caused me the faintest surprise . . .

Bob went on for pages with a mixture of sound advice and bombast. He was, in his terms, right, but he overestimated my good sense and underestimated Sarah's need for me as an anchor and her skill at manoeuvring me. On the same day, he wrote her a savage letter. Sarah dropped a reply at his flat, saying that neither of us wished to have anything more to do with him. He wrote again:

Dear Quentin,
  This is a rare bust-up.
  I am alone now, as I always feared I might be.
And can only echo, with Housman:

> 'The troubles of our proud and angry dust
> Are from eternity and shall not fail.
> Bear them we can, and if we can we must
> Shoulder the sky, my lad, and drink your ale.'

  In the crash of a civilization it is of no consequence to anyone but myself.
  But what I somewhat impetuously wrote, although purposely exaggerated and even distorted, was well-intentioned; and not without an element of truth. I was tired, and driven.

I wish you well.
Bob.

As the new year sped on a wavering course, Sarah's complexity grew and my folly deepened. There is so much that is confusing in a mad passion. I had believed that I was learning to understand my own nature, to know at bottom what was true and what was false; to recognize my motives, judging them a little less harshly, therefore allowing greater certainty. Later, I like to think, I got even better at it. But when I contemplate this period I, even now, feel sucked into the foaming whirlpool of emotion and unreason that hurled me round and round and from which there was no escape.

It became plainer and plainer that Sarah wanted something I could not give her. She sought a kind of wildness; she came to fear stability. Yet she could not quite cast off from the quayside. Her letters to me at that time spoke more and more of her need of me and less of how she loved me. The effect on me was to make my love more frantic. I can hardly believe the humiliations for which I offered myself up. Yet I could commit every one of those idiocies again. Then she wrote:

I am in love with Andrew. It is no good saying 'I'm sorry' obviously, but I am sorry for the suddenness of it. Please believe me, Quentin, had I known it was true all the times you questioned me about him, I would have told you. Perhaps it was true and I wouldn't admit it, even to myself . . . but I do mind doing this to you; so much I long to pretend, but I daren't.

I love you, Q, and in this way I always will . . . I have been happier during the last year and a half than ever before and it is all because of you. But this thing is new to me, and I can't just forget it.

And a few days later:

I have cried so much today I can neither think nor write properly . . . there are things I will never be able to do with anyone else in the world. I miss you – . . . I will never be so carefree or quite so happy again; because I can never forget you or what I must have done to your life.

For two or three weeks we did not see each other. I lived in a state of frenzy – crying to Lady Dorothy, abusing my friends in ways that I cannot really remember. A letter from Rosamond Lehmann gives a reflection of my state:

The awkwardness your disappearance caused me is infinitely negligible, so long as I can feel sure that my participation in your crisis plus my inability to do anything towards helping you resolve it have not caused you to turn against me. That would be so natural! Prolonged acute emotional tension operates in such unforeseeable ways. One tries to be prepared for that beforehand, but one never can put up any defences. Everybody closely involved becomes one more possible means of exposing oneself to suffering where one hoped to find relief, help, consolation. And in the end the vacuum becomes a temptation . . . I have had hideous experience of that state of trance you speak of, – it seems like possession by some daemonic force – and I dare say that is what it is. It works and destroys and finally wears itself out; but while it is in control it is a life-and-death struggle to counter it with love or faith. If one chooses not to give up – but if one's totally engaged, choice doesn't enter into it.

All I can tell you is that in the end one doesn't win *or* lose – one wins *and* loses. It is always oneself one saves or destroys, in the end. 'Il faut tenter de vivre.'

Possibly my derangement was not, in some ways, so great as I remember it. Earlier in the same letter Rosamond had written:

. . . you are one of the few people I know who seems whole emotionally, in the sense of not being split or self-destructive. I cherish and admire your

truth of feeling, maturity and generosity, more than I can say. I know you
are prepared, as I've always been and I suppose always will be, to go to the
very end to save or consolidate human relationships, so it is like finding a
kind of brother.

It may be that I had prepared some defences or that Rosamond's
estimation of my truth of feeling and the rest made me live up to it. I
did set out to preserve whatever might be saved of Sarah's and my
relationship.

A month later, Sarah said she was pregnant. It was July. Harold and
Lady Dorothy were due to go to Scotland. Bob was in Italy. He wrote:

> I am inclined to think that what has happened is the best thing that could
> have happened.
>
> Nature is sometimes cruel and sometimes merciful; but, when she
> intervenes directly in human affairs, the effect is decisive. As I see it, she
> has now said: 'Enough of this tom-foolery . . .'
>
> My gravest doubt is as to whether Andrew Heath is a strong enough
> character. That girl requires to be ridden on the curb, and no-one has yet
> done it – least of all, if I may say so, yourself . . . As for you, your eyes have
> at last been cleared of illusion; and, believe me, you will be better for it . . .
>
> I am glad you say you will do all you can for Dorothy. You will find that
> she is ready to play a fine part, as she always does in a crisis that is real . . .
>
> It is easier to deal with any given situation when there is no choice. There
> is only one thing to be done; and, as you truly say, everyone will have to
> make what they can of it.

My eyes had not been cleared of illusion, nor, in a sense, would they
ever be. There are aspects of love which other people can never guess
at. One of them, which Bob might have guessed at, had he understood
Sarah as well as he claimed, was that the child could just as well have
been mine as Andrew's.

It was not something I was going to tell Bob, Lady Dorothy or
anyone else. Sarah had decided that Andrew was the father. Even in
my turbulence, it seemed to me that a mother had a right to choose.

If Bob was wrong about me, he was even more mistaken about Lady
Dorothy. She saw the 'crisis' differently – as being a crisis for Harold.
The summer of 1951 was, politically, a period of excitement. The
country was facing one of its perennial economic disasters. It seemed
certain that Labour would have to call an election, and more than
probable that they would lose it. If the Conservatives won, Harold
would surely be offered an important job. Lady Dorothy decided that

nothing must be allowed to damage his prospects. She thought that Sarah's having a baby would be a threat; she must have an abortion.

At the time, abortions were legal if two psychiatrists could be found who would say that to have a baby was a grave risk to the mother's mental health. Given such a law, psychiatrists are easily come by. Nonetheless, there were endless delays. Sarah protested vehemently at first, but Lady Dorothy's insistence, coupled with her own perpetual sensation of guilt, induced by feeling that she was somehow an intruder, gradually wore down her resistance.

If the situation was to be kept from Harold, Lady Dorothy had to set off with him for their summer break as if nothing were happening. It was left to others to keep Sarah to her reluctant agreement.

Lady Dorothy wrote to me from the train to the north:

I do hope you won't say anything to Bob about any of the difficulties there have been. That would really make him angry. I simply said it was in Haire's [the gynaecologist's] hands. He'll quite likely switch round from having been violently anti Sarah to being violently pro so I don't think he need know, till later on, all about the pchycologists (that defeats me!) etc. I'd hoped it would all be over when I wrote to him next time. I shall leave dates vague and just say it has all been dealt with.

At last it was over. Lady Dorothy wrote:

We are *all* equally to blame but life is like that. It's a jigsaw puzzle and one has no idea that the things one is doing or the way one is behaving at a certain time will eventually produce a whole picture. The one we've all succeeded in making entirely against our wills has not on the whole been a very good picture. But that's now been taken to pieces, put away & will be entirely forgotten – except I'm afraid the hurt it has done to you. Now we've all got to start making another picture. We ought to know how to make a better one by now – but I don't expect we shall . . .

I had a *really* good letter from Sarah which has put my mind at rest about several things and I shall never mention any of this to her again.

Sarah wrote to me:

The baby has been taken away. No, no-one has failed anywhere, except me. And I; I have failed Mama, you, Andrew, and my child. . . . Oh Quentin, I killed it and I wanted it so much.

The threatened election took place. With three members of the family standing for parliamentary seats in different parts of the country, there was much to be done by way of canvassing, addressing envelopes, delivering pamphlets and all the menial tasks of the hustings. Sarah joined in with energy. When the election was over and the Conservatives had won and Churchill had given Harold the task of building three hundred thousand houses, life at Birch Grove resumed an easier course. Any recriminations were forgotten. Andrew Heath was working on the farm he had bought near Malmesbury and Sarah spent most of her time there. During the turmoil of the abortion, my relationship with Lady Dorothy had become closer and confiding, so it seemed natural that I should continue to spend most weekends at Birch Grove.

In the winter, Andrew fell ill with tuberculosis. He had to go into a sanitorium at Midhurst. Sarah came home and it was almost as if nothing had changed. But it had. Sarah's lark-like spirit was wounded; she had soared too high. I was still in love, sadder, if not wiser. In different ways, we needed each other and comforted each other. But, in the end, it was for me too painful.

Harold had sent me to his doctor, because my walking was getting worse. I fell down more and more and the knees of my trousers now looked like tea cosies and my ankles wept copiously. The doctor thought that my struggling on buses to work and the uphill walk each evening up the Haymarket was bad for me. I seized happily on this opinion and left my tedious job at the French Line.

In September 1952, I left for Italy. Lady Dorothy was in Scotland; she wrote:

I do wish I was at home to pack you up but I *hate* saying goodbye to people as you know and should only burst into tears . . . I shan't like coming home and not finding you there.

When I got to Italy, Sarah, who had come to London the night before I left and seen me off at Victoria, wrote:

For a mixture of happiness and misery your last night must hold the record for the past, and I think probably everything else that will happen as well.

CHAPTER EIGHT

AN ITALIAN APPRENTICESHIP

A memory comes late to me of a day in 1946, at Keats House in Hampstead, when I was to make an appeal for funds for the Keats–Shelley Memorial Association. I was nineteen, the newest member of the committee of this charity, which looks after the house in Rome where Keats died, and the poets' graves in the Protestant Cemetery. The first two speakers were John Masefield, the Poet Laureate, and Edmund Blunden. I had imagined that two such famous poets would illuminate some less understood aspects of the works of Keats and Shelley. I had learned by heart a speech of brisk practicality about roofs and damp courses and the ravages of war.

I listened, in despair, to Masefield and Blunden, neither of whom said a word about poetry, but talked about roofs and damp courses and of how the war came to Rome. From the platform, I looked down on expectant faces – Osbert Sitwell, Harold Nicolson, James Pope-Hennessy. I had nothing to say; the poets had said it all. A few days before, I had been moved by an account of Shelley's death, of his setting out to sail home to Lerici, of the burning of his body on the shore at Viareggio, of Trelawny's plucking his heart from the flames and of Mary's carrying the heart in a silken reticule till the day she died. In what I fancied was fine histrionic style, I launched into the tale, which was as familiar to my audience as 'Three Blind Mice'. I spun it out, wondering how on earth I was going to turn my irrelevant story into an appeal for funds. I could sense that they were wondering too. It was terrifying.

As I was on the verge of floundering, a ninety-year-old poetical baronet, Sir George Leveson-Gower, suffered a startling fit of incontinence. By the time everyone, including Sir George, had settled down again, my theme forgotten, it did not appear odd that I should quite simply ask the audience to give generously. I was never again so frightened of speaking in public.

Now, six years later, I came to live at Lerici. I was to read to Percy Lubbock, the author and literary critic, whose sight was dimmed to shadowy impressions. 'How did the man in St Mark know what trees looked like if he was blind?' Percy would ask. 'But that's how I see them – I see men as trees walking.'

The house lay a couple of miles to the south of the town. The way ran through groves of olive trees, casting their skimpy shade in speckled patterns on the dry brown grass of summer. The road rose and fell as it passed promontories jutting into a restless but friendly sea, wine-dark, as Homer had it, and trimmed with white where the waves broke on the rocks. Gli Scafari sat on one of these promontories, almost hidden from the road. In the next bay was a cluster of small houses belonging to fishermen whose boats were drawn up on a rare patch of sand or left to sway in the calm waters. Beyond that was a village, Tellaro, so steep that I never managed to get far down into it, certainly not to its tiny harbour. Not long before, the village had only been accessible by boat. There was little to draw anyone down this road before the days of the insatiable tourist.

The garden of Gli Scafari matched the near-wild feeling of the landscape. It was very English in its freedom – huge banks of mermaid roses, tumbling plumbago, a rhyncospermum climbing the yellow stucco of the house, its clean scent enhancing the whiteness of the flowers.

Percy's wife, Lady Sybil, had built the house in the 1930s. She was rich, the daughter of an Irish earl, the widow of an upper-class American. She had slipped into another marriage, been widowed again and then, for reasons too obscure to tax the imagination with, married Percy.

For a villa by the sea, in an unfashionable area, it was grand but without pretension. A wide marble staircase rose out of the plain, marble-floored hall. Off the hall were a large sitting room, a library and a dining room. Any formality had literally faded, as the covers on the chairs and the William Morris curtains wore thin and grew pale in the Mediterranean light. The great pleasure of the house was the wide loggia that ran most of the length of the front, overlooking the sea. Upstairs, Percy had a study and a bedroom. There were three or four guest bedrooms and a huge dark-blue room that felt cold and faintly sinister, despite a loggia matching the one on the ground floor; this had been Lady Sybil's. There was really no occasion ever to go in there, so there was nothing indoors or out to destroy the romantic image I had of Lerici from the days when I read of Shelley's sojourn there.

The front of the house looked out across the Gulf of Spezia to Porto Venere. I never supposed that the local legend that Byron had swum across the bay to the Cinque Terre had any substance in fact, but that he and Shelley were remembered even in myth by the locals was pleasing.

Often, Percy and I would sit on the loggia as the sun was setting. When it was gone, he would ask: 'Did you see the green flash?' The theory is that, for the briefest moment, owing to the curvature of the earth, the last of the sun reaches one's eye, for a brilliant second, through water. I never did see it. Not for certain, that is, but sometimes I would say: 'Yes, I think so.' At night, across the water, I would see the rising and falling lights of the fishing boats, drawing to them the still abundant mullet and sea bass, turbot and brill, until the growling of the waves sent me to sleep.

Unhappiness, it seems to me, has the edge over happiness in that it can endure for so much longer. Total happiness rarely survives for more than a fortnight. Happiness, on the other hand, is triumphant in the memory. After the first note of ebullience, prompted by the beauty of the place and the affinity, bred in childhood, that I have always felt with Italy, the letters that I wrote to Colin and to Lady Dorothy had a gloomy ring to them. Memory, allied with common sense, tells me that I was in many ways, even in most ways, unexpectedly happy.

Percy was unlike anyone I knew. He belonged to the same generation as my parents, yet his interest in young people and encouragement of them was so natural that he bridged the gap between us without my noticing that it had happened. It was not the same as it had been with John Hayward, who had revealed to me that adults had many of the same urges and vanities and feelings as I had. Percy was almost too fastidious, too unmalicious, but he had that quality of making one feel that one was a better or a more talented person than one had supposed. Perhaps he really made me better. He sought out my interests, even those that I had not known I had, and fostered them. He made me examine my opinions and hone them. He opened whole new areas to me, in the end to his disadvantage, giving a new direction to my life. In such circumstances, how can I have been, in truth, anything but happy?

My day of reading began immediately after breakfast. I went to Percy's sitting room. He sat in a small armchair. He was a big man, tall and imposing with a huge head, round as an orange, well covered by very straight grey hair which slicked close to his scalp. His face in the morning was overall a vigorous schoolboy pink. He wore a long Chinese robe, its brocade much patched, that fastened diagonally across his vast, indulgent stomach. His head leaned forward, tilted to one side as he held the envelopes of the day's post close to the thick lenses of his spectacles.

Until he knew me better and I had come to know his relations and friends, he struggled to read the letters himself. Over the months, he grew to have no secrets from me. After the correspondence, I read to him articles and stories from the Italian newspaper. Italian politics did not delay us much and, in any case, I had the choosing of which bits to read, preferring, for instance, a story of the *saponificatrice* that kept us amused for weeks, about a woman who murdered countless relations, friends and acquaintances and turned them into soap that she sold at modest prices.

Later in the morning, Percy came downstairs, dressed usually in a crumpled linen suit and tapping his way with a cane. I would read him articles from the *New Statesman* or reviews from the *Times Literary Supplement*. After lunch, Percy had a siesta. We would start reading again at about four in the afternoon. This was the time for history or for science, in particular for astronomy. Percy liked especially the works of Herbert Dingle, and a whole new world of black holes and whirling gases was revealed to me. Sometimes now, when new discoveries are made, I wish Percy were here to learn of them. He would have loved the thought of neutrinos tearing blithely through us and through the planet as if none of it existed.

Once astronomy destroyed a different interest. We were reading Laurens van der Post with enjoyment until we came to a passage in which he described lying under the African sky and seeing, I think, Aldebaran shining bright. Percy sat up.

'Orion over the Kalahari at that time of year. Nonsense. It is not possible. He's inventing. I won't hear another word.'

We would read until dinner. At six, the wine appeared – coarse white Elban wine – and we would drink, Percy's pink deepening as darkness fell to a rich brick red.

above) The family before I was born.
...t to right: Brian, Timmy, my Mother,
...h Colin on her lap, Shane, Terence,
...di, my Father.

...*ght)* As a child of two I had blond
...ls and the agility to climb into a cactus
...he Villa Igiea, Palermo.

...h Mlle Buricot and my mother (right)
...Palermo. The Marmon car, flying the
...sular Union flag, had a dickey in
...ich my father used to shut me up.

(Right) Playing my recorder on a better day at Drumore.

(Below) Drumore.

(Foot) Madeley Manor. One can see the house from the M6 on the left going north, soon after Keele service station.

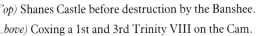

(Top) Shanes Castle before destruction by the Banshee.
(Above) Coxing a 1st and 3rd Trinity VIII on the Cam.
(Right) Colin served in the Irish Guards during the war, until taken prisoner.

Sarah Macmillan at a
Sussex point-to-point with
myself and Michael
Rutherstone.

(Right) Lady Dorothy
Macmillan. *Copyright
Popperfoto*; and *(far right)*
Rosamond Lehmann.
*Reproduced by kind
permission of Roland
Philipps.*

(Above) Percy Lubbock with Willy Mostyn-Owen on the loggia at Lerici.

(Above) Bernard Berenson. *Copyright Popperfoto.*

(Left) Sir Harold Acton at home, with his Donatello relief. *Copyright Christian Banfield.*

(Left) Lord Beaverbrook with his grand-daughter, Lady Jeanne Campbell. *Copyright Express Newspapers.*

(Below) Professor Derek Jackson F.R.S.

Engagement party at Londonderry House, 1956

(Below) A general party scene, including Tom Wiseman, Venetia Murray, Robin Warrender, Anne Massingberd-Munday, Margaret Philipps, Robin Fedden and Timothy Jones.

Dancing with Martha. Bare feet made it easier to balance, but it was the last time I ever danced.

Right) Mark Boxer, Ingrid Guinness and ny brother Colin. *(Below)* Antonia Fraser,)sbert Lancaster, Jane Sheffield and)celyn Stevens, Henrietta Crawley, Evelyn Lothschild, and Billy Kaye.

(Right) Moku Yanagawa, the young man who taught me Japanese; and *(far right)* Shigeo Imamura, the reprieved Kamikaze pilot.

(Above) Martha, with Sebastian and Sabrina.

(Left) Beatrix Miller, the most civilised editor I ever worked for. *Reproduced by kind permission of Beatrix Miller.*

After dinner we read fiction, usually classics. With consistent reading, even aloud, it is surprising how many books flow by. It is hard to recall what we read – all of Jane Austen, much of Tolstoy, *Vanity Fair*, Hardy (rather grudgingly on Percy's part), no Dickens. Of course, we read Henry James, for Percy as a young man had been his amanuensis. He used James to illustrate so much of what he was, by stealth, teaching me about writing and, above all, fiction.

After writing *The Craft of Fiction*, still probably the best book on its subject, Percy had wearied of novels. It may also be that the failure of his only novel, *The Regent Cloud*, depressed his interest. He knew it was a bad book. 'Don't bother to read it, but you must admire the title.' He had read practically no novels since the early 1920s. I decided that this was absurd and insisted on reading a selection of later books. He was determined not to enjoy them. What he did enjoy was pointing out the flaws in Hemingway, Graham Greene or Scott Fitzgerald. Some authors he managed to destroy for me, for instance Aldous Huxley. Others, like William Faulkner, he sat through in silence, which I took to be qualified admiration. Curiously, considering Henry James, he seemed more prejudiced against American writers. He spoke well of E. M. Forster, but he was roused to fury by Carson McCullers, complaining unreasonably, I thought, in view of what he had taught me, of the subject matter. There came a day when I was cross with him for what I felt was his intransigence. I decided to punish him and told him that I was going to read him a really new book. I was sure that he would detest it.

'How does it start?' Percy demanded, polishing his sarcasm. 'With a conversation? Or with a description of the way up to a house?'

I couldn't see why either of these was impermissible.

'It starts like this: *If you really want to hear about it, the first thing you'll probably want to know is where I was born, and what my lousy childhood was like, and how my parents were occupied and all before they had me, and all that David Copperfield kind of crap, but I don't feel like going into it.*'

After five or six pages, 'Stop.' Percy poured another glass of dark-yellow wine. 'You know what? This is a real book. Let's go on.'

We finished the whole of *The Catcher in the Rye* that night and went happy to bed at three in the morning, no longer at odds.

On occasions, I used to read for eight or ten hours a day. It became so automatic that, when bored by something, I could read on with perfect inflection while thinking about other things, quite removed.

'I can't agree with that, what do you think?' Percy would ask, and I would have to admit that I was not listening.

When not reading, we talked endlessly, but not really in any way that I was accustomed to. We exchanged experiences; his always by allusion, mine with the narrative gush of gossip, until I learned to moderate the abruptness which offended his sensibilities. He showed me how little, when people are in tune, needs to be said. He paid such attention to the exactness of a phrase, to the precise quality of a chosen word, that I had almost to learn a new language.

Some areas were forbidden. Even when I had become more skilled at the oblique methods of conversation, I could never learn anything of Lady Sybil. He spoke of her with something like detached worship, but I concluded, as I found his dependence upon myself growing, that there was in him a streak of masochism. From other people's accounts, she was odious, using him and tormenting him without mercy. When he had friends to stay, she would go to bed early, pleading a headache. Percy and his companions would sit smoking on the loggia until Lady Sybil sent her lady's maid, Edmonds, to complain that the smoke from their cigars was wafting up and into her bedroom, worsening her headache.

Life at Lerici was very far from dull. Percy had a good sense of humour and he had a storehouse of anecdotes; but as with everything else they were brought out usually to make a point.

When warning once about the dangers of reported speech with the tone unheard, he told of going to the music hall in Windsor with Henry James and their being taken backstage to meet the chorus girls. Later, someone asked Henry James what he had thought of them.

'One of the poor wantons was not wholly lacking in a certain cadaverous charm.'

The flavour, Percy pointed out, would have been very different if one had not heard in his voice that he was joking.

Talking of observation, he told me how Edith Wharton had come to write the two books he considered her most interesting – *Ethan Frome* and *Summer*. Her car broke down in a small village in Vermont. She had to wait all day for it to be repaired. The only warm place was the public library and Mrs Wharton sat there. It was a good meeting place for a chat and no one paid much attention to a woman sitting reading. From the gossip that she overheard, Mrs Wharton built two novels of amazing power and verisimilitude, far removed from the fashionable world that she lived in and that formed the base of all her other novels. Percy's politics hovered near the comic. He believed himself to be a Communist, though anxious to point out not a Stalinist, while he was, in nearly all that he expressed, manifestly an ordinary liberal. He did not mind being teased about this, but became indignant when people doubted his beliefs, asking how he could justify living in such comfort if his opinions were so radical. He pointed out that his inability to live according to the principles that he professed did not mean that the principles were wrong, rather that he was weak. Had he had a vote, he would unquestionably have voted against his own selfish interests. He was amused by how many people were unable to grasp this concept.

With the people who worked for him, Percy was certainly true to his principles. Mario, the cook, was allowed to get away with shameless fudging of the accounts. Maids came and went, their length of stay depending on how much they enjoyed sitting on Mario's knee. Andrea, the gardener, I am sure sold any produce he grew in the *poderi*, while Percy helped with the upbringing of Andrea's beautiful son, Clemente.

There was also Edmonds, the one who had been Lady Sybil's lady's maid. She was one of those sad, elderly, dispossessed people of whom there were many at that time, who had come out to Italy or France or wherever, full of hope, to look after their employer and then had got stuck. Never having met the *principe azzurro* of their romantic dreams, they stayed unmarried. Their families at home died off. All they could do was hang on. Not surprisingly, Edmonds had become a woman of sour disposition, which she concealed behind an unctuous manner. Her hair was coiffed in an Edwardian style, and her dark print frocks hung thin and loose from her crabbed shoulders, her feet wobbled loosely at the ends of her legs, as if held firm only by rubber bands. She regarded everyone as a trespasser – new guests on the memories of earlier days; the servants on her domain.

She busied about, snooping into everything, sneaking on the maids and Mario, stirring trouble wherever she could. She exasperated me. She even appeared to be becoming rather dotty. When Rosamond came to stay, Edmonds resented her glamour and the interest she inspired in Percy. One of Rosamond's rings disappeared. She was certain that Edmonds had taken it. Percy was patient and kind with her. In a phrase I have often since used to myself, he reproved my intolerance – 'You cannot put a quart into a pint pot.'

Willy Mostyn-Owen was living in Florence studying under Bernard Berenson. He had taken me once to I Tatti, Berenson's villa at Settignano, just outside Florence. The visit had disappointed me. Berenson was not there, and I had been taken around by adoring acolytes of the great art historian. They rehearsed every minute of his day.

'This is where B.B. sits in the morning. You see, his rubber cushion is waiting for him . . . After lunch B.B. takes a walk, he is so brave and we worry as his shoes are not strong like your English shoes . . . B.B. speaks Russian, English, French, Italian, German and understands so many more . . . In the evening we listen to what B.B. has to say . . .'

In the end, I quite disliked the idea of this pampered old man.

On our first visit to Florence, Percy and I went to dinner at I Tatti. We assembled in a sitting room of no great grandeur. A Sassetta of St Francis hung on the wall and a fifteenth-century Annunciation, attributed to no particular artist but of memorable beauty, on another. In the middle of the room was a large, square table covered with magazines and journals in many different languages.

Berenson appeared, a diminutive figure with a faintly rabbinical look. He went straight to the table and started to leaf through a journal, ignoring his guests.

'B.B., I don't think you have met Quentin,' said Willy.

'I'll meet him all in good time,' said B.B. and he went on reading.

After a while, he melted – greeting Percy and being introduced to me. At dinner, for some reason, Willy and I sat on either side of Berenson while Percy was some way down the long table. At first, B.B. made general conversation.

'Percy, I did not invite Harold Acton tonight, because I know you don't like him.'

A splutter came from Percy, in protest at so direct an assertion.

'Is it because he is effeminate that you do not care for him?'

A further expostulation satisfied B.B. for the moment. He even soothed the tension by saying in tones of convincing admiration:

'You know, Percy, when I think of how you stay nearly all the year on your lonely peninsula, I do not envy you your life, but I do envy you your ability to live it.'

Then he turned to ask me how I found life on the lonely peninsula. It happened that at that moment the butler, Vittorio, brought the vegetables to Berenson's left. Intent on what he was saying to me, he did not see Vittorio, who stood waiting for long minutes. After a time, Willy could not bear it. He spoke to Berenson, who looked round, saw the vegetables and helped himself. Then he said: 'Willy, another time, if you have nothing better than that to say, please do not interrupt.'

He resumed talking to me. 'I am so glad that you came today. This morning I took a walk through the olive groves that I have not taken for twenty years. The last time I took that walk was with your mother.'

I was touched, and B.B. went on to charm me that evening and, on other occasions, to give me pleasure of a singular kind. There was never anyone (with the exception of John Berger, who guided one sometimes for the wrong reasons) who could so illuminate a painting for me that I felt I could understand, to their full depth, the purpose and the inspiration of the artist. The suggestion that he was a fraud is, I think, absurd.

He was a conjurer but not a charlatan. On a later visit, I sat next to him at lunch. That day he was teasing Mary McCarthy, who had just brought out a forthright feminist book. He had invited her to visit him after reading a chapter of it in a review. He met her in Venice and, she told me, as she stepped out of the launch he greeted her with a whisper:

'And, Miss McCarthy, have you brought your pessary with you?'

He continued the joke a little more gently in public. To me, he said: 'This morning I took a walk through the olive groves that I have not taken . . .'

At first I was shocked, even angry. Then I realized that he had hit upon a way of pleasing me and had forgotten, at the age of ninety, that he had used it before.

The accusation that he plotted with Lord Duveen to use his reputation to sell falsely attributed paintings was possibly prompted by envy that a man should use his academic skills to make money. There was really no need to cheat, there were still at the time of their collaboration so many wonderful paintings awaiting discovery.

Sir Harold Acton put it to me not long ago that 'it was an anti-Jew thing – Berenson was a Jew and so was Duveen. Berenson was honest, and why should he not make money? Brought up in the ghetto in Riga, wouldn't you want to make sure that you never went back?'

More astonishing, to my mind, is how few wrong attributions he made in the days before scientific tests of all sorts, when an expert had to rely only on his eye, careful research and his experience. Nor did Berenson claim infallibility. Asked, in a court case, why he now said a painting was by Titian which he had before said was by Giorgione, he answered: 'I never stand by my mistakes.'

Percy was happier in Florence with a few, more sedate friends and was always glad to get back to his lonely peninsula. To me the city was fascinating both for its beauty and for the variety of life there, mostly found for me by Willy.

There were echoes of the kind of Florence that E. M. Forster wrote about. There was still a large British colony that mixed rather little with the Florentines, several of them relics of the days when it was possible to live more comfortably in Italy than in England on a small income.

Reggie Temple was a very small person, who lived in an apartment not far from the Arno. He was scrupulously neat and his shoes were as highly polished as the little varnished boxes he used to make to supplement his pension.

Reggie had been an actor and had trained, in the 1890s, at Sarah Thorne's academy in Chatham. He used to describe the involvement of the audience at a level that I found hard to believe until years later when I saw a Masai warrior throw a spear through a cinema screen, aiming at a Red Indian creeping up behind John Wayne.

If Reggie were playing the part of a pauper, he would get offers from women to do his mending, and if the part of a villain, he would be showered with rotten eggs and vegetables. For the most part, the plays were absurd melodramas, made even more ridiculous by the improbable casting of the diminutive Reggie opposite Constance Collier, an overwhelmingly large actress, who went on to achieve great fame. Reggie, standing on a step to make him look taller, would have to address her as 'Thou cast-off plaything of an idle hour'.

His favourite play was one in which he had to stalk on to the stage, looking nervously around, and deliver the opening line: 'Here I am in this wood, with £40,000 disposed about my person. What would my mother and father up at the Hall say if they could see me now?'

Reggie's life was almost a symbol to me of how I did not want to end up. He had had an existence full of fun and entertainment. He was amusing, and it was a pleasure to go to see him and to hear stories of what, he said, were the grand days of the theatre. I was, on the other hand, made miserable by the effort to maintain a standard of gentility, by the feeling that nothing was as good as it used to be, that the world was on a downward course, that the only things worth living for were memories, represented by the nostalgic varnished boxes. I would always want to believe that the world was getting better.

At the opposite end of the scale from Reggie, both in fortune and in outlook, was Harold Acton. I had naturally heard of Harold, if only as the original, or at any rate substantial part of the character of Anthony Blanche in *Brideshead Revisited*. He was spoken of by many people as a disappointment, having been considered among such contemporaries at Oxford as Evelyn Waugh, Cyril Connolly and Raymond Mortimer as the one with the most promise, but having never fulfilled it.

He is in fact a brilliant historian. One might wish, perhaps, that he had turned his talent and his harmonious prose to broader, more familiar subjects than the Neapolitan Bourbons, but he is a Cellini crafting a jewelled, delicate masterpiece, rather than a Rubens, splashing a huge canvas.

But I knew none of that and was both terrified and mesmerized when Willy first took me to lunch. Everything was imposing. The high iron gate swung open and the drive, lined by dark cypresses, stretched straight for a quarter of a mile, dipping then rising, like a study in perspective, to the solid block of the sixteenth-century Villa la Pietra.

A white-coated butler and footman ushered us into the dark interior, through the domed stair hall, frescoed with nymphs and peopled with statues, and on into a large sitting room, cluttered with velvet-covered chairs, still dim but not unfriendly.

I was prepared for Harold's manner, for Willy had imitated almost too well the carefully enunciated speech, each syllable being given an exaggerated emphasis, so that it sounded nearly like a foreign accent – and yet it didn't. It was not camp; it owed nothing to anyone else. It was his and nobody else's way of speaking, slow usually but capable of little darts of wit slipped into the narrowest gaps. The timing of each minutely chiselled sentence was exquisite.

Willy had captured the tilting of the head, the slight leaning forward, but he had overlooked the curious walk with the toes pointing out so that it became a waddle, and, fortunately, the sheer impact of Harold's courtesy, that stilled any temptation to laugh.

Harold's mother was a surprise. She was an American, short and not very striking, except that her make-up was laid on to such a thickness that it was risky for her to smile lest it should crack. So she did not smile. That she was a woman of prodigious self-control I knew from the stories of her arrest during the war. When America joined in, she was taken to the police station for questioning. They kept her for forty-eight hours, shut up with prostitutes and thieves. Never once during that time did she take off her gloves. She never ate, she never peed. She just sat.

That day of my first visit, Mrs Acton made the cocktails – socking dry martinis. It was difficult to sort out what I had heard of the Actons from the highly civilized, very formal atmosphere at lunch. I watched as Harold choreographed the conversation. It was beautifully done. Only very occasionally, in response to some slipshod thought, did he allow himself a mannerly, but deadly, shaft of demolition.

Lurking in his eye, one could tell, was a measure of good-humoured mischief, but not much of the Anthony Blanche extravagance. Was it true that during the war in the Air Force he had been transferred for turning to his commanding officer's wife and saying to her: 'Aha, Mrs Robinson, with those ruby-red lips of yours you could conquer any man'? And on arriving at his new post that he was greeted by the general with 'Acton, you don't look to me like the sort of man who, if his lorry broke down, could get underneath it and do things'? And that his reply, in tones of precision, was: 'That, General, very much depends who with'?

After lunch as we went round the garden, the air filled with the scent of *oleo fragrans*, and we looked at the statues. Harold, now unrestrained by the presence of his mother, became a little racier, telling stories of his days in Peking, of opium and stranger indulgences. We came to a figure of a satyr chained to a rock.

'You know, my dear, I sometimes feel a little like a chained satyr myself.'

How different it was with Mrs Trefusis. She was the daughter of the beautiful and cultivated Mrs Keppel, the last mistress of King Edward VII. Violet liked people to think that she was his daughter. But she wasn't; her mother's affair with the King had not begun when she was born. Her own affair with Vita Sackville-West had, on the other hand, given Violet a certain notoriety.

'It will be rather a grand dinner, there will be royalty,' she said in lofty tones on the telephone.

I protested that I had no dinner jacket.

'Never mind, they are not fussy royalty.'

As well they might not have been, as it turned out to be someone called the Archduke Robert of Austria.

My memory of that particular evening is of a mixture of beauty and farce. Violet's villa at Bellosguardo lay in the hills to the south of Florence. It was in that house that Galileo worked three hundred and fifty years ago to prove that the earth moved round the sun. So many interesting people had lived in the Villa Ombrellino – Florence Nightingale, the Brownings, James Fennimore Cooper, Nathaniel Hawthorne, Henry James, Ouida and many others. Everything in the house was in perfect taste, except the hostess.

The evening was still and warm. It was a fairy-tale delight to wander out among the statues on the terrace, to look over the perfect view of Florence by moonlight – the dome of the cathedral and Giotto's tower proud above the silvered red roofs of the city, the Arno threading through, bordered by great palaces, the Ponte Vecchio a glowing band across the river.

Violet was dressed in billowing orange. Her shoulders were bare except for a light chiffon scarf. She was an ugly woman, her face like an inflated prune, yet she had an air of command.

There was at the dinner a good-looking young man of about my age. Violet fastened her interest on him. Some time after dinner, she led him to the further end of the terrace. She peeled back her scarf and, in her husky voice said: 'You may bite my shoulder.'

Hugh Whitaker was the uncle of my brother Terence's wife, Jean, but she hardly knew him for he was the black, albeit rich, sheep of the family. It was another nephew of his who proposed that we should meet. Mr Whitaker wrote to me in Lerici and invited me to stay at his villa in San Domenico, just outside Florence, adding that he might be able to help with my health.

I wrote saying that, as I made few visits to Florence, I wanted, when I did come, to see as many people as possible and that I would not like to treat him as an hotel. He wrote again to say that that would be quite all right and that I would be free to come and go as I pleased. I made another attempt, suggesting that my disability might make it difficult if there were many stairs. He insisted; and I went.

Mr Whitaker was waiting in the hall. He was a towering man, well over six feet, and not thin. He whined a greeting in a surprisingly high voice. Then he stood, looking me up and down, saying nothing. To cushion the moment, I remarked on the four eighteenth-century portraits of extremely pretty girls. Were they French?

'They are not girls, they are boys,' Whitaker said with squeaky

95

satisfaction. The only other portrait was of my host when young – a full-length in an arrogant pose, with a long riding whip.

The house was vast and steep with stairs. My room was on the second floor, but Whitaker summoned three handsome young footmen to carry me up the broad stone stairway.

At dinner, Whitaker wasted little time on small talk about his niece Jean or his nephew. He announced: 'I shall cure you and you will walk. You must take one of these three times a day and you must eat exactly what I say and do what I say.'

He produced a box of enormous, torpedo-shaped pills of a nasty grey colour. He had had them made especially, according to the prescription which had been 'revealed' to him. One of the footmen brought me the box.

'Take one now,' said Whitaker. He gazed at me, his pale-blue eyes unblinking chips set in his pudgy face. The table was long and we sat at opposite ends in high-backed Florentine leather chairs. The room was lit only with candles. Even those fixed eyes could not be sure whether I had really put one of the huge pills into my mouth. I spoke thickly for a moment, made a gulping noise and finished with a clear 'Ah' of triumph. It was a charade at which I became skilled over the next days.

Below the dining room was a crypt. After dinner, Whitaker told me to go down and to wait there. The minute chapel had three pews and an altar. Two tall lighted candles stood on the altar. A narrow beam of electric light shone to one side. To the other side was a door. I sat in the middle pew and waited, wondering why I had ever got myself into all this.

Whitaker came into the chapel from the door on the left of the altar. He wore a resplendent cape of red velvet covered in gold filigree. He had an air of majesty. He stood to the right so that the thin shaft of the spotlight fell exactly on to an exercise book from which he began to read in questions and answers. His shrill voice assumed a clerical lilt.

'Tell me, Master, what didst thou mean when thou saidst, "Render unto Caesar that which is Caesar's"?'

Whitaker's voice shifted down a semitone.

'My son, you tell me what you think I meant.'

From where I sat, I could see into the exercise book. The questions were in blue ink on the left-hand page, the Master's answers were on the right in red ink, albeit in the same handwriting. A long, muddled reading followed, from the blue side.

Then, from the red: 'Well done, my beloved son, no man before has ever understood so well my meaning.'

When it was over, the beautiful youths carried me up to my bedroom. I locked the door and slept uneasily.

For the sake of politeness, I spent far more time at the villa than I wanted to. Whitaker told me at length about the place he had on Elba that he was turning into a rest home for tired statesmen. When the burdens of office became too great, the leaders of the world would go there for a few days to relax. There they would meet other politicians all in a carefree mood, so that they would solve all world problems while, in effect, being on holiday. Whitaker subjected me to more readings in the chapel and many severe quizzings as to whether I had strayed, sinful, from the prescribed diet. I lied respectfully. On the fourth afternoon, I met, by chance, some friends from Rome. They were having a party. I telephoned to say that I would not, after all, be in for dinner that night.

When I got back, not very late, the drive gate was locked. At last, I roused the gatekeeper. The house was dark. Only a lantern burned in the hall. Beside it was a letter:

The Corsini rang up to say . . . would you dine with her tomorrow, or else lunch on Friday?

I feel sure therefore that you will be able to keep these engagements more easily if you are staying in town. So I will send you down in the car in time for lunch tomorrow.

I had hoped to be able to help you with your trouble, but see that is now impossible . . .

I had to clamber up the stairs alone; but I slept peacefully.

I did not see him in the morning, but he pursued me to the hotel with another letter.

My brother in Christ,

. . . I wanted to put my powers of Healing at your disposal. But evidently this was completely misunderstood, though, as you saw, I had special remedies prepared for you, which, if you had taken regularly, would have completely healed you. This was certain, as I had worse cases than yours.

So, naturally, as you showed that the social side of life appeals more to you than the complete recovery of your health, I could only facilitate you in this choice by arranging for you to stay in the centre of these activities.

Yours sincerely
Hugh Whitaker.

As it happened, a little light healing might have been useful. My walking was getting worse. I took no exercise, because the way down to the sea was precipitous and rocky – I had to be carried and there was no one to do this, and for swimming I really needed two people to get me in and out of the water. I could not reach the road as the drive was too steep for me to walk up. I ate a good deal and the Elban wine, I dare say, took its toll.

The doctor who came from Florence to see Percy was inevitably unable to help. He was obsessed with sex and had somewhere gained the impression that orgasms were especially tiring to muscular dystrophy sufferers. He questioned me closely as to whether this supposed exhaustion was greater or less after real love-making or after masturbation. He wanted to enquire further as to whether I thought there would be a difference in fatigue between heterosexual and homosexual affairs. At this point I allowed my Italian to fail me.

In revenge for this pauciloquence, he prescribed a rigid diet and banned alcohol. Percy, on the other hand, arranged for a car to pick me up every day and take me to a point on the road from which it was all downhill on the way back to the house.

I think it likely that the deterioration was due as much to restlessness as to any other cause. As the months passed, I found Gli Scafari more and more claustrophobic. Percy encouraged and inspired me, but the more I responded, the more possessive he became. The pleasure that my being an excellent pupil gave him made me half-afraid that I would end up like Tony Last in *A Handful of Dust*, reading in Amazonas to Mr Todd, unable ever to escape.

I came also to dislike my power over Percy. There is something intensely disagreeable about being loved too much, especially if one is fond of the admirer. The temptation is to see how far one can push it. I could make him do things that I knew he did not like doing. For instance, Willy and I forced him to take us on a visit to Max Beerbohm in Rapallo.

For Willy and myself it was an interesting occasion. It was mystifying that so fastidious a person could live in such a horrible house, literally on the main road, so that when the BBC had been the week before to record one of his soft, nostalgic discourses, they had to hang blankets all round the room to deaden the noise of the traffic. Sir Max produced for us his copy of Queen Victoria's *Leaves from my Highland Notebook*, which he had improved by adding to the drawings and by writing extra captions in a skilful imitation of the Queen's handwriting. He had put a cross on an oak tree in a picture of a wooded glade. Under it he had written: 'This was my favourite tree, alas now cut down. But I have by me as I write some chips from its bark, painted black, which are a *great* solace to me.' Sir Max was a performer and we laughed a lot.

The two old men hardly spoke to each other. Sir Max, Percy and Berenson were staging posts on a kind of intellectual sightseeing tour. People coming to Italy in the summer would call on each of them in turn, and there grew to be a measure of rivalry between the three. Each was at his best on his home ground. Percy hated the whole outing, and I felt ashamed of the unkindness on my part in having taken advantage of Percy's affection for me. It was the element of desperation in that affection that goaded me.

Percy would promise to leave me Henry James's gold watch, or at any other times a Tang figure of a horseman. I suppose he felt my wriggling in his grasp. Unfortunately, from his point of view, he had shown me a new possibility.

He had been asked by the *Times Literary Supplement* to review some books on the novel. He refused, but recommended that I should do them instead. The editor accepted this idea and I wrote my first published article. I had already started to write some short stories and even embarked on a novel, though that never progressed much beyond five thousand words. Other reviews followed and I decided that I wanted to be a writer.

I did not have such confidence in my choice of career that I gave any thought to the idea of leaving Percy at once. I had, after all, wanted to be a sailor, an actor, a barrister, a bookseller, an antique dealer, even an MP, and not much had come of those ambitions. There was no reason to suppose that my latest enthusiasm would endure.

When Lady Dorothy suggested that I come home for the Coronation in 1953, I went, with every intention of returning and, come to that, having given sworn promises that I would come back in a month.

CHAPTER NINE

FIRST STEPS IN FLEET STREET

Harold Macmillan had written:

> Your room is ready and you will not find things much changed . . . the
> pheasants turned out pretty well. Life goes on – but it will be more
> agreeable still when you rejoin.

Lady Dorothy had written many letters, telling me news of all the
family and other pieces of gossip. Her sister-in-law, Mary, Duchess of
Devonshire, was

> . . . very nervous about being able to manage the Coronation as it is such a
> long stand, and she has to kneel with nothing in front of her for a long time
> too, and her robes are very heavy. As she is 'Gone' in the feet, the back, the
> knees and the tummy, and her shoulders ache anyway, it is going to be
> rather a trial. Anyway the Queen's butler used to be our pantry boy, so he is
> going to be asked to give Moucher Coca Cola, which is the only thing that
> revives her. It somehow seems rather inappropriate for a Coronation. My
> Mother [the Dowager Duchess of Devonshire] is now furious because as
> Queen Mary is not going, her Ladies were not either, and now Old Lady
> Airlie wants to go as a Member of some order to which my Mother also
> belongs, and she never thought of it . . . Did I tell you we had the Eden's
> for a Sunday. It was so funny. Mrs E. quite obviously did not like us and
> was bored to tears, and we did not know how to get on with her. He was all
> right and fairly easy.

I got back in time to go to the Coronation Ball at Hampton Court
with Lady Dorothy, and I watched the Coronation procession from
Harold's flat in Piccadilly. It was so easy, and indeed agreeable, to slip
back into life at Birch Grove. Harold gave me his wartime diaries to

read. Lady Dorothy and I found that, through our correspondence, we had formed a closer kind of relationship, in which she treated me as a cross between a favourite son and a fellow conspirator or perhaps confessor. She would in the mornings come and sit on the end of my bath and chat. She loved sleeping out on the terrace and sometimes dragged another bed out for me to sleep on, and she would talk long into the night – often about Bob and about Harold.

Sometimes I was uneasy about the amount of trust that she placed in me. She asked me to sort out a chest of drawers that sat in her sitting room, full of letters. There were none of Bob's; those, I think, she destroyed. But there were several of such intimate pain from Harold that she should never have allowed anyone to see them. There was a quality of ruthless innocence about Lady Dorothy. The letters had evidently not moved her. So she could not see why they mattered – yet she had not thrown them away. (They did, incidentally, contradict with finality any nonsense about Harold's being homosexual.)

Sarah was mostly away, living with Andrew on his farm. They were at last to be married in July and we all arrived at a *modus vivendi*. It promised to be a lazy summer before I returned to Lerici.

Then Bob asked me to lunch in his flat. The only other guest was John Junor, a restless red-faced Scot, who looked too hot in a suit. He had an easily dazzled naivety that would one day turn into a studiously homespun spade-calling prudery. He had just been made deputy editor of the *Evening Standard*.

When he asked what I did, I mentioned my reviews for the *Times Literary Supplement*. John was impressed. 'I could na' do that.' He asked if I would write for the *Standard*. I hesitated. I don't know what Bob had told him, but he was very persistent. 'At least come to see me in my office.'

Of course, I went. Fleet Street at that time was still rich and whimsical in the style of *Scoop*. John believed that Prince Rainier was about to hand over his principality of Monaco, or at any rate the port, to Aristotle Onassis, who would turn Monte Carlo into a Mediterranean Liverpool.

I spoke French, I knew Monte Carlo, I was the man to bring back the story. So John said. It would only take a day or two. Then I could go back to Italy if I wanted to. As surprised as William Boot, I found myself on an aeroplane to Nice.

Naturally, I had not the faintest notion of how to conduct such an investigation. As far as I remember, I resorted to the ruse of telling

101

everyone I met, shopkeepers, taximen, croupiers, that what John had heard was in fact about to happen. Their reactions were spirited.

Back in London, I was given a desk in the *Evening Standard* office next to a portly man with a sympathetic, unselfish nature. John Clarke wrote a daily Court Casebook, vivid vignettes of cases in the magistrates' courts.

He looked at what I was writing and gave me my first lesson in popular journalism.

'Go twice as far as you think the farthest barrier is. Embarrass yourself thoroughly and you may get somewhere near what they want.'

His own writing was far from florid, but he knew that mine would be impossibly chaste for a melodramatic article of this kind, with no substance to support it. Grateful for his advice, I added phrases about my footsteps echoing in the parqueted halls of the deserted casinos and some lively sooth about the clanking chains and oath-filled cries of the teeming stevedores soon to flood the former haven of the great playboys of the world. They printed it.

John Junor then offered me a job as a leader writer. I refused on the grounds of my promises to return to Percy. My refusal urged John on. He could not believe that anyone could turn down such a chance. He offered me more money – £15 a week. I gave in. I forgot easily all the things the doctors had said before I left the French Line. The fact was that I had been excited by the days when I was working on the Monte Carlo article.

My conscience troubled me and Percy knew exactly how to pluck its strings.

Aug 13

My dear dear Quentin

I know well that it cost you not a little to write that letter (I had it yesterday evening) – and you know well that it cost me no less to read it – so we utterly understand each other – and this is really and truly and essentially what matters. I feel this very strongly.

More than this I can't write now – for thoughts and feelings churn too deeply – though with nothing in any of them that is not understanding and affection – mind that.

I shall write again soon – and you will write to me . . . I will only think that we each gave the other something while you were here – and something that neither of us will forget.

We do understand each other very well, don't we? – and ever shall.

Your Percy

He wrote often, struggling with his wandering pencil, and it was two or three years before the always denied note of reproach faded from his letters. But he was right that I would never forget, and even now I still refer some problems to the memory of his judgement.

I crushed my conscience because for the first time, at the age of twenty-six, I had a job that I really enjoyed. I was fascinated by Fleet Street, or rather, Shoe Lane, where the *Evening Standard* lurked in a shabby old building.

The editorial department was on the second floor in a huge, crowded room filled with ugly desks in jumbled rows. There were windows on two sides of the room, but they were not for looking out. One side faced a blackened brick building thirty feet away; the other a murky street. They let in a filtered, fuzzy grey light. Telephone wires trailed from the ceiling on to the desks, where the telephones sat next to typewriters that looked ancient even then, sturdy relics from before the war. There were only two enclosed offices – the editor's, which had rippled glass so that one could not see into it, and John Junor's.

The news desk occupied a far corner. The features desk the centre. The critics and leader writers ran parallel with them, and the Londoner's Diary had a cluster of desks to one side. The noise was prodigious, the clatter of typewriters, cries of 'boy' to summon a youth to take copy to the printers' chute, reporters yelling down telephones to distant countries.

My first impression was of the extraordinary variety of my new colleagues. Many of them were like John Clarke, unassuming, cultivated people who may in youth have aspired to literary heights, but had settled for a steady respectability. A few were positively intellectual, such as Ken Tynan, Alan Brien and Philip Oakes. Then there were mavericks like Milton Shulman, who had once been a crooner on the boards in Canada, and Morris Finer, a distinguished lawyer, who wrote most of the leaders. Milton had written a book, *Defeat in the West*, that had much impressed Lord Beaverbrook, who ordered his minions to 'find Shulman and offer him a contract to write for us'. Through his publishers they discovered that Milton was already working in some comparatively modest position on the *Evening Standard*. The editor had actually just decided to make him redundant and had to say to Milton that he had changed his mind. They saw no reason to tell Beaverbrook any of this, but produced him, as it were, out of a hat.

At the other end of the scale were people of almost unbelievable ignorance, devoid of all taste. The languid, urbane news editor had as his deputy a cross-eyed gnome of a man who seemed unable to be other than rude. I stood beside him in the newspaper's library.

'Get me that new book on Duff Cooper. It's by a guy called Talleyrand.'

The features editor was a dour Scot, Charles Curran, who spent most of the day with his feet on his desk and did nothing. He later became an MP, though how he got anyone to vote for him was a puzzle to me. His assistant, another Scot, shook my faith in the excellence of Scottish education. He entranced us during a discussion about the musical *Kismet* and whether it was legal to use Borodin's music, by asking: 'Why do we no ring up Borodin?'

There were few women. I remember only three. Evelyn Irons, an intrepid person, who was happiest reporting from the front line of any small war. Anne Sharpley, who combined an Irish physical generosity with the North Country practicality of Macclesfield, where her family had a silk factory. She had an unspecified relationship with Lord Beaverbrook, based as much on her skill as a journalist as on her warm beauty. Joyce Rackham worked on the Londoner's Diary and knew a lot about wine and all about etiquette.

There was one mystery figure who used to come in once a week. He wore the clothes of a character in Dornford Yates – in the summer a striped blazer and a boater. He would sit for half an hour with the literary editor and then go again, speaking to no one else. When I asked who he was, they told me to look at an *Evening Standard* of about 1923. Every week at that time, spread over two pages, was Horace Thorogood's column. He was famous. Now, still once a week, Mr Thorogood came to collect the short stories submitted by readers. He read them at home and brought in his selection of the three best stories. It was his pension, this small task. 'I never pay a blind bit of attention to his choice,' said the literary editor.

I soon realized that journalists have few traits in common. The only certain one is a delight in gossip. Then, possibly, an appalling sentimentality. Hardly a week went by without a collection being got up for somebody's wedding or leaving present or for even less likely causes – 'You know poor Phil's aunt is sick.' And drink, of course.

The excitement for me lay in the immediacy of journalism, in the variety and in the unpredictability. At that time, at least six editions of the *Standard* appeared in the course of the day. Not every page changed every time, but the Londoner's Diary, for instance, changed its early morning collection of stories at midday and again at about four in the afternoon, so a piece of gossip gleaned over coffee at lunchtime would be on the streets in time for tea.

I liked having to mug up everything possible about, say, the trees of London for a fancy of Lord Beaverbrook's. He wanted a picture of every species growing in the parks and gardens of the capital, one a day for about three weeks, with a poem about the tree in question. It was easy to find poems for commonplace trees – oaks, elms, chestnuts. We were defeated by the catalpa, which had evidently inspired no poet. The problem was solved eventually by, I think, David Holmes, who wrote: 'A thousand glorious ages have sounded through the trumpet flowers of my catalpa. *From the Chinese'*. Fortunately, Lord Beaverbrook did not know that the catalpa came from the Americas and that its flowers were not trumpets.

My nomadic instincts were all well nourished by the knowledge that I might, at ten minutes' notice, be sent off to Scotland or Paris, Madrid or Penzance.

With the pleasures came many dangers and the uncomfortable realization that, at its humbler levels, if one wants to keep a job, journalism asks for many compromises with principles. When a reputation is established and they need one more than one needs them it becomes easier, but there are still moral decisions to be taken every day – about privacy, about when reasonable enquiry ends and persecution starts, about what is confidential and where lies a breach of trust.

The leader writers were all of a liberal turn of mind, but were obliged to follow the policies of Beaverbrook. We did have an agreement that none of us would write a leader in favour of hanging, but that was all. I was not much good at leader writing and was transferred to the Londoner's Diary, where the problems were less about opinions and more about betrayal of friendship.

I could never decide whether the man who ran the Londoner's Diary, Tudor Jenkins, was on the side of good or evil. I liked him, for he had great charm and a broad smile which used all of his face, and he was a storehouse of strange anecdote. Against that, he was ruthless in pursuit of a story and was scathing in the face of any hesitation. Quite quickly I learned to say that I had rung people with some question or other and that they had either been out or had said 'No comment.' He probably guessed that I had not rung at all. Many times he told me that people were really pleased to see their names in print and that Lord Castlerosse, who had had a column in the *Sunday Express*, had said that friends who were offended weren't worth having as friends.

105

A year went by. The office was a peaceful place after the last edition had gone and everyone had moved over to the Two Brewers. I sat there alone writing letters. The telephone rang and I answered.

'Who's that?' said the familiar voice of Lord Beaverbrook.

'Crewe.'

'Ah, yes. Well now, I have a great story for you. You know Crowther's down at Syon where they sell statues and gates and garden urns? You do. Good. Poor Albert Crowther died. He died in prison. He was in prison for receiving a stolen mantelpiece.

'It is very sad. Everyone loved old Crowther. You will go to see Mrs Crowther and you will write a warm, human story about Crowther for tomorrow morning's paper. The funeral was this afternoon. You go off now.'

'But I can't possibly go.'

'What do you mean, you can't go? You have an important engagement?'

'No, I mean I can't go and disturb Mrs Crowther on the day of her husband's funeral.'

There was a long pause, timed with care.

'And I thought you had a great future in journalism.'

It was my turn to pause. Colin and I had a new flat in mind. My life was fun. I had bought a car. I did not dare to think of Percy.

'All right, I'll go.'

'You will write a warm, human story. I am sure of it.'

Together with a photographer I got to Syon Lodge while it was still light. Everything was shut, the house locked. The photographer needed some pictures. He nipped over a wall, while I trembled in the street terrified that Mrs Crowther would come back and catch him. When he had taken his photographs, he climbed back. We waited. It grew dark and no one came. I suggested abandoning the job.

'If the old man asked for it, we stay all night if necessary,' said the photographer.

Mrs Crowther got back at about eleven. There were four or five people with her. I asked one of the men to ask her if I could have a couple of minutes' talk with her.

He protested. I told him Lord Beaverbrook had particularly asked for this. He went to speak to her. When he came back he said, 'Mrs Crowther says she will see you if you insist, but I think you're a shit if you do.'

I did. I needed only two minutes, just to be able to say that I had

106

spoken to her. She told me that the business would go on, run by the family. I went back to the office and wrote a story, sympathetic and tactful. It appeared in the morning, covering a whole page, with one of the photographer's stolen pictures of a row of Roman emperors' heads lying on the ground.

Beaverbrook left it for about three days. Then he rang.

'That was a fine, warm, human story you wrote about Crowther.'

'Thank you.'

'But I recall you were reluctant to do that story.'

'Yes.'

'Ah. And have you perhaps heard from Mrs Crowther?'

'Yes.'

'She telephoned or maybe she wrote a letter?'

'She wrote a letter.'

'And what did she say in that letter?'

'She said she was sorry if she had been rude when I went to see her and that she was very grateful for the kind things I had said about her husband.'

'There you are. I told you it would be a fine human story, did I not?'

He had known of course, exactly how I would behave and just how she would respond.

'Yes,' I said, 'but never again.'

He chuckled and put the telephone down.

Inexperience plunged me into a whirlpool which I would later have viewed with more caution from calm waters beyond the lip. Humphrey Brooke, the Secretary of the Royal Academy and an old friend, asked me to meet Graham Sutherland. They told me that curious things were happening at the Tate Gallery. Humphrey had been the Deputy Director of the Tate and Graham was one of the Trustees.

Sir John Rothenstein, the Director of the Tate, had already been involved in something of a storm in a teacup over a photograph that had appeared in the press of Zsa Zsa Gabor in the Gallery, her skirt pulled up above her knee and her foot resting on a piece of sculpture. In 1952, such a thing was thought disgraceful and Lady Davidson asked a question in the House of Commons about it.

What they now suggested was more serious. They accused Sir John of breaching the conditions laid down by people who had left money to the Tate. They hinted that worse was to come, but that this would be a good opening salvo in a campaign to oust Sir John. I put a paragraph in the Londoner's Diary asking why the labels which had always said that certain paintings were bought with money from one fund had been changed, attributing them now to different donors.

When this paragraph produced an evasive response, my informants provided me with a further group of shuffled funds, then another and another. In the end, the Tate had to confess to a long list of errors. Funds left for the purchase of paintings had been used for sculpture. Others intended for English paintings had been used to buy French pictures. Money meant to be devoted to pictures of fluffy cats and dogs had acquired Giacomettis and Modiglianis.

For me, who had been a journalist for only a matter of months, the whole thing was intoxicating. As a result of my paragraphs, more questions were asked in the House. The national press took up the campaign. Through Graham I met art historians and art critics, all of whom endorsed his view of Sir John's administration.

The publication of the list of sins was by no means the end of the hunt. Sir John had bought a Degas bronze, *La petite danseuse de quatorze ans*, for what turned out to be £9,000, when the Trustees believed he was paying only £8,000. The suggestion was that £1,000 had somehow slipped into Sir John's pocket. In any case, it was said that there had been another copy on the market for half the price.

Graham resigned from the Board of Trustees. My standing grew because I published the news of his resignation first. Kingsley Martin, the distinguished editor of the *New Statesman*, invited me to lunch, to ask me for my version of the whole story. I remember pouring out to him all the malicious tales my informants had brought me – ones that I could not publish for fear of libel.

Art paper was still rationed at the time. Sir John, they said, had invented a large series of mythical publications in order to be able to claim a vast amount of paper. Getting it, he immediately sold it on the black market for a huge profit. There was no strong suggestion that he pocketed this money. There were stories about his private life; of how he kept a fur coat in his flat and insisted to any girl he took out that she wear it, because he liked to be seen with pretty girls in fur coats.

Kingsley Martin listened to all this and then warned me of the dangers of becoming too carried away, of being too involved, of the risks of not being dispassionate. In a way, this was odd because years later, in his autobiography, Sir John singled out Kingsley Martin as having been particularly vindictive in the affair and having carried it on long after others had tired of it.

In any event, Kingsley Martin made me think, and I came to recognize that nearly all the information came originally from one source, the fairly recently appointed Deputy Director, a South African called Leroux Smith Leroux. What he had conducted was a smear campaign, with the primary objective of his replacing Sir John. I did not fully appreciate the mendacious nature of this man until much later, but I became more cautious.

The mythomane is a familiar figure to most of us, best depicted perhaps in *Billy Liar*. The male versions are usually salesmen, journalists or politicians. It is rare to find mythomanes in the gentler calling of the arts, where truth is of greater importance, even, as Keats had it, the sole aim.

That gave Leroux a greater latitude than he might have had in any other field. No one could imagine that a man dedicated to the arts could weave such fantasies from such slender material. An art dealer might invent things, but not a museum director. Leroux had all the beguiling persuasiveness of the real con man. That he should have deceived me was not to be wondered at when he could convince Lord Jowitt, an ex-Lord Chancellor, Lord Harlech, the chairman of a bank, Lord Crawford, a shrewd and careful man, of almost anything.

Gradually a certain balance returned. It was plain that while Sir John was a slapdash director, while he was vain and not very lovable, he was genuinely devoted to the Tate. While he had, as it were, cooked the books and for all we know even cheated the Board of Trade, he had done so in order to buy what he believed was best for the Gallery. Indeed, we can be very glad today that he bought that little dancer for so little money and be thankful that we have the Giacomettis and the Modiglianis rather than a lot of pussycats snuggling in their baskets.

The Trustees dismissed Leroux, and the diminutive Sir John punched the gross, fat, vicious art critic Douglas Cooper on the nose at a soireé. The affair was over.

A year or so later Lord Beaverbrook sent for me. A large painting was propped against the wall of his sitting room. Beaverbrook stood at his lectern with his back to me. Every so often he screwed up a piece of paper and threw it on the floor. He did not turn round.

'What do you think that picture is?'

'It looks like a Constable.'

'That's right. I paid £30,000 for that painting on the advice of your friend Leroux Smith Leroux.'

When Leroux had left the Tate, Beaverbrook had asked me what I thought of him. I had some doubts, but Leroux's charm still worked. I believed much of his hard luck story and told Beaverbrook that I thought he knew his job. Possibly he did, but how he used that knowledge was another matter.

'Not my friend, my acquaintance,' I said, foreseeing trouble.

'Hmph. Today Agnew's came to look at the picture. What do you think they say that picture is worth?'

I waited.

'They say it's worth £30. What have you got to say to that?'

I thought of suggesting a second opinion. It seemed pointless.

'I'm very sorry.'

Beaverbrook turned at last, and smiled.

'Oh, I suppose it's not your fault. Now I'll tell you something. Do you know which is my favourite painting in all of my collection? You don't? Well, it is this Constable that they now tell me is worth only £30.'

CHAPTER TEN

MARTHA

Colin and I had a flat in Dolphin Square. We decorated it in appalling, rather theatrical taste, but it was an unexpectedly pleasant place to live. It was on the eighth floor and had a sixty-foot balcony, overlooking the river and Battersea power station. By day the light was bright and clean, and at night the sounds of the river, the hooting of the barges and the rattle of anchor chains, made me dream of foreign lands.

We lived well compared with the days in Sloane Street. There was a small spare room and, beyond the kitchen, a maid's room and bathroom. We advertised for a housekeeper, the advertisement starting: 'Two bachelors . . .'. From the 136 replies we chose Eva, who was Polish in origin and a superb cook. At breakfast, her long auburn hair fell loose over her shoulders and her bare nipples poked through the holes of her broderie anglaise shirt. After dinner, she would ask with lingering emphasis: 'Are you sure there is nothing else you want?'

There wasn't really, because in the middle Fifties there was already an easy-going spirit that foreshadowed the permissive society. It no longer occurred to us to take a girl to one of those restaurants where there was a band and one could dance between courses. Instead we went to small bistros and to nightclubs. I don't think we were unduly promiscuous, but life became gradually less complicated.

At the same time, much of our social life followed the old pattern of dances and country-house weekends, so that my life especially became more and more divided into compartments with several different groups of friends who never met and who would in many cases have been so incompatible as to be intolerable to each other.

The idea that one could like Oswald Mosley was one that I would hardly have cared to mention to many of my friends. But I did like him in many ways and I was certainly fond of Diana, his wife. Quite separately their children by their first marriages were friends of mine, but Mosley came into my life because of his friendship with Lady Jeanne Campbell, Beaverbrook's granddaughter, with whom I shared a desk at the *Evening Standard*.

Their friendship had a comical ending. Beaverbrook got to hear of it and summoned Jeannie to Cherkley, his house in Surrey. When she arrived, she was shown into the library. The long table in the middle of the room was piled with press cuttings about Mosley, and propped up on the shelves round the walls were all the pictures of Mosley from the *Daily Express* photo library.

Jeannie took one look round the room and said: 'All right, Grandfather, I give in.'

Of course, Mosley's views were unacceptable, but it was only beyond a certain point, something like a sound barrier, that they became so. Up to that point, they were often far more politically perceptive than those of many who have muddled our affairs since the war. There was, as Beatrice Webb, much earlier than most, pointed out, something flawed in his character. It was partly that he was impatient, extremely intolerant of people less intelligent than himself and unable to take criticism; all symptoms of his fundamental incapacity for understanding other people. He had simply no idea how other people felt and no pity for their shortcomings. His gift for mob oratory gave him the illusion that he had a rapport with the working classes, whereas what he really had was the power to arouse the thug. It is hard to say whether he really was anti-Semitic, which he always denied, or whether he used anti-Semitism as a means to attract support, which is possibly worse. There was also a streak of shallow frivolity about him, a playboy quality that meant that he was never truly serious, even at his most brilliant.

Nonetheless, I found him interesting and, this side of the sound barrier, instructive – perhaps learning as much what to beware of as what to embrace.

Mosley occupied such a peculiar position on the political and social scene and somehow aroused the very worst side of British humbug. His career had not made it easy for anyone to associate with him, but so much of the disapproval was for the sake of appearances rather than genuine feeling. Mosley came from an establishment background. There were, after the war, still many MP's in both parties who had been in the House of Commons with him. There were many who had toyed with the idea of joining the New Party, which he launched in 1931, such as Harold Macmillan, Bob Boothby and Aneurin Bevan, and one or two who had actually done so like John Strachey. They knew him as Tom, spoke of him in private with a casual intimacy, even in some cases affection. In public they would vilify him. I went up the stairs to his daughter Vivien's wedding reception with Violet Bonham-Carter.

'I hope Tom won't have the bad taste to be in the receiving line. If he is, there will be a Gadarene scamper down the stairs.'

'Surely no one would ruin Viv's wedding just for that?'

'No one will shake hands with him.'

Tom knew the rules of humbug better than anyone. He was not in the line.

I admired more those who did not let public opinion dent their principles, for instance Lord Sherwood, the Liberal peer, who battled for the restoration of the Mosleys' passports at the end of the war, and even more Professor Derek Jackson, who in 1943, when the Mosleys were released from prison after three years of internment, lent them his house.

They had hardly moved in when Herbert Morrison, the wartime Home Secretary, telephoned to say that they must move out as they could not stay in the same house as Jackson, who was involved in secret war work in the Air Force. Derek told Morrison that he would not take orders from a civilian. 'Mr Home Secretary, when you have won the DFC, the AFC and the OBE for valour, you can ring me up again.' The Mosleys stayed until they found a house.

Derek Jackson was a diminutive man who moved with oddly jerky gait and gestures. His voice had a gravelly, strained quality as if each word had to be squeezed past recalcitrant vocal chords. His face could assume a grave expression, even a wise one, but mostly twitched with mischief and an excitable charm. Conventional wisdom played no part in his character, which had been formed by unusual circumstances.

He and his twin brother had little parental guidance, as their father died when they were fourteen and their mother, who took scant interest in their education, when they were eighteen. They were, however, enormously rich, their family owning a very large share in the *News of the World*. In Derek's case, this upbringing left him with a certain emotional instability and an ambiguous, although happy, sexuality. He was married six times – to the daughter of Augustus John, to one of the Mitford sisters, and to four others of varying fame, the last time very happily.

Derek was an amateur jockey of skill. He rode three times in the Grand National. Each time he completed the first round safely. In 1935, on Princess Mir, he fell at Beecher's; in 1947 his horse Tulyra fell fairly early in the second round; and, in 1948, he was lying second when Tulyra refused at the last-but-one fence.

As if this were not enough, Derek and his twin both became physicists. Vivian died in a sledging accident when they were thirty, but Derek by that time, had already established a high reputation in the field of spectroscopy, and was University Lecturer in the subject at Oxford.

He was a superb teacher, having that strange ability to make obscure things clear even to the layman. I remember sitting with Derek one rainy afternoon near Paris, when he explained exactly how a nuclear bomb worked. For at least a week afterwards, I felt that I could have built one. He told me that day that there were only twelve people in the world with whom he could have a serious conversation about his work in physics.

People thought that Derek was arrogant, but it was more that he was completely fearless – if he had an opinion he saw no reason to conceal or moderate it, either for convention or politeness. Being so rich gives some of this kind of courage. Lord Beaverbrook once said to me as his wife left the room: 'There goes a woman of strong character and strong opinion – strong opinion backed I dare say by two million dollars a year.' With Derek there was the further element of being the eternal naughty child.

In Paris, he used deliberately to upset people with his atheism, referring to Christ as 'the bearded monster' and growling jerkily: 'You're not going to tell me that that Mrs Joseph wasn't covered.'

But his courage was not only of this kind, it was physical as well as intellectual.

Derek had believed, for whatever reasons of his own, that the war should never have happened. Before it, he would say that if there were a war he would go to America, but when it came he joined the Air Force, pulling strings with Churchill himself to be released from scientific work for the Admiralty.

MARTHA

The Admirals may have been relieved, having been teased by Derek on an occasion when they summoned him to give an opinion on a piece of equipment. Derek could not be bothered to explain the merit of it to people who had no understanding of its workings.

'It's so lovely I could stroke it,' he said in a rather coy growl.

'Come now, Jackson. We don't want that sort of talk, do we? This is serious.'

Derek was not used to argument and criticism.

'What sort of "we" is that, Admiral – a royal we, an editorial we or just you and your tapeworm?'

He trained as an air gunner and wireless operator. At the moment that his training finished, it happened that the Air Force needed urgently to improve the radar on its fighters, first assessing the problem in actual battle. Derek flew at least sixty missions in Beaufighters, as navigator. The pilots liked him because he worked the radar equipment so much better than anyone else and because he was always calm in a crisis. His seniors were at first suspicious of his unusual remarks, uncertain whether he meant it when he used to say: 'I haven't laughed so much since Dunkirk.' He made them still more uneasy when he was asked after one night sortie how many planes he had shot down.

'Three and a half.'

'What do you mean, a half?'

'Oh, that was one of ours.'

They soon came to recognize his courage, however, and his scientific advice was invaluable. He went on to develop 'Window', the strips of metalled paper which frustrated German radar, and also to save many lives with his acute judgement of what the enemy were doing in the field which was akin to his own speciality. At the end of the war, he was a wing commander, having more than earned the decorations that he had flung in Herbert Morrison's face.

Derek went back briefly to Oxford and became Professor of Spectroscopy, but he was unhappy with the Labour Government and even more with British taxes. He went to live in Ireland, and for a time was Visiting Professor at Ohio State University. Eventually he settled for working in France at the Aimé Cotton Laboratory, with which he was associated for nearly thirty years until he died in 1982, one of Europe's most respected atomic physicists. He was, however, never above teasing. At one solemn conference, an American scientist finished his paper with the words: 'This work has been supported by the US Navy.' Derek came next. He ended: 'This work has been supported by my horse.' It had won a race.

Derek's fierce brand of independence had about it an interesting element of almost perverse tenacity. When technological advances made the measurement of the spectral lines of atomic beams far easier, Derek stuck to the older methods. He enjoyed the challenge to his skill – 'a somewhat similar challenge', his colleague H. G. Kuhn suggested, to the 'challenge he had enjoyed in his earlier activities, riding in a steeplechase or acting as observer-gunner in a night-fighter'.

He was supremely British, but Britain lost him, possibly, in the words of Michael Foot writing about Mosley, because of the British 'deep-laid middle-class love of mediocrity and safety-first which consigned political [in Jackson's case scientific] genius to the wilderness and the nation to the valley of the shadow of death'.

John Hayward was always urging me to get a wheelchair. I was falling over more than ever. The slightest unevenness under the heel of the leg my weight was on would push my knee out and I would crash down. I looked once to see what had unbalanced me and saw it was a cigarette butt. It took an effort to see that that was funny.

I resisted with fury the idea of a chair for several reasons. In the first place, I thought that John was somehow anxious to reduce me, as I thought of it, to his level. Of course, vanity played a large part; I thought that people would treat me differently – feel sorry for me or look with some contempt on a cripple. I also feared that it might imperil my job. A year or two before, Sir Christopher Chancellor, the head of Reuters, had explained with perfect kindness that mobility was the prime requirement for a journalist. As it was, the editor would send me off, without any apparent thought that it might be difficult, on stories anywhere in the country or even abroad.

I had at one point become the paper's helicopter correspondent. It was very tricky getting in and out of it, but no one had thought of this and I was determined to manage, as it was fun even if of little use journalistically.

Lord Beaverbrook had bought the helicopter thinking that this would make the *Evening Standard* the first with the news. Of course, it did nothing of the sort. By the time the photographer and I had got to where the helicopter was kept, flown to wherever the event might be, found a place to land and hired a car, the local correspondent had telephoned a story to the paper and nobody wanted anything I wrote.

Trying to think of uses for it, the editor sent us to fly over the most popular beaches where Londoners might be having their holidays. The circulation department thought that this would promote sales of the paper. The helicopter had *Evening Standard* in large letters on the side, as well as the embarrassing registration G-ANAL.

Probably we annoyed more potential readers than we seduced. We flew low over the sunbathers, our fierce down-draught puffing sand-filled gales over oiled bodies and into lunch packets. Merrymakers cresting a rise on the big dipper would be confronted with the sight of our whirling blades seemingly about to decapitate them. As we could not land and talk to anybody, I found it hard to make Clacton sound very different from Margate.

This difficulty was exacerbated when we were for once to be first with the news, sent to fly over the troop-carrier bringing back the boys of the Glorious Gloucesters, heroes of the Korean War. We flew from Guernsey and found the ship. We waved, they waved. Vic Drees, the photographer, hung out and took his pictures and we waved again and they waved again – and then I had to write a thousand words.

Some less than friendly people had suggested that the Gloucesters were perhaps not so courageous after all, and that they had been troublesome rather than glorious.

It is odd to remember now that I was reproved not for writing a boring piece about all that waving and smiling and possibly hurrahing, if I could only have heard the cheers from the noisy helicopter, but for saying that the boys didn't look bloody-minded to me. 'Bloody-minded,' said the news editor. 'What sort of newspaper do you think this is, that you can use language like that?'

Larks in the helicopter, trips to Paris or Oporto or Edinburgh, suited me well, and I was afraid that the sight of a wheelchair might set them wondering. In the end I gave in to the inevitable. I bought a hideous-looking thing that I later came to realize was, in comparison with others equally ugly, poorly designed. It is still a matter of astonishment to me that, despite numberless projects in design schools and universities of many countries, the design of wheelchairs has advanced so little. However, I did discover that John was right; it was a relief to surrender to a chair. I had not realized how much the fear of falling had been making me not do things – going across to the pub, to a museum, to the races. I had been making excuses to avoid the risk of falling yet again. In a sense, the chair was a liberation.

It brought with it, on the other hand, a whole new lot of problems. I had been right in my fear that people would see me differently. If one is in a wheelchair, a large proportion of the population assumes that one is idiotic, probably incapable of speech, let alone of making a decision. 'Does he want a window seat?' I had to learn how to make people forget the wheelchair, almost not to see it. This is difficult, because I believe a part of the predicament lies in the difference in height. Talking to someone in a wheelchair means looking down on them, and Jungians, I have no doubt, would find the phrase significant, even inspirational of disdain.

People sometimes do ask me questions about skiing or climbing or playing tennis. Then they look embarrassed and apologize, whereas I am delighted for it means that they have forgotten and are treating me normally. It is those who make a fuss of me who offend me.

At first, I could wheel myself around a certain amount and, as I could stand and drive, I was still independent. My fear about my job was unfounded – I was still sent off on interesting journeys, although the helicopter was quietly sold off.

I knew very little about Martha when we decided to marry. She was American, she had studied comparative religion at Columbia University. Her father, who came from Kentucky and who had been in the Marines, was dead. Her mother lived in Connecticut with an elder daughter by an earlier marriage. Beyond that Martha talked very little about herself, except to say that she was sure that I would like this or that one of her friends.

It was staying with friends of mine in Oxfordshire where she was working as an au pair that I met Martha. She was tall and beautiful with a soft, soothing voice and a laugh of unusual innocence and warmth. I fell in love at once.

There was a generous quality about her nature that I found irresistible, but it was perhaps the difference from the kind of girls I knew that drew me more than anything. She had a bubbling enthusiasm, with none of that false restraint which so besets the English, and she was far better educated than the majority of my girlfriends. She preferred talking of books or paintings or music to the rattle of gossip that I was more used to; although that may have been partly because we had no friends in common.

Within about three weeks we were engaged. When we are young, it rarely occurs to us to wonder why other people love us; we find it perfectly natural that they should do so. Martha is not a passionate person in the way of demonstrative affection, but she is given to extremes of feeling or sensibility. I think she saw my disability as meaning that I was vulnerable and in need of protection, and herself in a Jane Eyre role.

We were to be married in America, so to celebrate our engagement, in March 1956, I gave a party in London. It is marvellous to give a large party for which you alone are responsible for choosing the guests. Martha knew only three people in England, so I was able to invite three hundred or so. It was also an occasion on which I could muddle up all my disparate kinds of friends without having to explain them to each other.

The only problem was money. To hire Londonderry House in Park Lane, with its copy of the Waterloo Chamber at Windsor Castle, was surprisingly cheap – £30 for the night. A band was out of the question. Colin and I happened to know an engagingly roguish jazz musician in Soho, Billy Kaye, who undertook for £36 to provide some friends who would play. It seemed to me that if there was enough to drink, food would not matter much. I asked Searcy's how much three hundred people would drink, bought one hundred bottles of champagne, doubled their estimate on everything else, and got barrels of beer for the musicians. In case anyone was really hungry, I ordered a few hundred sausage rolls. The whole party cost about £350.

I cannot remember what I put on the invitation about dress but, whatever it was, people interpreted it very differently. It happened at a time which was the watershed between the ending of automatic, conventional formality and the insouciant freedoms of the Sixties.

Some of the rigorously correct among my friends like Lord Thurso, the wartime leader of the Liberals, and Lord Waverley, famous for the Anderson shelter in the Blitz, came in white tie and tails. Harold Macmillan, then Chancellor of the Exchequer, arrived off a train from Scotland in a pin-striped suit. Many of the younger people wore jeans or catsuits or anything. An elderly cousin, who had been a lady-in-waiting to Queen Mary, hailed a taxi and asked the driver to take her to Londonderry House.

'Oh, to Mr Crewe's party.'

'How do you know?'

'I am going too.'

Billy fulfilled his promise with gusto. He had put it about that there was an opportunity to play some exciting jazz. More and more players turned up. The noise soared. Every so often a beautiful girl sang – it was Annie Ross, who, someone said later, sang for the first time in public that night. At about one o'clock, there was a further influx. These were Stan Kenton's band from America, who had been performing in Bedford and had heard of the chance of playing with some British jazz men and came straight from their gig. At one point there were eighty musicians. The noise drove away the older members of the party and the jazz grew more and more progressive.

Any party has a kind of tension which must not slacken. The incongruity of the guests and the improbability of the music kept this one going at almost too high a pitch. Only Robin Fedden was unaffected. He slept curled in a corner of the lift, riding up and down for two hours. The music began to grate into the brain so that, rather than slackening, the tension felt as if it might snap. Then up the stairs came a new sound as soothing as cool water. As a last gesture Billy had conjured up a steel band – Russ Henderson.

The mood changed, the other musicians drifted away and a new energy carried us on. I took off my shoes to balance better and danced for almost the last time in my life.

At nearly six in the morning, Londonderry House had had enough of us. In any case, Martha had to catch the boat train at eight-thirty, as she was sailing that day to America. Russ Henderson insisted that he wanted to give her a real send-off. We all went back to Dolphin Square, Russ and his band drumming in the lift and in the flat.

Then to Waterloo. The commuters were beginning to arrive. Russ's drums beat their loud calypso rhythm. Martha was still in her rose-coloured ball dress. Raymond Carr kept on inviting people getting off the trains to dance, eventually leaping on to a trolley and whirling a struggling porter round and round, finally letting go of him saying: 'You may be a success as a porter, but you're a dreadful failure as a dancer.'

The train jerked, then pulled away. Russ beat on until the last coach faded.

Pork Hollow Farm lay below the narrow country road. It sat among the maples and beeches of the Connecticut woods, newly in leaf. Near the house were some fine elms rising above the other trees, and dogwood flickered white in the undergrowth. The house itself looked almost too perfect; its windows with neat dark green shutters were set in perfect symmetry in the white clapboard, a classical pediment lent an air of grandeur. A large red barn stood above the house, and a rustic well between the drive and the front door suggested a more rural way of life than was the case.

Inside there were not many rooms – a large drawing room with a conservatory beyond, a dining room and a small library. It was all furnished and decorated in perfect taste, but with that rather untouchable quality of American houses.

The three women who greeted Colin and myself could not have been more different both from Martha and from each other. Martha's mother, Ruth Sharp, was fastidious, well-dressed in an old-fashioned and expensive way. Her grey hair was curled and rinsed with blue, which fitted well with her lively eyes. Her voice was faintly husky and she had an unusual but pleasing laugh that started with a kind of bark. Her air of confidence came from having travelled a good deal, having been a nurse in Europe in the First World War, from reading and from an unexpectedly broad acquaintance. Her sister had been a friend of Howard Carter and been with him at the opening of Tutankhamun's tomb. At first, I took her to be a cross between a character from Edith Wharton and one of the staider figures from Scott Fitzgerald.

Nancy Carroll, Martha's older half-sister, was tall and broad. She was proportionately noisy, argumentative and hard-drinking. She did not so much move as transport herself in huge displacements, shaking the floor as she went. She was a member of the State Legislature, the benefits of which I saw when I took my driving test – once round the yard of the police station, with completely unfamiliar hand controls, and I passed. Nancy did not live in the house but in the barn, which she had converted for herself and the huge Great Danes that she bred.

Then there was Aunt Martha, the widowed sister of Martha's father. She had one of those long, plain American faces that shine with kindness, so familiar from movies about hardship in the Midwest. Aunt Martha came really from Paris, Kentucky, and was full of Southern ways. Mrs Sharp usually addressed her as Martha Green. She had a house in Kentucky but spent at least six months of the year with Mrs Sharp, keeping her company. Aunt Martha thought the best of everybody and her only wish in life was that everyone should be happy, to which end she was free with much advice of the proverbial sort.

Fortified by the unaccustomed strength of American whisky, I tried at dinner to thank Martha's mother for her welcome, explaining that I had no idea whatever as to the kind of family I was going to meet, as Martha had never told me anything of what to expect, and what a pleasant surprise it had been. Mrs Sharp gave me a severe and puzzled look. She said: 'But aristocrats can recognize one another anywhere.'

However that may have been, I soon came to realize that the difference in marrying an American was possibly greater than it would have been had I married a French girl or an Italian one.

I grew fond of Martha's mother because she was a generous-spirited woman and she had an admirable fortitude. Although she was rich, she was never idle, turning her hand to improbable enterprises that might prosper or founder, eventually building a doll's house for our daughter Sabrina that quite equalled Queen Mary's. She also had a sense of humour, laughing at herself when her less probable undertakings failed hopelessly.

At the same time, her political opinions were so extraordinary that I found it hard to believe they were serious. Never having been to America, it took me some time to realize how many people shared them, even after the excesses of Senator McCarthy. I don't think she was a member of the John Birch Society or the Daughters of the American Revolution, but she subscribed to a number of extreme news digests and wild tracts arrived by every post.

Fluoride in the water supply was a burning subject at the time. Ruth was convinced that it was a plot conceived by a combination of Jews and Communists specifically to poison brave young American fliers, so that they would be weakened and unable to take off when the Russians attacked. It was the latest version of the medieval or even older myth of Jews poisoning the wells.

One day, I mentioned Graham Sutherland. 'He's a Commie', said Ruth. I explained that a less political person could hardly be imagined but that, if he did hold any opinions, they were more likely to be conservative. 'It's in the Congressional Record,' she said as if that settled the matter. There was a Senator Dondero from some Mid-western state who made extravagant assertions about British public figures, particularly anyone to do with the arts. He hated Herbert Read, for instance, and I would guess that Graham came into his fire as a result of the portrait of Churchill. I had not realized that it is not necessary actually to make a speech in the Senate for it to go into the Record, the equivalent of Hansard in Britain; any Senator can just send in what he wants to have printed. It seems an odd system, but I suppose it spares others the boredom of having to listen to the wafflings of such people as Senator Dondero.

It took me years to see Aunt Martha as anyone but a warmer

character from Tennessee Williams, with her deep drawl and her aura of better days remembered. When I did, I found a woman with a rare capacity for perceptive affection.

Nancy Carroll fitted no literary matrix. She held the same political views as her mother, often in a more violent form. 'I stood next to a dreadful Jew in the travel agent's, he held up everybody else with all his fidgeting and changing.'

'How did you know he was Jewish?'

'Oh, I did the eye-to-ear test. It never fails.'

She was also beset by a puritanism that was far removed from her mother's more sophisticated ideas. Even after we were married, once when Martha had to go away it was suggested that I might stay in the barn for a weekend with Nancy Carroll – out of the question, she could not possibly be alone in the house with a man, even her brother-in-law.

It was so surprising to me, this disparity between the modernity, the material progress, the artistic experimentation that I had always associated with America, and the rigid conventionality of the vast majority of Americans. As the preparations for the wedding went forward, I became more and more astonished by the formality of the arrangements. We moved to New York – Martha and her mother to a ladies' club, Colin and I to an hotel.

There were set occasions – the bride's shower, at which all Martha's girlfriends gave her presents, and the bachelor night. Martha's male cousins offered to take me out for this. Both Colin and I wanted to go to Harlem to hear some jazz. This idea was met with surprise and alarm. None of the young men had ever been to Harlem. Out of politeness, they pretended to look into the possibility, but said a day or two later that they had been strongly advised against it. I cannot remember where we went in the end, except that wherever it was Patrick Kinross, who was to be my best man, sat on the floor. They all felt it very wrong for a Lord to sit on the floor.

The peak of the pre-wedding events was the rehearsal dinner. We all met at the church – St Bartholomew's on Park Avenue – and learned our parts. That over, we went to a restaurant, where we sat in appointed places and had drinks but did not eat. After a while we moved to another restaurant where we sat according to a different seating plan and the waiters sang arias from Italian opera.

The wedding itself was equally formal. Everyone wore tail-coats and the ushers had gloves, literally offering women their arm to escort them up the aisle. And afterwards at the reception there was dancing. But that is not what I remember of that afternoon. What went on outside was merely happening. It might as well have been a film that I watched only because it was there on the screen. What went on inside was quite different, inside me that is – an agonizing turmoil. We had discussed the wedding service at length. I wanted to put in 'with my body I thee worship', which I believed and which American propriety left out. The clergyman had agreed, though Martha's friends thought it 'raunchy'. I had given no special thought to the vows. They were the standard vows that I had heard people pronounce a hundred times or more.

Suddenly I was making them, thinking them, believing them, meaning them, and my brain began to spin in throbbing echo of the words. I loved Martha, I wanted to be married to her, to fulfil all that I was saying. I felt as solemn as my words spoken in this dark church with its Byzantine shapes. I had felt solemn in this way only once before – at my confirmation. And what had become of that, of the vows I had made then? I was terrified, but the film went on, implacable and unnoticing. I must be looking mad, I thought, as the words echoed round and round, but Martha was calm, smiling at me with an ivory beauty, and the priest looked benign. It seemed to go on for ever, something like the sound E. M. Forster's Mrs Moore heard in the cave. Those earlier vows in Eton College chapel reproached me as *I do, I do, I do* rang now in my head. Would these new vows mean any more than those had done?

We drove away to the South in the airy, yellow-and-white convertible Martha had given me as a wedding present. Late in the evening, we ran over a skunk. It took a long month before the smell faded from the car. At about the same time, my head finally cleared of fear and guilt.

Our honeymoon lasted a year. The first six months we spent wandering round the United States. The impressions I formed then have become so overlaid by later visits that it is impossible to recapture that excitement which was the basis of a lasting affection for America and Americans. It may be that I am wrong in thinking that America then was so different, so much less harsh, less violent, safer, more friendly, while really it was just that we were in love and that the warmth was a response to our evident happiness. The bitter problems of America – Cuba, Kennedy's assassination, the race riots, Vietnam, Watergate and all the rest – were yet to come.

Of course, there would be hiccups. I had an introduction to Colonel Schulz, the military aide to President Eisenhower, who gave us a private tour of the White House at the unhoneymoon hour of eight in the morning. As we left, he said: 'No matter where you are, night or day, if you're in trouble, just you call me.'

That night we drove aimlessly round Washington, looking at the sights. Always in America I seem to find myself on roads that carry me inexorably in directions I do not want to go. We appeared to be going right out of town when I saw a slip-road where I thought I could turn. It led to a large building slightly below the main road. The turning space was small, but there was a convenient arch in the building. I drove in, planning to reverse out.

There was a loud clang as a portcullis slammed down behind the car. Men came running with guns. 'Get out.'

This moment is one that I always find frightening: will the man with the gun think I am being dificult? Getting out of the convertible was comparatively easy, but even so I used to have to kneel on the seat and put one leg out and then come out backwards. The gun made me nimbler than usual. 'Walk.' I demurred. 'I said, walk.'

I got my stick and stumbled after the first soldier, the others came behind, ready with their guns. After about eighty yards, we came out into a vast courtyard. I noticed with some alarm that the building had five sides. In the guardroom they were suspicious. We had no papers, we had left everything in the hotel. Martha's accent was so gentle that they asked, more than once, whether she was sure she was American.

Time went by, hostility mounted. I asked if they would ring the number Colonel Schulz had given us. The officer took it from me.

'But this is the White House.'

'Yes. If you ask for Colonel Schulz, he will vouch for me.'

'If you're kidding me, you're dead.'

Colonel Schulz sorted it out and we were led back from the Pentagon to our hotel by a military jeep with siren blaring.

Surprising gentleness was my more general impression. In North Carolina we were hungry. There was a bar advertising food. We went in and asked for a hamburger. The man behind the bar stared.

'Do you know where you are, lady? This bar is for black people.'

Martha explained that we were just hungry and asked whether it really mattered. Of course, we would go if they wanted us to, but it seemed a nice place to us. They let us stay and we all had drinks. Other people came in to look at us and we had more drinks. Then someone started to play a piano and the party grew. In the end, everyone was dancing and it was four hours before we drove rather hazily on, puzzled at the forgiving nature of black people.

Colin joined us in Charleston and we followed a tourist course through New Orleans, Texas, the Grand Canyon, Arizona and the sequoia forests to San Francisco, where he left us.

Neither he nor I could get used to American speed limits, despite Martha's agitation when we went over sixty-five miles an hour. We were driving through New Mexico at night, in that odd way that one always does when one has plenty of time and means to stop while it is still light. The road was straight and endless, there were no villages. Colin was driving steadily enough at eighty-five miles an hour when we were stopped and taken twenty miles to a court that apparently sat all night. The walls were covered with photographs of fearful accidents. The judge was a small elderly woman.

'Where were you born?'

'Abyssinia.'

'Abyssinia? Is that Alabama?'

'Yes,' Colin said, thinking that was simpler.

'You were going seventy-five miles an hour and the speed limit is sixty at night. Pay fifteen dollars, one dollar for every mile over.'

Afterwards, Colin asked the policeman why he had reduced his speed limit by ten miles an hour.

'I didn't want to give that little old lady a heart attack.'

From San Francisco we made our way to Canada, where we had been lent a house on Vancouver Island. Qualicum Beach was a small village, populated entirely by millionaires. The difference between rich Americans and rich Canadians, I concluded, was one of enjoyment. The people of Qualicum Beach were not beset by the worry of being rich. They loved it without being conscious of status symbols. In many ways they were modest.

Mr Brown gave a party. Before flying off to work in the morning, he did most of the preparation himself. He dipped several large jugs and one hundred and fifty glasses into water and then put them in the huge deepfreeze – together with many bottles of gin and Noilly-Prat.

When the guests arrived in the evening, he made dry martinis of which I have never tasted the equal. More and more of them, 'so many and so many and such glee'. It was a good party.

There were no thieves in Qualicum; people generally left their keys in the car. When the time came to go home, we found all the keys had gone. Mr Brown had taken them, so that no one should drive home drunk. Instead fifty brand-new bright-blue bicycles stood in the drive and everyone wove home.

We got back to Connecticut in time for the Suez crisis and the unpleasant feeling of having one's country abused, while agreeing with the abuse. It was made worse by the attacks launched on me by Nancy Carroll, whose political opinions on everything else I found so abhorrent.

It was a relief to fly off to Jamaica, where we spent the next six months. We were spoilt to see that most beautiful of all the Caribbean islands before tourism gobbled up so much of its charm. Our life was an idyll. At first, we were lent a house near the Blue Grotto. It sat alone on the beach where now a hundred houses hide the shore, and nearby a stream wriggled through the palm groves that were later bought by Garfield Weston to build a swank hotel. I used to swim for hours, masked to watch the Technicolor fish, once following an unrecognized beauty over the reef until I saw ahead an enormous barracuda and, terrified, clawed my way back over the razored coral, arriving on the other side safe, but lacerated and bleeding.

This peace was interrupted by a telegram from the *Evening Standard*. The Prime Minister, Sir Anthony Eden, had resigned. He was coming to Jamaica to recuperate and would be staying at Goldeneye, Ian Fleming's house near Port Maria. I knew the house because my eldest brother Shane's widow was now married to Fleming, so I was able to send descriptions of the house and some endearing chat from the maid who looked after the place, before the police sealed off the house from all outsiders. The press arrived in force. The Edens refused to see anyone.

All the journalists, with one exception, put up in the most dreadful hotel simply because it was the nearest. It was my first experience of this kind of journalism and I thought it extraordinary. The journalists all knew each other, drank with each other but watched one another with suspicion, in agony lest someone else should get a story. Martha retreated to our house by the sea.

Everyone had sent in a letter to Eden to explain why he should be the one journalist that the shattered Prime Minister ought to see. No replies came. There was nothing to write. Then came a spate of telegrams. 'WHY HAS *MAIL* LARGE PIC EDEN BATHING PARTY. YOU NOTHING?' The answer to that was that the one journalist not in our hotel, Don Iddon, had thrown a number of coconuts into the sea and photographed them from a distance and written a piece to go with the pictures.

Also in the hotel was one of Eden's detectives, Inspector Harwood. He was an amiable man and we ate together quite often. One night he told me of a rat hunt they had had at Goldeneye, with some entertaining details. In my naivety, I repeated the story to the *Daily Express* correspondent, Ronald Singleton. He asked if I had already sent the story to the *Evening Standard*. He was generous enough, instead of pinching the story himself, to explain that in such a drought of news from Goldeneye I was sitting on a scoop. I filed the story and, sure enough, congratulations poured in, and cartoonists in London, who had nothing to illustrate, drew rats for three days.

Such a good turn deserved another. The one pleasant thing about the hotel was the receptionist, Estelle, who was pretty, a beguiling child of nature. Singleton was captivated by her and took her out whenever she was off-duty. He came back with accounts of visiting her family, somewhere inland, taking them a goat as a present and how readily they accepted him. He took her to Kingston and was enchanted by her laughter in a bookshop when she pulled out the bottom book of an elaborate castle built of books and the whole display collapsed. The man was besotted. He told me he wanted to marry her.

I pointed out all the obvious disadvantages, but nothing would dissuade him. I explained that she did not love him but was just dazzled. He would have none of it. In the end, I said that I could easily seduce her. Singleton was most indignant.

'All right, if I can seduce her, will you give up the idea of marrying her?'

He agreed, if I would promise not to cheat. I took Estelle out for the afternoon in the yellow-and-white convertible that we had brought with us. I had relied to a large extent on the charms of the car. Estelle surrendered without a murmur of guilt. It was I who had to draw back, affecting a sudden reluctance to cuckold my friend Singleton. He accepted my word and disentangled himself with the gift of another goat.

Martha and I moved to another house, in the hills above Ocho Rios. It was little more than a cottage and it only cost £5 a week, but we lived agreeably. People came to stay and we made many friends. We even had a little calypso band who attached themselves to us. There were Buster, Aston, Ron and Cabbage. Buster had a beautiful deep voice and was a real musician, while the others were just happy guys who could play a chord or two or beat a drum. It was a mystery how they survived as none of them had a job. They were, I suppose, what we would now call streetwise. Going once to see Buster in hospital we found him inexplicably cheerful, until he pointed at the ward's window boxes where flourishing plants of ganja grew.

The explosion of Jamaican music that was to lead to reggae had not yet happened. There was a little mento and perhaps the beginnings of ska, but all that we were aware of was calypso, which was Trinidadian in origin, and we wished that we could do something for Buster. A friend who arrived to stay recorded Buster's voice and promised to get him a job in a nightclub in London or Paris. But he did nothing, and the shame of it haunts me still.

We sailed back to England and, on the strength of the rats, the security of a new job on the *Evening Standard*.

The learning of a craft is to a great extent an unconscious process. On becoming an apprentice, one soon feels as if one has mastered whatever it may be and cannot understand why everyone else does not recognize the fact. It is the urge to do things in one's own way before the fundamentals have become instinctive that creates the difficulty, and the fundamentals are hard and slow to learn – something I wish more painters, singers and cooks, let alone writers, would appreciate.

I had now been a journalist for four years and was beginning to have more of what I wrote published. I was fortunate in having David Carritt, the art expert, as a friend. He was forever discovering extraordinary paintings – a Dürer in Sir Edmund Bacon's house, a Tiepolo on the ceiling of the Egyptian Embassy, some vast Guardis in Ireland. He would tell me about these and I would have a front-page story. Berenson said that David had the best eye for painting of anyone he had ever known. After the disaster of Leroux Smith Leroux, Lord Beaverbrook took David on (this time really at my suggestion) as his adviser, but one of his odder discoveries was for Lord Rothermere.

When Rothermere bought Daylesford, the house built by Warren Hastings, the local schoolmaster brought him some paintings that had been stored in the school and said that properly they belonged to the house. John Fowler, who was decorating Daylesford, told Rothermere that they were completely uninteresting and advised him to bundle them off to Sotheby's. Rothermere had a canny side to his nature and he arranged that the van should stop on its way to Bond

Street at David's flat in London. David had to clamber into the van with only a cigarette lighter to illuminate the pictures. He could not really see what they were. One appeared to be of a large goat, but there was something about the painting of the goat's hair that David found interesting. He recommended Rothermere not to sell the pictures but to have them cleaned.

The goat proved to be a yak. Warren Hastings had brought one back from India and it roamed in the park. He commissioned Stubbs to come to paint it and, while he was there, he painted Hastings's horse as well. Either of these two paintings was worth more than Rothermere had paid for the house.

There had long been a daily column in the *Evening Standard* giving accounts of parties and happenings of the previous evening. It was turgid and uninteresting. I was surprised to be asked to take over this page, and even more surprised to be told that the staff of about six reporters was to be disbanded and that the column would carry my name, instead of being anonymous as before. I would have one assistant, Jeremy Campbell. Luckily he was both intelligent and presentable, so that it was not an embarrassment to be represented by him, which would surely have been the case with some of the others.

At last I could do things in my own way. Nonetheless it was a terrible job. I would arrive at about five in the evening at the office, where an optimistic lady called Connie produced a list of things that were happening that night – publishers' parties, gallery openings, first nights, cocktail parties, dances, cabarets. Connie would have telephoned all the hosts or organizers to ask whether we could come to whatever it was.

Often she would say:'The Duchess of Somewhere is giving a ball at Claridge's. We're not invited, but I'm sure they wouldn't mind if you went.' The last editor had had no objection to gatecrashing. I was relieved that it was I who chose which things to cover. The interesting thing was how very few people did not want to have the *Evening Standard*. In many cases there was no need for Connie to ring up the hostess, she would have already rung Connie to make sure we would be going. I began to understand what Tudor Jenkins of the Londoner's Diary had meant when he insisted that nearly everyone likes to see his or her name in print.

The previous aim of the column had been to get in as many names as possible. I thought this dull and meaningless and decided that I would try to give a point to the column. Primarily it should entertain, but it could be in some way a comment on social behaviour and also endeavour to tell readers what it felt like to be at whatever event it was. It was an amazing success. It offended some people, for instance Kenneth Tynan, who did not speak to me for a year after I wrote an account of the party in a cellar in the King's Road to launch *Declaration*, a collection of essays by the Angry Young Men. I started the piece:

Down in a deep dark hole sat an old cow munching a beanstalk;
Out of her mouth came forth yesterday's dinner and tea.

I had a fall and hit my head on a kerbstone. The doctor said I had concussion and for me this was a convenient excuse. I was exhausted after a month or two of doing In London Last Night, because I had to go to two or three things every evening, five days a week. By the time I had enough material, it might be three o'clock in the morning and I might well have drunk far too much. Then I had to go to the office to write it up and rewrite in my style what Jeremy had done. Everything had to be finished by seven in the morning. I gave up with no regrets. It was this column, however short-lived, that established me as a journalist; I never again had to worry about getting a job.

Almost at the same time Martha, rather to her surprise, had a baby. I think that she had pictured our marriage somewhat differently and she had not included children in her imagined tableau. The arrival of our son, Sebastian, meant revising the picture in a more realistic manner. She was always to be the most conscientious, self-sacrificing mother, but never an instinctively maternal one.

A few days before Sebastian was born, Colin got married to Sally Churchill. Our half-sister Midi always maintained that he waited to get married until I was settled in life. Our father had died while Martha and I were in Canada, but Colin had delayed telling me until it was too late for me to go to the funeral. As with the death of my mother, I felt little grief, but in his case a shrivelling guilt that I had not made more effort to understand a man in many ways so estimable, when I could with thoughtfulness have bridged the lack of common interest. With his death and the inheritance of some paintings, I now had a cushion against any financial difficulties, so perhaps Colin did feel freer. What our parents had left us they had divided two-thirds to

Colin and one-third to myself on the grounds that, if I were unable to earn a living, he would support me, whom they considered entirely feckless. It was typical of Colin's extraordinary generosity to me that he rearranged the proportions to half and half.

CHAPTER ELEVEN

A YEAR IN JAPAN

I remember neither our real reasons for going to Japan nor what we told ourselves and each other. For me it must have been in part the restlessness that always overtakes me when life is just rumbling along, coupled with my need always to have a project, the lure of something new ahead. For Martha it was a keen interest in other cultures, religions and art forms with, lurking below, an incipient dissatisfaction with our marriage that a change of scene might remedy. However unclear the reasons, they must have been strong to impel us to fly off to the Far East with a five-month-old baby.

George Weidenfeld had commissioned me to write two books – one on Japan and the other on Thailand. Our plan was to spend six months in each. In Europe, in 1958, most people knew very little of Japan, apart from memories of the war. They envisaged a ferocious, militaristic people, inscrutable and cruel.

At first sight I disliked Japan. From the air I looked down on Tokyo, a brown fungus spreading over the flat land below the rumpled mountains. Driving into Tokyo was depressing – longer than an hour, down potholed, half-paved streets lined with battered wooden houses that formed a grey dusty wall on both sides. Not even the ideograms could make attractive the profusion of notices and advertisements, stuck everywhere like a fallen shower of huge playing cards. In the centre, Tokyo was beginning to sprout high-rise buildings in imitation of the worst of Western cities, but the mess and the noise of hooting cars, clanking trams, pedlars' horns and street cries made it hideous in every other way as well.

I learned quickly the first rule of travelling in strange, as opposed to familiar, foreign countries; that almost no one can help – one must do it all oneself. I planned to buy a car. At the British Embassy they told me that this was folly. The roads were so bad that one could go nowhere, the maps were so unreliable that it was impossible to find the way, the people were so unhelpful that they would deliberately mislead one. I soon found out that, as is so often the way with Foreign Office officials, most of them had never seen the countryside or even stayed in a Japanese inn. They lived in a diplomatic cocoon, meeting only officials and a few token outsiders who trotted round as if hired from a sort of diplomatic pet shop. I bought a Chevrolet. It is almost impossible to believe, but there were, in 1958, no Japanese cars on the road. Toyota produced a three-wheeled van, but everything else, apart from a few European cars produced under licence, was American or a pre-war relic.

The frustrations of trying to deal with Japanese ambiguities, with no knowledge of the language or understanding of the customs, were enough to make me regret the whole undertaking. I had planned to try to find a house in a village and to live there, studying the way of life of the people. Later I realized that this would have been nearly impossible, but instead of someone's explaining this in terms that I would have thought rational, politeness meant that officials and even professors from the university fabricated the most improbable excuses. Babies did not grow well in one area, in another the sun never shone, a third was dangerous and the island of Shikoku, the fourth largest, was 'such a backward place, lived in by such barbarous people with no manners'.

We decided to move to Kyoto. Of course, there had been pleasures in exploring Tokyo – the sight of a band of Shinto priests with their strange headdress walking down the commercial streets, the glimpse of a geisha in a closed rickshaw drawn by a trotting man, the comical signs saying 'cigalettes'. There were surprises of all kinds – the public telephones that just sat on wooden boxes outside shops with people shouting '*moshi-moshi*' down them, the absence of beggars, the refusal of taxis to take tips, and for sheer confusion the bizarrely logical system of numbering houses in a street not according to where they stood but in the order that they were built, so that Number 1 might be next to Number 326, while Number 2 was far away down the other end of the street. There were unlooked-for charms – the phallic statue in the main park, the extraordinary honesty. I remember being taken round a big department store where, incidentally, you could get married. I was carrying a heavy camera. My guide told me to put it down in an empty space on a counter. I hesitated. 'If it's not there when we come back, I'll buy you another.' It was.

But I was thankful to get out of the city. As soon as we were in the countryside, the incomprehensibilities became amusing rather than irritating.

We spent some days near Mount Fuji, soon understanding why it is, with the possible exception of Kilimanjaro, the most beautifully mysterious mountain in the world. The landscape round it was small and fierce. The contours of the lower mountains were sharp and rocky with, in betweeen, little bites of valley shining green and neat with work, but Fuji rose serenely smooth, with the confident stroke of an artist's brush, up and up unimaginably higher than all around it, so that on some days the peak appeared to belong not to the earth but to the sky. The gods might well live at the top.

The familiar Japanese woodcuts do not lie. Those spikey prints with their improbable lines and twisted hills, their slanting threads of rain and their spiralled mists, are not a stylized fancy but almost pure realism. This discovery robs them of their imagined invention and, for a time, altered my view of them so that it was not until my own memory of the landscape faded that their full enchantment returned.

In the early morning, the mists slid grey over the valleys and crept into the gullies of the mountains like pale ropes on the steep hillsides. The morning was the time when the country seemed most like the prints. The hillsides hung in the air as if they were a firmer kind of cloud; everything was fluid, nothing earthbound. As the mists moved and wandered, so the land itself seemed to change shape. The ruffled rims of the mountains stretched restlessly in the fashion of a rough sea. Nothing was permanent, nothing definite; all was lightly sketched, leaving solidity to the imagination. The colour was a grey mono-chrome, taking its lead from the clouds, but tinged with green. The spiny pine trees echoed the shapes of the mountains in their black-green outlines. The morning was a time of fleeting, unmarked beauty – the time which represented most clearly Japanese ideals. For them it was a mild pity when the rising sun began to furnish the scene with colour.

The sun up, the land took on the harsh reality of a grudging soil from which too many people had to coax a living. The light showed up the pinched, bitter terrain with great expanses of unyielding rock, acres of heights on which only a tree would grow, rushing rivers liable to flood, the fresh scars of earthquakes, woods flattened by wild winds – a countryside and a climate perpetually opposed to settlement.

During the day the sun beat with scorching heat and etiolating brilliance into the depths of the valleys, revealing the struggles against this forbidding nature. So small a proportion of the land of Japan was arable that to look at these valleys was at once to understand the precariousness of the people's lives. Every particle was used, no space wasted. Nothing ever lay fallow. The houses huddled together with never more than a few square feet given to a garden. The paddy fields were separated only by thin strips of embankment to keep the water in; even the telegraph poles were set on the actual roads so as not to take an inch from the rice crops. In front of the houses there were no pavements, and in many villages it was possible to reach out from the car and touch the buildings on both sides.

The paddy fields rose from the bottom of the valleys in terraces, clawed out of the hillside until it was no longer possible to grasp another few square inches of space. The farmers thought it worthwhile to build a wall four feet high in order to create a triangle of flat earth on which nine stalks of rice would grow.

In the evening, a lambent glow spread over the land as the setting sun returned new colour to the fields that it had bleached throughout the middle of the day, making the young crops prematurely golden in the fading light. I soon came to love the beauty of the countryside and to understand the Japanese absorption with the seasons.

We drove to Kyoto and found that everything we had been told by the people at the Embassy was wrong. The roads were appalling, even the main road, and the Tokkaido Highway made famous by Hiroshige, was in places a muddy cart track, but they were improving. The journey which now took three days, I covered a year later in a matter of hours. The maps were adequate, if occasionally outdated by this progress, and the people were immensely helpful, though unsurprisingly, as many of them had never been more than twenty miles from their homes, often wrong about the way.

Kyoto was as pleasant as Tokyo had been disappointing. Our brief excursions had shown us that we had to learn the language and at least start to understand the rudiments of Japanese culture before attempting to live too far from a city with some familiar point of reference. In a sense, we compromised, living at first in a traditional inn, where no foreigners had ever stayed before. To reach it we had to walk through a small copse and across a footbridge over a stream. One of the delights of Kyoto was that the country often came far into the city and, from almost anywhere, one could see the surrounding mountains.

A young man of twenty-six used to come every morning to teach me Japanese. He was what he called very *apuré*, which meant *après guerre* and thus modern and worldly-wise, not hampered by tradition. He would bounce in, snatch what he called his hunting beret off his head and nod with four or five jerks rather than bows. The beret sat oddly on the top of his head and, when he took it off, his hair sprang up straight in a wild brush style and his face crinkled in smiles so that his eyes disappeared. His nickname, Moku, was knitted into the bottom of his pullover. When the weather became really hot, he exchanged the beret for a linen golfing cap with a suppressed peak. This he called 'my promenade hat'.

Japanese is an easy enough language to learn badly. I was soon sufficiently fluent to shop and to travel, but there was so much more to it than that. The grammar was tricky, adjectives, for instance, having tenses like verbs, but it was the spirit of the language that was interesting. Tenses were in a way not important. The gist of a statement was all that was needed, especially if it involved the future. The future tense was used only to mean 'Let us do something'. To say 'We shall go on Tuesday' was impossible, for who could say what might or might not happen between now and Tuesday? Everything was kept vague. 'Name is Watanabe, but . . .' No one introducing himself ever used a personal or relative pronoun, though he would always add a 'but' that just hung in the air. What the 'but' meant was not clear, any more than you could be certain what was implied by the 'however' that innkeepers always added when you asked if they had rooms. 'Yes, we have rooms, however . . .' However, you may not like them? But it won't matter in a hundred years?

For Moku I used to write down sentences that I had needed the day before. One night in the inn there was a fearful disturbance. I wrote down: 'What happened last night? Was something wrong?' Moku wriggled and grunted, which meant that he was embarrassed.

'It can't be all that difficult, they are two simple questions.'

'Ah, yes, simple for you.'

At length, he wrote a very complicated sentence in Japanese which I then read out and asked him if I had pronounced it correctly.

'Yes. Very good. But we would never say that, of course.' He had spent ten minutes preparing it.

137

'Well, whatever would you say?'
'*Yube do shita no*. Last night - how was it?'
'What about the second question: was something wrong?'
'Ah, we would never ask that. It would be much too rude, implying that the inn was not a good one.'

People always read into what one said so many more meanings than one could possibly expect. 'We would just repeat the question – *do shita no*.'

The vagueness and mistiness of the language matched the landscape, but its quality also had a direct effect on the character of the people, as is the case with any language, but with Japanese more obviously.

Much later I went to a lecture at a seminar for Japanese teachers of English. The organizer, Shigeo Imamura, was a lecturer at Shikoku University and one of the very few people at that time who spoke perfect English. He had been born in the United States, where his parents had emigrated. When war threatened, the family moved back to Japan, where Imamura, who was ten, finished his schooling at the time when Japanese imperialism was at its strongest. Everything that one supposes he had learned in America was wiped out by the all-pervading militarist doctrine.

When he left school, he volunteered for the Air Force and, at the very end of the war, he trained as a kamikaze, a suicide pilot. The day came when he was to go on his first, and necessarily last, mission. He dressed in his best uniform. They all stood on the tarmac for the final ritual. Unflinching, Imamura drank his formal cup of *saké*. The pilots waited for the order to climb into the planes. It did not come. The Emperor had declared the ending of all kamikaze operations. Five minutes later would have been too late.

The war over, Imamura went to Michigan University to study English and teaching. Meeting him one could have had no inkling of his fanatic past. He was a gentle person, with the soft, pliant face of the southerner that appeared to be fired only with boyish enthusiasm. He was passionate about the teaching of English, and fascinated by the by-ways of etymology and dialect, giving good imitations of an Indian accent long before Peter Sellers isolated its curiosities. He did have an air of authority, almost perhaps the assurance of a mystic. I thought, at first, that this, coupled with a love of precision, was all that remained of what must have been an overpowering certainty that had possessed him in his youth.

When I knew him better, I asked him how much of his earlier belief still lingered within him. Did he, for example, still believe that the Japanese were the chosen race of the gods and superior to any other race?

'It depends on which language I am thinking in. If I am in an American mood and thinking in English, I believe all men are equal. If I am in a Japanese mood among only Japanese people, then I can still believe, half and half, that we are superior to white people, and know with absolute certainty that we are infinitely superior to black ones.'

Almost the hardest aspect of travelling is ridding oneself of prejudice so that one may see other people clearly. I sat with Kawakani San, another teacher, talking about the difference between the exquisite manners of the Japanese in circumstances for which traditional rules had long existed and how rough they were in the modern mechanized culture which had been imposed on them from outside, for which there was no code of politeness. At a crowded festival no one would ever jostle or bump into one, whereas when boarding a train, even when there were plenty of seats, everyone would shove and kick to get on first.

'But you must not be misled into thinking that all Japanese behaviour in public is rude, much of it is rude by Western standards, but polite by Japanese standards.'

'When my wife pushes me in my wheelchair around Kyoto, we come sometimes to a steep step which she cannot manage. There may be half a dozen young men standing about, but none of them ever offers to help. Can you call that polite?'

'Definitely. It is a perfect example of what I am saying. To you it may seem rude that they do not help. To us it is excellent manners to ignore you. First of all, to go to help you would be to draw attention to your disability, and secondly it would place you under an unbearable obligation to the helpers, which you would have no way of repaying.'

'That seems to me a monstrous distortion of common sense.'

'Of course it does, but you will sit there and judge us by your values, and they simply do not apply.'

There were so many values that were directly opposed to ours. There was no disgrace in getting blind drunk at a party and passing out. Homosexuality was not much disapproved of, although, when I talked to Moku about this, he said that, while he would not be scandalized to hear that I was living with a man of my own age, he would think it preferable that I should have a relationship with a boy of fourteen. The contrast that most surprised me was personified by a Tokyo professor who told me that, when he was taken prisoner by the British in Burma, he had served on Mountbatten's staff as an interpreter. No one regarded Professor Nishioka as a traitor; he had behaved sensibly. It was common among Japanese prisoners of war, those at least who did not commit suicide, to reveal anything to their captors. For them the victor was right, an attitude that made the task of the occupying Americans unexpectedly easy.

I struggled more than somewhat in using my imagination to encompass these cultural opposites, but was comforted by the thought of Lafcadio Hearn, the most famous Japanophile of the nineteenth century. He worked, much respected as a foreign teacher, at Tokyo University. He was married to a Japanese and knew everything about the country and loved it so well that he applied for Japanese citizenship. They were much surprised but, in the end, his wish was granted. The following month his pay cheque was for one tenth of the usual amount. When he protested, they bowed and said: 'But you are Japanese now. You get Japanese pay.' He had known not quite everything.

There were opposites, however, that I found wonderful. I do not think anyone could live in Japan without his visual appreciation being altered. Their every sense was so different from what I was used to.

In building, our tradition is to consider the external. We build crescents and squares and make fine façades. We like symmetry and decoration, to show off to the outsider. With the exception of temples and palaces, the Japanese give little thought to the exterior of a building. Their houses present blank faces to the passer-by.

The European ideal of my childhood was for there to be a great clutter indoors, with many pictures on the walls, a mass of furniture, and collections of objects on every surface, while out of doors we liked space – a broad park dotted with trees.

The traditional Japanese house is virtually empty. In one corner of a room hangs one painting in a niche with, below it, a vase of perhaps three flowers. The few bits of furniture – the table for eating, the *futon* for sleeping on – are put away as soon as their purpose is served. Outside, the little space that is available is crammed with plants, stone lanterns, tiny pools and small paths that lead nowhere. A Japanese garden is as cluttered as an English mantelpiece.

Of course, we are all now used to space, encouraged by designers who have been to Japan, but for me it was a revelation and a source of pleasure to learn to see things in a new way.

On one of our many journeys, we went to Hiroshima. It was August, the month in which the first atomic bomb had been dropped on the city thirteen years before. We spent the day visiting the museum and the hospitals and the American medical research centre. It was so moving and distressing that, in the evening, I found it impossible to write my notes with any self-control. Instead, for almost the only time in my life, I wrote a poem:

Today they crowd thick in the Peace Park of Hiroshima
And they remember.
Thirteen years ago it fell, at eight-sixteen a.m.
With passive pride they most remember this:
I was one kilometre five away and I nine twenty metres.

The vault beneath the shabby arch is open this one day
And, dankly dim, the roll with unread names
Serves for two hundred thousand graves.
All manner of believers peer,
Bombers and the bombed,
Half reconciled in comfort with these symbols.

The Buddhist Phoenix, on the cathedral roof,
Stares unaccustomed at the Christian Cross –
Mere symbols to be argued by the Vatican.

Nor does the living dying evidence have more to tell.
In the hospital, the housewife shows her photographs
And, crying, claims:
'My son won prizes in our baby show.'
Then, laughing with the laughing doctor, waits to die.
The burned schoolgirl strips her kimono for the thousandth time,
With innocent gladness baring her useless flesh.
The bank clerk cannot count his white corpuscles,
But smiles, 'I'm well – it was one kilometre two.'

The naive brochure extols the broadness of the streets
Peace Boulevard, it says, adds beauty one hundred metres wide;
Aside, it makes an 'effective firebreak in case of major fires'.

Japan at this time was suddenly interesting to the British. The house we took in Kyoto seemingly became a stopping point on every visitor's tour. Lady Violet Bonham-Carter, Stephen Spender, Sacheverell Sitwell, Arthur Koestler, Harold Nicolson and Vita Sackville-West, Gavin Astor, John Foster and many others. We guided them round the temples and the gardens of Kyoto, answering always the same questions again and again about cruelty, geishas, hot baths and other clichés, which made me realize how narrow one nation's perception of another is bound to be, and therefore made me more tolerant of the Japanese who always put the equivalent questions to me, although what they were usually more concerned with were a foreigner's impressions of their country.

The visitors provided entertainment as well. Gavin Astor, the owner of *The Times*, wanted to know what to buy his wife as a present. At first, he rejected the idea of cultured pearls, on the grounds that he had given her real ones as a wedding present. Then he thought for a bit and said: 'I suppose I could buy her a few strings of these and they'd do for travelling.'

John Foster, the Conservative MP, came with a Russian princess. I took them for dinner to a beautiful inn by the river at Arashiyama. I had asked for a carp, which we ate raw. It was a glistening, fresh fish and delicious. We ate the whole of one side and wanted more. The kneeling maids turned the fish over, at which it started to open and close its mouth and gills. It was still alive. The giggling girls poured sake down its throat and it lay still. Most of the guests would have no more and even regretted what they had already had. John ate happily on, only sending a nervous postcard from England on his return to say that Miriam Rothschild, the great expert on all kinds of parasite, had told him that carp were especially liable to a vicious liver fluke and that to eat them raw was folly.

The Nicolsons were reluctant sightseers, disliking the idea of getting out of the car, which meant that they saw little. They were on a cruise and only in Kyoto for one day, so I felt that Vita must see at least one garden and took them to one I was fond of. They bumbled round quite quickly and sank gratefully back into the car, Vita saying: 'Well, now we've seen a Japanese garden in Japan and it's really much more like a Japanese garden in England than we expected.'

Sacheverell and Georgia Sitwell arrived in a state of indignation. They had heard that Stephen Spender was staying in Tokyo in rooms above a rather saucy bar.

'It is a disgrace that he should behave like that,' said Sitwell, 'and I think he should have his passport taken away. I have never trusted

142

him since the Spanish Civil War when he supported the wrong side, a traitor to his class.'

Sitwell was in Japan doing research for a book that he published a year later called *The Bridge of the Brocade Sash*. When it came out, I was asked to review it. It had all the flourish of his famous books of travel, but it was almost a work of fiction. He described seeing from the window of a train the castle of Himeji, standing proud above the town. It had actually been bombed flat during the war. He wrote of the long red-lacquer bridge in the Heian Shrine, whereas it was of plain wood. I counted 208 errors of fact. We met at a party soon after my review was printed. I was sitting with a large glass of whisky in my hand. Sitwell came over: 'My dear fellow, how nice to see you again.' He took the wrist of the hand that held my glass and shook it with vigorous warmth. I was soaked. It seemed a fair revenge for what he no doubt took to be a betrayal of my class.

Arthur Koestler was also researching a book – *The Lotus and the Robot*. Like many other former Communists, he spent long years searching for a replacement for the god that failed. Eventually he was to settle for the paranormal, but at this time he was examining, and rejecting with an over-reasoned fury, the religions of the East.

We made many expeditions together, which were fun, but always threatened by Arthur's irascibility. There is often in people who care passionately about humanity as a whole an amazing insensitivity to individual feelings. Bertrand Russell, for instance, treated his wives with a cruelty that was startling, yet his concern for the world was genuine and moving. Arthur was an extreme example of this phenomenon.

In Tokyo, he had gone with a teacher and translator of Japanese, Professor Ivan Morris, and his Japanese wife to a Kabuki bar, the Otowa. The manager, Fumio San, a disappointed actor, was impressed at having such a distinguished visitor, for the newspapers had been full of articles about the arrival of this foreign writer, who was much admired in Japan.

Kabuki actors are all men and very often homosexual, so there was little likelihood that Fumio San's attentions to Morris's wife, Yaki, were other than amusing. Arthur decided that Fumio was trying to seduce her. He flung a glass of whisky in the actor's face.

I had not heard about this, but happened to go to the bar soon after. Fumio San, when he learned that I was a writer, asked me: 'In England are writers good or bad men?'

143

'Good and bad, like everybody else.'

'Mr Spender, he is a good man, is he not?'

'Yes.'

'But not all writers are good men like him?'

'No.'

'Do most English writers hate the Japanese?'

He then told me about Arthur and the whisky. Fumio had done nothing. He had just ignored Arthur, who then left. Two nights later, Fumio took an overdose of sleeping pills. He did not die.

'Did he hate me because I am Japanese?'

Fumio and his vanity could not believe he was disliked for himself but, in a kind of national humility, felt a keen disgrace. I could not explain it to him.

Nor could I explain Fumio to Arthur. When I told him about the suicide attempt, he just growled: 'How could he be so stupid?'

We went with Arthur to the south. Japanese respect for learning and particularly the teacher runs parallel with their belief that the victor is right. I used to teach a few students and could never get them to discuss a book with any spirit of disagreement. My opinion, as teacher, must prevail. So as we left Tokyo, several professors came to see us off and, whenever the train stopped, academics from the local university would come on board to pay their respects to the famous *sensei*.

All this aggravated Arthur. We broke the journey at a small town near the Inland Sea. As soon as Arthur stepped out of the train, two young men from the local radio station rushed up asking for an interview. Arthur said he was on a private visit and would rather not make any statement. The journalists persisted and begged for a few words. Arthur gave in. They switched on their tape recorder.

'What are your impressions of Kurashiki?'

Arthur pointed out that all he had seen of Kurashiki was the station platform.

'Go away and think of some more intelligent questions.'

After ten minutes, while we arranged the next stage of our journey, the boys came back, bubbling with new confidence, and said that they were ready with their questions.

'What are they?'

'First, what are your impressions of Kurashiki?'

I grabbed Arthur's arm as he raised it to hit the boy, and distracted him with some financial matter. He liked to reckon up any expendi-

144

ture as soon as possible, so that we could be 'straight', as he put it. About four times a day, he would start muttering Hungarian numerals and then either hand over, or demand from me, a few yen to get us 'straight'.

Possibly more successful were our visits to monasteries so that Arthur could learn more about Zen. He thoroughly enjoyed the day when, trying to understand the philosophy that lay behind Zen's interest in archery, after listening to much stuff about the 'itness' of the arrows and the selflessness of the aim, he discovered that the archer stood only twenty-five feet from the target.

In Kyoto, I arranged for Arthur to meet the head Abbot of Daitokuji, the largest Zen temple. We knelt on rather thin cushions facing the Abbot, who had an enviably fat one. It was soon plain that neither he nor the monks who accompanied him were going to answer in any helpful way the questions Arthur put to them.

'Is there a metaphysic in Zen?'

'No.'

'Is there judgement between good and evil?'

'None.'

'Why, then, is Zen not immoral?'

'By Zen you cross into a world where good, evil, and beauty do not exist and, having seen this, you are free to come back to this world and see that they do not exist here either.'

The monks threw out little parables:

'A horse in Tokyo eats and a horse in Osaka feels full.'

'But that is totally meaningless.'

'It is no more unreasonable than when a Sputnik goes up in Russia, the stocks go down in New York.'

Arthur was quite equal to this. He transposed the problems of guilt by omission raised in Camus's *La Chute*, with much irrelevant elaboration of the kind with which the monks decorated their parables.

'A man is on his way to prayer. He is crossing an elegant, red-lacquer bridge. From beneath the bridge comes a cry from the deep, still water. A man is drowning. The Zen monk is so intent upon his prayer that he does not hear the cry for help.'

The Abbot was angry; having answered logic with parables, he now switched to a definite reply:

'We are not like that. He would hear, and he should go to him.'

The Abbot soon reverted to evasion. Discussing whether they were a mendicant order he said: 'Two or three of us go out into the street, but we don't beg. We happen to have a bowl in our hands into which people happen to put money.'

I asked whether Zen was a religion for everyone.

'We press nobody. If I decide to go to Tokyo, I do not insist that everyone should come with me.'

I tried Arthur's tactics:

'A man is living in poverty. In tending his aged mother and mixing her medicines, he discovers the panacea for all ills. Should he cure only his mother?'

'Zen is open to everyone to find for himself. Your logical questions merely embarrass us.' He stood up and left the room.

We abandoned our original plan to go on to Thailand, because Martha became pregnant again. It had been difficult enough settling into Japan with a small child. The idea of going through all that again with Martha expecting a baby was too daunting. We thought of moving to America or going back to England, but it seemed easier to stay put. Six months, in any case, had not been enough to penetrate the mists of Japanese culture. It was really in the second half of the year that we learned to understand more of the country.

Sabrina was born in a hospital not far from our house. The Japanese doctor had trained in America, but was quite horrified when I suggested that I might be there when the baby was born. It had not been allowed when Sebastian was born because there had been a fear that it might have to be a Caesarean section.

Martha was amazed by the Japanese mothers in her ward. From the first moment that their babies were put into their arms, they started to chatter to them – telling them how welcome they were and what wonderful lives they were going to have. Perhaps this was the explanation for the fact that Japanese children talk so much earlier than European ones.

I wrote to Colin that the emotions one feels at the birth of a daughter were quite different from those when one had a son. I did not expand on this. Now, I cannot recapture any differences in feeling. What I most remember is that Sabrina howled without cease for the first three months of her life and then settled down to be the quietest of all my daughters.

Japan stays with me as an experience that altered my life. Not only did

146

I look at everything with different eyes, but I began to accept the idea that there were attitudes, ways of behaviour and standards that were neither better nor worse than ours, merely different.

It was a beginning, but not enough. I came to feel that I would never make a real friend in Japan. It was easier to form a relationship with the women, whose spirit was freer, despite the outward patterns of male domination, but we met so few of them.

It was an incident with Moku that made me despair. It had always seemed to me that we were on easy-going terms. In fact, he often used to surprise me with confidences about his private life that in Europe would only be usual between extremely intimate friends. He grumbled a lot about his wife and, when I asked why he had married her, said: 'Her insistence was greater than my refusal.'

Long after I had any need of his help, Moku used to rattle in to see us and make us laugh with his accounts of other tourists and of the regular misfortunes that befell him. One day, he told me that he had lost his watch when mountain climbing. He had never let me pay him much – the equivalent of £3 a month for five mornings a week. (Our nanny and cook each had £7 a month.) Here was an opportunity to make up for this. I bought a watch that was good enough to give anyone pleasure, but not so expensive as to be alarming to him.

I prepared the way with care, even with someone nominally so uninhibited by tradition. I reminded him how *apuré* he was and how *modan*, which meant modern. I said that between us the usual rules of obligation did not apply, especially as I was a foreigner. He would owe me nothing in return for this small present. Moku agreed with all this. I gave him the box. He unwrapped the watch and, when he saw it, his face tightened and his eyes disappeared into two straight lines. He bowed right down to the ground, coming up with a sharp hiss. I had never seen him bow before and now he did so four times. He ran from the house and we did not see him for nearly a week. When, in the end, he came back, he bowed again, and gave me a small box. It was a cultured pearl ring for Martha that must have cost about £4, a month's wages for his afternoon job at a blood bank.

'Why did you do it? Why, when I had begged you not to?'

Moku bowed: 'The burden of my obligation was too great.'

Now, I would view it differently. I was expecting the rules of friendship to be the same in Japan as they were in Europe. I had failed to see that I had made friends – ones who would have been, in all probability, more constant than many on whom I counted at home.

I spent the last fortnight of our stay in Tokyo and boarded the liner that was to bring us home in Yokohama. Martha had gone to the Japan Alps for a week before packing up. She and the children joined the ship in Kobe. Everyone had come to see us off and they all came on board – the Abbot of a small Zen temple in grey robes, fascinated by everything on the boat, most of all by how many American cigarettes I could buy for him merely by signing a chit. The students that I had taught came in succession throughout the day, all pledging friendship.

'And you too, please always be my friend, and if I ever come to your country, please honour me by receiving me as your one-time Japanese companion.'

The cook and the nanny, both suddenly tiny and cowering in the passageways, cried as I had never seen people cry at parting.

Moku had not come by the time all visitors were asked to leave the ship. Martha and I sat in our cabin. She told me that she had fallen in love with someone else. At that moment, Moku, wearing his hunting beret, romped in. With his wide-boy expertise, he had got on board late and without a pass.

I had a lot to learn.

CHAPTER TWELVE

THE POWDER MAGAZINE

Jocelyn Stevens had recently bought *The Queen*, then a faded magazine dealing with women's fashions and the fringes of Society. Jocelyn, whose mother had died when he was born, was on that account not on very good terms with his father, who resented him. He was more attached to his maternal uncle, Edward Hulton, the founder, more by good luck than shrewd judgement, of *Picture Post* and *Lilliput*, two immensely successful magazines. From him Jocelyn acquired an enthusiasm for publishing and, from that side of his family, quite a lot of money and a certain instability of temperament. He also had, from somewhere, golden good looks and a boyish charm, coupled with amazing energy.

Jeannie Campbell, Beaverbrook's granddaughter, Vere Harmsworth, Rothermere's son, Jocelyn and I had often talked of the possibility of starting a magazine, but nothing had come of it. Now, Jocelyn had written to me in Japan and asked me to join *The Queen* as one of the assistant editors.

The team that Jocelyn gathered round him and that I joined in 1959 reflected not only his character, but his own understanding of the weaknesses and strengths of that character. It revealed, too, that instinct for what the public that he was aiming at wanted, but did not know they wanted, that is the key to much successful journalism.

He was devoid of taste. I remember a particular painting that he bought and loved of a baby that had apparently fallen through a window frame and lay surrounded by broken glass. To remedy this deficiency, he employed Mark Boxer, a friend from his days at Cambridge, who had more than enough taste or at least visual

149

imagination for two, and who could be depended on for outrageous opinions of all kinds.

The editor was Beatrix Miller, a person of wonderfully balanced judgement, who Jocelyn recognized would never be frightened of him, who could not be bullied and who would always save him from the excesses to which he was prone. Her knowledge of fashion was unerring; her ability to smooth out troubles pretty to see.

Jocelyn did not understand writing, although he could come up with a forceful phrase. This lack was filled by Francis Wyndham, whose literary talents and learning were impeccable, so that the magazine published much good writing and criticism. I was employed to tease the Establishment without causing too much hurt.

In other fields Jocelyn was canny. He kept on from the old magazine a Miss Holmes and a Mr Pemberton, who watched over the finances with careful thoroughness. He also enticed Mrs Kenward, who wrote Jennifer's Diary, away from the *Tatler*. Everybody else groaned at the idea of her long lists of names and perpetual praise for every function she attended. Mark, who saw himself as a romantic radical, having been the first person since Shelley to be sent down from university for blasphemy, even threatened to resign if she came to the magazine.

She did come, bringing with her large numbers of readers, so that Jocelyn was proved right commercially, and we all came to like and admire Betty Kenward for her courage and her honesty. As a widow, she had worked during the war as a boys' maid at Eton in order to earn money to educate her son. The fact that she never said anything disparaging in her column, except in the most general terms, did not mean that she did not have strong opinions. Her methods were subtle. Girls whose hair was dirty would never be mentioned, boys whom she thought mannerless were left out. There was a kind of code of omission that she operated fearlessly. It may not sound much, but I have no doubt that most of those she disapproved of were pained at not being mentioned, being those sort of people. Her approval, on the other hand, was far more direct. She was always thoughtful about anyone who worked for her, and extremely helpful to young people, sympathizing with those whose parents' failings she detected with shrewdness. Her stamina was as unusual as her integrity – she kept dreadful hours, always being up by six-thirty in the morning, never being late at the office, missing nothing, never tiring. She has only recently retired at the age of eighty-five.

The beginning of any new enterprise is exciting, particularly in a field where results are so immediate. Within a year of Jocelyn's buying *The Queen*, it became fashionable and, in limited ways, influential. It was the time when at last the war could be forgotten, when the old conventions were being broken. Harold Macmillan's boomtime was in full swing. A new irreverence was abroad, but also in our minds there was the idea that life was not so compartmented that a magazine must be either serious or frivolous but not both, that fashion could not mix with politics, that good writing was too sacred to lie beside nonsense. It was a new approach that set a pattern that has been copied by glossy magazines ever since.

We carried articles teasing the government and the Establishment, pieces about anti-Semitism, rising violence, the horror of the gossip columns, the Hanratty murder, interviews with Harold Macmillan, President Kennedy and Harold Wilson and, as a result of Francis Wyndham's influence, writing by Truman Capote, Tom Wolfe, Graham Greene, Dom Moraes, Colin MacInnes, Frank Tuohy, Angus Wilson, Alan Sillitoe and many others.

Television very often picked out articles in the magazine and followed them up. The Profumo scandal was set off by an oblique question asked by Robin Douglas-Home in his column.

Perhaps more than anything, it was Jocelyn's enthusiasm for good photography, coupled with Mark's skill at layout and design, that brought such success. Jocelyn had that kind of meanness that the poor most resent in the rich, of quibbling over the trivial and yet splashing out on big things. While the previous owner had thought that 19s 6d was a lot to pay for a photograph, Jocelyn would spend thousands of pounds on a set of pictures by Henri Cartier-Bresson, Richard Avedon, Helmut Newton or whoever he happened to admire. Tony Armstrong-Jones made his name on *The Queen* before he married Princess Margaret.

It was a tempestuous place to work. The offices were in a tall Victorian house in Burleigh Street, off the Strand by Covent Garden. Our editorial discussions often took place in the Savoy Grill, where Mark would draw layouts all over the tablecloths. Then we would go back to the office and Jocelyn would call a general meeting to complain about how much was being spent on taxis, scourging himself into a state of manic rage. His pale face would gradually suffuse with red and he would rise up and down, bending at the knees, so that he looked like a furious cockerel on a carousel. His voice would soar higher and higher, until it broke in a sob at the pitiable thought of how our extravagance was ruining him.

Sometimes he would beat with his fists on his desk and at others lie on the floor in a stiff anger, thumping and thumping on the thin carpet so that the plaster on the ceiling of my room below fell in flakes. We learned to pay little attention to these passions which were, I suspect, more alarming to him, who had insanity in his family, than to us. Mark Boxer's ice-cold spikiness, very telling in its accurate cruelty, was far more unpleasant. His was no blind lashing out, prompted by some sad inadequacy, but a desire to hurt, with neatly trimmed darts sharpened mostly by envy and jealousy. He was always afraid that someone might supplant him in Jocelyn's affections, although Jocelyn had a concept of loyalty unrecognized by Mark. In the end, it was Jocelyn who felt betrayed when Mark left after four years.

Jocelyn was always himself, either up or down, while Mark was at times unrecognizable. He stood once round a passage corner when Colin, who knew him well, came to pick me up. They did not see each other. Mark was ranting at me. As we went, Colin asked, 'Who on earth was that going on in that extraordinary way?' Mark. Colin had to go to see, not believing me, and came back bemused.

And yet I had a far greater everyday rapport with Mark than with Jocelyn. In fact, I was firmly fond of him, liking him almost whatever he did, in the way that one can love some unlovable friends. If one is disabled, one is very conscious of people's reactions to helping. Jocelyn hated it. He never expressed this and would, if necessary, carry me up the stairs but, if there was somebody else strong enough, he would always let them do it. Mark who was far weaker was always ready to help, giggling as he stumbled and we teetered on the steps.

It may, of course, be that the reluctance really lies in me. I certainly divide people into those I am happy to ask for help and those on whom I would much prefer not to make any demand. I tell myself that it is what I sense in them that decides it, but perhaps it is my instinct that is at fault. Either way I should forget it. If the hesitation is theirs, they should know better. If it is mine, it is silly. It is one of the problems of disability that I have never learned to ignore.

The one thing that always restored Jocelyn's good humour was a crisis. There was a printing strike soon after I joined The Queen. Jocelyn flew to Germany, found a clandestine printer who would print the magazine secretly at night, in defiance of the German printers' solidarity with the British strikers. He took all the manuscripts and photographic blocks with him and set much of the type himself. Once the copies were in England, he and all the staff humped the bales onto lorries for distribution. For three weeks *The Queen* was the only magazine to appear.

It was all fun. Francis Wyndham made us laugh in the middle of all disasters with his whimsical air of bemused common sense. Many of our contributors were exotic. Jonathan Miller, working at the time at the Middlesex Hospital, would send round notes hastily scribbled on the nearest piece of paper headed, 'Coffin and Shroud ticket'. Tony Snowdon was given to practical jokes. One weekend, he bought from a totter in the King's Road a pile of old exhaust pipes. He took them to Jocelyn's house in Chelsea, knowing that he was away. The maid hardly liked to turn away Princess Margaret's husband. On the first floor landing, Tony welded the exhaust pipes into an enormous sculpture with waving arms, far too big to be moved down the stairs.

After about a year, we moved from Burleigh Street to modern offices in Fetter Lane. Somehow, the fun was much diminished. Instead of a kind of undergraduate romp, it became a more grown-up undertaking. Jocelyn was always brave, particularly in defying advertisers, but he had got engaged at my wedding party and his responsibilities were greater. When Harold Wilson took over, Jocelyn interviewed him and came away impressed by what needed to be done in the wake of Macmillan's premiership. He commissioned sombre articles about the plight of those who had not flourished in the boom. He printed an issue on ration-book paper. The advertisers fled. The froth soon returned.

My role changed. Jocelyn had bought a travel magazine called *Go!* I edited it for a number of issues, all of them beautiful, with the finest writing by such authors as Patrick Leigh Fermor, Raleigh Trevelyan, Patrick Kinross and Robin Fedden and also the best photographs. The advertising plummeted and the pathetic circulation remained the same. The places that I liked to have articles about were usually on no airline's route and surely not those that travel agents wanted to promote.

Discreetly, Jocelyn suggested that I should write a history of *The Queen* for its centenary in 1961. It had been founded by Samuel Beeton, the husband of Mrs Beeton. Sam was a monster. One of his descendants, the journalist Nancy Spain, when she heard what I was doing, took me to the British Museum to show me the collected correspondence columns from another of Sam's publications, *The*

Englishwoman's Journal. Oddly, they were in the 'Private Case', that is among the naughty books, not available without special permission.

Had one seen an occasional copy of the *The Englishwoman's Journal*, one would not have noticed anything strange about the letters page. It was when one realized that the correspondence about the spurring of horses had gone on for three years that suspicion arose; tight-lacing lasted four or five and chastising of young girls was a hardy perennial. Closer reading revealed the same phrases about, for instance, 'the glorious, stern look in his eye as he raised the cane to beat me', recurring at intervals, until it was plain that all the letters were by the same hand. Hearing that Nancy had been to see me, another descendant, Mrs Patsy Fisher, who had been an MP, arrived in my office to beg me not to pay any attention to the lies that Nancy would have told me. I hardly liked to tell her of our visit to the British Museum.

Apart from the fact that proofs of the magazine were always sent to Queen Victoria before publication, Sam was the only object of interest in the magazine's history. It would have made a dull book. I hit on the idea of doing a light-hearted study of the attitudes of Society over the previous hundred years, as reflected in *The Queen*.

I had four young researchers, one of whom was Auberon Waugh. I gave them each some volumes from each decade to read through, in order to get a different point of view on every period, for their selections of what they thought interesting varied according to their characters.

Katharine Sachs, the respectable daughter of a judge, was excellent on domestic questions; Judy Innes was good at historical and literary things, pointing out, for example, that there was no mention at all of the General Strike in 1926; Terence Griffin loved the bits about servants and eccentrics; but Auberon had a special genius for finding the least expected but often the most telling things – many of them to do with disasters, of which the Victorians were particularly fond. Only he could have found a reader's letter about mice:

> Can you inform me whether singing mice are very uncommon? I lately heard one in my room and it made quite a flute-like musical noise, almost like the singing of a bird. (The so-called singing in mice is really only an asthmatic wheezing, arising from an obstruction of the air passages. When captured the singing can always be produced at will by putting the cage in cold air – Ed.)

The book, entitled *The Frontiers of Privilege*, was beautifully designed by Charles Rosner. It had friendly reviews, but met with little success, which was a pity because it shone an interesting sidelight on history.

By this time, I had also landed myself with a task that was to occupy part of my life for the next twenty years. We used to publish every fortnight a list of restaurants with one-line comments about each. It took up about half a page. We had not noticed one day that the girl who was responsible for it was ill. When her list was meant to go to the printers, we had an empty half-page and only an hour or two to fill it. I was on my way to lunch and suggested that I write something about the restaurant I was going to. It happened to be Wilton's, a famous fish restaurant in St James's, very popular with the aristocracy, and run by a former club servant, Mr Marks, who had formed the opinion that what the upper classes liked was for their servants to be rude to them.

I had no idea how to cook anything, but I was greedy and enjoyed food. At the same time, I had always thought that food writers who described in detail what they had eaten were rather disgusting. They could not be sure that their description of some rich dish might not be read by someone with a hangover or jaundice. Furthermore, they used awful words like 'tasty', 'morsel', 'portion' and 'condiment'. I decided to say, in decent English, only what there was to eat and whether I liked it. But that would not fill half a page, and I had to write about something. I thought I would include some remarks about the decoration of the restaurant, do a pen portrait of the egregious Mr Marks and describe the waitresses and the other customers – rather as if the whole thing were a bit of theatre.

Wilton's was a gift from this point of view, with the aristocrats, the simple cooking, like nursery food plus caviar, oysters and lobsters, and the waitresses dressed like nannies. It might have been a play by William Douglas-Home. I was able to end my piece by saying that the prices, as befitted the clientele, were like death duties, aimed at capital rather than income.

No one had ever written about restaurants in this way. I became the restaurant correspondent. For a long time I blundered about having no knowledge of my subject, justifying this to myself on the grounds that I was an average restaurant-goer. I did not need to know anything other than whether I had enjoyed myself.

The column became popular. Mr Pemberton's alarm that my frequent rudeness would frighten away advertisers proved groundless. Restaurants, knowing that mine was the most read column on the subject, flocked to place their advertisements near it.

All at once, I was an expert – a situation that has made me very wary of experts ever since; the more so because, after thirty years, I still know very little about it and have never pretended that I do, yet I have become even more of an expert since I virtually stopped writing about food.

My power was extraordinary, fortunately mostly for good. There were two or three restaurants that I rescued from disaster by writing about them and filling them with customers, one run by a future brother-in-law. Filling them was sometimes unhelpful, because a rocky restaurant that had cut down on staff to save money might not be able to cope with a sudden influx. There was only one restaurant that I wrote about that actually closed as a result. I cannot remember its name, but it was appalling. The waiter, when I asked for ice, brought a sackful, put it on the floor and jumped on it to break it up. Our dirty plates he piled on to the next table, which was empty. For two weeks people flocked to see if it were truly as bad as I had said. It was. The following week it shut.

Sometimes there were unexpected results from my articles. I always enjoyed Chez Luba, a nominally Russian restaurant, though the owner, Niki, was I think Polish. His *koulibiaka* was the best I have ever tasted and everything else was good, helped I dare say by the rowanberry vodka. I did tease him about the red flock wallpaper and his Edwardian style of decoration. Goaded by this, he ripped it out and half the building collapsed; it had been supported by the wallpaper. When he reopened Niki, plonking a two-kilo tin of Sevruga caviar on the table, told me how many thousands it had cost him to rebuild the place and to redecorate. Of course, he put in red flock wallpaper and it all looked exactly the same.

I don't know what went wrong for him, but the restaurant closed a year or two later and Niki stood in Walton Street giving away pots and pans and china and glass and silver to any passer-by.

My favourite headwaiter was Luigi at the Savoy Grill, a man of much greater distinction than most of his clients, a great actor, who moved with a grace that Jeeves would have envied, and a fine fly-fisherman. For some reason, he was moved to the restaurant at Claridge's, where the food was never as good as at the Savoy. As if enquiring about something of no particular interest, he asked me one day why I was never so polite about Claridge's as I had been about the

Savoy. I lifted up a lettuce leaf under which I knew there was, by good luck, a fat slug lurking. I had been wondering whether to make a fuss about it and, if so, what sort of fuss. Now there was no need. I said nothing. Luigi said nothing. He tilted his head to one side and gave a little bow. Then he picked up my salad (he was never too grand to do things himself) and walked away with a little smile round his eyes. We never spoke of these things again.

By that time, I was also writing about restaurants for the *Evening Standard*, so that I had to go to at least ten a week. It was impossible to maintain anonymity, as the waiter population of London is nomadic; in any new restaurant there were always one or two who knew me from some other establishment. It made little difference, because a mediocre chef cannot suddenly cook well, indeed he probably makes even more of a hash of it if he knows he is being tested, and as for service, I paid no attention to what happened to me, but watched how people at other tables were treated.

The early years of my restaurant writing were ones in which a great deal was happening. Restaurants, like everything else, had been stuck in a pre-war mould. There had been in my youth four things that were never talked about, being unmentionable for reasons of decorum or because they were taken for granted – sex, money, decoration and food. Now, no one talked of anything else. Gradually there appeared small bistros that produced something approaching French food. Then came an Italian revolution – the old Italian restaurants, largely run by Cypriots, were superseded by noisy trattorias run by Neapolitans who dressed up their peasant cooking as if it were a form of *haute cuisine*. The success of both the bistros and the trattorias coincided with the spreading of the expense account lunch.

I became, if not knowledgeable, much involved in this sideline, as I always regarded it, of my work. The trouble about getting to know the restaurateurs was that I found myself feeling sorry for them, because I could understand their difficulties. Before, I had not cared if staff were hard to find, taxes readjusted or whatever – I just judged.

Restaurateurs, I discovered, were for the most part exceptionally charming people. There is in the nature of their work an element of generosity and a desire to please, which are essential if they are to be successful. Naturally, there are some who achieve success without these traits.

Many became real friends. Nick Clarke ran what he called a diner in Fulham, but it was a very serious restaurant that had a considerable influence. Nick was exuberant and fat. He was also naive in the most attractive way, believing that the world could be made better for everyone – a view, incidentally, shared with less naivety by Raymond Postgate, the founder of the *Good Food Guide*, whose hope it was that socialism would mean *haute cuisine* for everybody. Nick became the Liberal candidate for Chelsea, but, as may be imagined, not much came of that. And Nick, who had never done anyone anything but good, with too much food and too much drink died young.

Mario and Franco were two Savoy waiters, who launched the trattoria revolution. They opened the Terrazza, a small place in a basement in Soho. Mario was the expansive one, who burst with Italian bonhomie and created muddles. Soon after Tony Armstrong-Jones married Princess Margaret, Jocelyn took him to the Terrazza. Tony had no tie. Mario, used to the Savoy, would not let him in, until Franco explained who he was. After that Mario would hardly let anyone in who was wearing a tie. Franco came from a rather grand Neapolitan family with princely connections, and was as privately melancholy as Mario was extrovert.

A large part of their success was due to the designer of all their restaurants, Enzo Apicella, one of the funniest men I know, if one can understand anything of what he says, whether in Italian or English. He cast out the dreadful pictures of Vesuvius in eruption and the Bay of Naples by moonlight that Mario loved, and created a style entirely his own that has served well ever since.

From this small beginning, there grew a whole family of Italian restaurants, started by waiters who had worked for Mario and Franco, though there was also a thread of tragedy that ran beside the successes. After Mario and Franco sold their large business of a dozen or more restaurants, they fell out. Franco went back to Italy and died soon after. The third partner in the restaurants, another Luigi, also retired to Italy, and was murdered. Mario, bored, started another restaurant on his own, but it only caused him trouble and a heart attack.

Joseph Berkmann started as a restaurateur in 1958, opening the Genevieve. Ten years later, he owned a total of nine restaurants, scattered all over London. They were not outstanding, but mostly above average. It was Joseph who first made me understand the problems of restaurateurs and contrived to soften my unyielding approach to my subject. He was a good employer, demanding, but generous, encouraging his young managers to take responsibility. Yet every time I saw him he would have some frightful story to tell of how one or other of his staff had cheated him, fiddled the books, or left him in the lurch.

Joseph, really, was more interested in wine than in food, eventually getting rid of all his restaurants except for the Jardin des Gourmets and concentrating on his wine business. He taught me much that I am grateful for. In the 1960s, he used to give dinners in one of his restaurants that can have had no parallel then and would be impossible now. Each dinner was devoted either to a château or to a chosen year. The wine was always claret. The dinners that I remember most clearly – which, as you will see, could not be all that clearly – were for Mouton-Rothschild, for 1945 and for 1949. When the dinner was for a château, we had roughly a dozen different examples of the wine in question. In the case of the Mouton-Rothschild, we started with the 1893 and then progressed through the Twenties and Thirties, admiring the 1928 and pondering the 1934, and adoring those wonderful, unevenly numbered years of the Forties until we got, I think, to 1953. If the dinner was for a year, we had a dozen different châteaux to compare – 1945 Lafitte, Latour, Margaux, Haut-Brion, Cheval Blanc . . . it is hardly possible to believe. We swigged away at bottles that would sell today for £1,000 or more – not just in sips but in glassfuls. I think it was Bernard Levin who described one of these evenings as 'the most elegant piss-up' he had ever attended.

On occasions, I went with Joseph to France on wine-tasting trips during which he taught me as much about burgundy as he had about claret; and I still turn to him to hear of unknown vineyards that will produce, at a reasonable price, the kind of wine he taught me to enjoy.

I got to know David Levin when he opened the Capital Hotel in 1968. I had had a press release about the hotel and was intrigued by the statement that, if customers put their shoes outside the door at night, they would not only be shined but also resoled if necessary. Such service, I thought, needed investigating. What I was not prepared for was to find that the restaurant was the equal of any in London at the time.

David turned out to be a delightful Scotsman, a man of exceptional kindness and generosity, with the most beautiful wife. He likes to pretend that my article in the *Evening Standard* produced his first customers for the restaurant, which had been completely empty for six weeks after it opened. Over the years, he has helped me far more than I ever helped him.

After twenty years, I decided that I had said all I had to say on the subject of food and today only very occasionally weaken in my resolve.

Martha and I bought a house in Chelsea. Our married life continued in a rather formal manner for about a year, but Martha was not happy. For the sake of her Aunt Martha, who was coming to stay with us, venturing abroad for the first time in her life, we endeavoured to put on a brave show. She was not deceived, demanding to know why the laughter had gone out of her niece.

I could give no answer, because I had not then understood how much of a burden it is for a young person to live with someone who is disabled. At that point, I could still walk a little, enough to get around the house and to and from the garage, but whenever we were going out we had to work out whether there were any steps, whether there would be someone to help. It meant that Martha had to do so many things that a husband would normally do, such as loading the car or parking it in the rain.

Often she and someone else would carry me, making a seat with their crossed hands. With Alan Brien's wife, Nancy, two majestic girls in white gloves, she bore me up the broad stairs of Covent Garden for the first night of an opera. It was, as you might say, all right for me.

Martha moved out.

As *The Queen* prospered, the new offices in Fetter Lane were soon crowded. Jocelyn put into my office, according to him in the face of vociferous protests from both of us, one of the junior girls – Angela Huth. Within a year, in August 1961, we were married.

The theory that divorced people often marry the same sort of person again is not true in my case. The three people I have been married to have nothing whatever in common – except, of course, me.

Angela was the opposite of Martha in almost every way. She was pretty rather than beautiful, bouncy and short, moving with rapid steps, rather than stately and tall. Her education was dismal.

She was, on the other hand, a person of great strength of character and varied interests. She had decided when young that she wanted to be a writer. She had studied for a while at the Beaux Arts in Paris. She had composed songs and she played the piano in a style that might be called 'after Charlie Kunz'. She was a good photographer. These other activities, however, were sidelines to be practised for pleasure, while writing was the supreme objective. She had got her job on *The Queen* by writing little articles and slipping them into Jocelyn's pocket whenever she saw him at debutantes' parties.

160

Any shortcomings Angela may have had were more than counter-balanced by the most attractive qualities of optimism, curiosity in the best sense and resilience. She enjoyed life, laughed more at herself than at other people and she had a singular capacity for loving.

Angela's father, Harold Huth, had been a film star in the Thirties, with a large following of excitable women, who would write to Angela whenever she published an article, telling her how they had loved him. He was a most friendly, but sorrowfully weak, man who wished everyone well, and so surrendered his one talent to the whim of his wife, Bridget. She did not like his being an actor and persuaded him to become a producer, for which he was not so well suited, although very skilled at dealing with the unions, so that any film set he worked on was always a happy one.

He was embarrassed when we got engaged, having been told by Bridget to ask me what my prospects were. We sat forlornly, drinking whisky, not knowing what to say to each other, I having no prospects to speak of and he not wishing to convey that sort of news to Bridget. At length, we hit on a formula and thereafter we were on fine conspiratorial terms.

Bridget was at heart a generous, unselfish woman, who had been filled with much nonsense by her extraordinary mother.

The family was somehow dominated by Bridget's mother, a raucous Irishwoman of more than eighty, who lived in what had been Harold Macmillan's flat in Half Moon Street. She was rich, having been married to two millionaires, and owned the largest pearl in the world, so famous that it had had a book written about its strange history. It had been stolen more than once and was found in a matchbox in a gutter in Stanhope Gate, at least that is what the old woman said. Angela's grandfather bought it for her in 1913 for £13,000.

For some reason she had an account at the Bank of England, the only woman at the time to do so. Apparently, she had always to keep £10,000 in this account. When it sank nearly to this figure, she would go to the Westminster Bank nearby and ask for the manager. 'Give me £10,000, my man,' she would say, striking him on the behind with her umbrella. When she got it, she would board a Number 9 bus and give the ticket collector threepence, saying: 'Take me to the Bank.' She would never pay more than threepence and, I suppose to avoid an unbearable fuss, conductors always let her stay on the bus. At the Bank she would deposit the cash and then take a threepenny bus ride back to Piccadilly.

161

She talked a lot about her will, often at the top of her shrill register at lunch in the Ritz. She sat always at the same table by the entrance to the restaurant, commenting on everyone who came in. Whenever I lunched with her, she would shout to know how much money I earned. She held up her fingers, one by one, to represent thousands. I always waited until she ran out of fingers before I nodded. She was one of those people who appear amusing until you are related to them.

The pearl, by the way, was stolen again. When she was over ninety and bedridden, she had a nurse to look after her. Two men in stocking masks rang her bell, tied up the nurse and burst into her room. She thought that they were nice young men who had come to tea. When they asked where she kept her jewellery, she told them and explained the value of each piece. The men left with it all. None of it was ever seen again.

Angela and I were married at St Bride's church in Fleet Street. I did not, at this time, have such trouble with the vows, partly because it was hard not to laugh. The Rector, Mr Armitage, had told us that he could not marry properly someone who was divorced, but that he would conduct a service that would sound as if he were marrying us. We had to get legally married the day before at a registry office. When we got to awkward sentences in the church service, he would slur them a little, but nobody would notice. 'From this day forth . . .' would be a hastily spoken 'From yesterday forth. . .'. And for the most important line, he would not say, 'I pronounce you man and wife,' but instead, 'I announce you man and wife.'

Nobody did notice, because, on the day, Mr Armitage forgot our arrangement and spoke the full words of the normal service. I managed to walk down the aisle and the passageway to Fleet Street, the last time that I walked so great a distance.

I left *Queen*, as it was now called, soon after we got married, although I continued to contribute my restaurant column. Much of the fun and excitement had gone out of the magazine. Mark Boxer had gone. Lacking the courage to tell Jocelyn to his face that he was leaving, he waited until Jocelyn was on holiday and wrote to him. This depressed Jocelyn more than his going. Some time later, for reasons that I never fathomed or for possibly no reason, Jocelyn asked Beatrix to leave. That depressed me. The *Daily Mail* had been urging me to take over their gossip column. I was very reluctant to do this, but when they suggested that I become their film critic I went.

CHAPTER THIRTEEN

A QUESTION OF GOSSIP

Being a film critic was a pleasant occupation. It took up only half the week. We saw about five films in three days, and on Wednesday afternoons I wrote my column for Thursday's paper. Setting off at ten in the morning to go to the cinema gave me a delicious sensation of mild decadence. The other film critics were nearly all sympathetic and good company. My only reservation was on account of Cecil Wilson, who had been the *Daily Mail*'s critic for many years, who knew more about the subject than I ever would and who remained on the staff. Accustomed to the capricious ways of Fleet Street, he showed no resentment and was rewarded for his natural kindness by getting his job back within six months.

The editor of the *Daily Mail* was William Hardcastle, a large, amiable man. He was an excellent editor, but a hopeless administrator, because he was bored by everyday routine. His desk was piled high with letters and memoranda awaiting answers and decisions.

Ever since *Queen* had published an article by Penelope Gilliatt denouncing the intrusive and dishonest practices of Fleet Street's gossip columnists, editors and for that matter newspaper proprietors (with whom, it had been pointed out, lay ultimate responsibility for the squalid misdemeanours of their employees) had been nervous and embarrassed.

The *Daily Mail* column, entitled Paul Tanfield, had been one of the worst, and its editor, Alan Gardner, being a man apparently driven by some spur of envy, had printed and had to apologize for scores of calumnies, exaggerations and downright inventions. He had been labelled by Mrs Gilliatt as a 'florid-faced little man who specializes in broken marriages, lost jobs and petty rows in the film world: he noses out failure with the same single-minded concentration that Hickey brings to the pursuit of success'. Both Bill Hardcastle and Lord Rothermere, the *Mail's* owner, were anxious to erase the stigma of his tenure of the column. Hardcastle kept on at me to take over the page, eventually agreeing to accept any conditions I wanted to impose.

I made them stringent. I insisted that the name of the column should be changed. I refused to write about royalty, divorces, family rows, pregnancies, and irrelevant misfortunes. My column would be about people of all kinds who were doing things, preferably worthwhile and of intelligent interest.

Esmond Rothermere asked me to lunch. I had known him for some years, because my eldest brother Shane's widow had been married to him for a spell, before exchanging the comforts and power of being a newspaper proprietor's wife for the more precarious arms of Ian Fleming. We agreed with enthusiasm on the terms I had laid down.

On Alan Brien's recommendation, I recruited from the *Evening News* Julian Holland, a person of rigid principles, absolute reliability and penetrating humour. In the spring of 1962, Charles Greville, as the column was called, replaced the old Tanfield.

When I look at the few cuttings I have of the column, I do not feel much pride. It had about it an aura of earnestness that reflected my priggish determination not to yield to the pressure put on me by the old guard, who wanted to see more titles and were missing the cardboard figures of the imaginary Chelsea set, not to mention a bit of scandal.

Julian produced plenty of material that fitted my criterion of intelligent interest, especially in the field of music. We had interviews that could have claimed to be of some importance.

One interview probably bored many readers. It was with an engineering salesman who was developing trade in Eastern Europe, much of it with Romania. This I deemed commendable, well within my other criterion of worthwhile activities. The salesman was called Greville Wynne. A month or two later he was arrested in Bucharest. He was a spy, the 'cut out' to MI6 for Penkovsky, the Russian traitor. They were tried the following year in Russia. Penkovsky was shot; Wynne was sentenced to eight years hard labour. He served about four years and was then exchanged for Gordon Lonsdale. He died in 1990. He must have been pleased that we took his cover seriously.

But the column lacked a real voice, and what merriment there was

was inclined to be stilted. Much of the trouble lay in the near impossibility of shaking off the old patterns or rather the expectation of them. In eschewing the fabric of a popular newspaper's gossip column, we had nothing to build with that might not perfectly well have appeared on other pages, in the news columns or among the features.

Hardcastle, having pressed me so hard to take over the column, now pressed me to change it. He himself was being attacked by the circulation and advertising departments. There was a downturn in the women's readership figures. Advertisers had liked Paul Tanfield, because the scandals, the family disputes and the midwifery items were, they believed, read eagerly by women. They placed their advertisements for feminine things on that or the opposite page.

We argued. The editor would put pictures of royalty into my column, on the grounds that I had only said that I would not write about royalty. It was a photograph of Princess Alexandra that ended the matter. I refused to have it on my page. Bill said it was a good picture. I agreed that it was charming, and suggested that he put it somewhere else. He said that mine was the right page. I maintained that it infringed our agreement. He fired me. I was to leave at once. It was six o'clock in the evening. He had barely an hour in which to fill an empty page. It was quite brave. Julian, with equal courage, stuck by me. We sat together in a bar in Fleet Street, wondering what would become of us.

A couple of days later, Esmond rang me at home and asked me to lunch again. He wanted to know what had happened. Feeling aggrieved, I gave a lively account of Bill's behaviour and made a number of general criticisms of the way he ran the paper.

'He must go,' said Esmond, with what, in anyone else, one would have taken for determination. He said that I was not sacked and invited Angie and myself for the weekend at Daylesford.

Sitting under the Stubbs of Warren Hastings's yak, we mulled over the possible replacements for Bill. The chief contender, it seemed to me, was Mike Randall, an energetic, personable man, who was the deputy editor.

Esmond had considered Gordon McKenzie, who at one time had been editor of the *Sunday Chronicle* and had once been called before the bar of the House of Commons to be reprimanded for contempt. He had printed the home telephone number of a Minister who was planning some fatuous move, and suggested that readers should ring him up and abuse him. Gordon later told me that he had been asked to lunch by Esmond, but it had not gone well despite his smart new blue suit. First, he had refused a dry martini and asked for whisky instead. Esmond was pained. 'But, McKenzie, my dry martinis are famous.' Then his eye, lowering in sorrow, fell on Gordon's shoes. Brown suede with that blue suit. It was the shoes that decided it.

Esmond suggested that I go away for a holiday. He kindly offered us his villa in the South of France, but I thought that my colleagues on the *Daily Mail* might think that that was going too far. When I got back, so he said, Hardcastle would be gone.

When I got back, Bill Hardcastle greeted me with a warmth of forgiveness that revealed his true nature, but the atmosphere was rich with intrigue. Everyone knew that it was only a question of time before Esmond would muster the energy to dismiss him. Both Julian and I became feature writers and, like everyone else, we waited.

Mike Randall invited me to lunch to sound out what I thought his chances were, and to ask me to speak well of him to Esmond. Ambition glittered at me over the coffee cups, as he seemed to me to hint that I could choose my own role on the paper, if he were the editor.

At last Bill left and Mike replaced him.

I stayed with the *Daily Mail* for a while with little to do. Julian and I, at this time, wrote occasional sketches for the television programme *That Was The Week That Was*. Mike somehow or other never found for me the kind of job that I thought he had hinted at. Indeed, when he had been established for some time he fired me for, as far as I could see, no reason. I concluded that he did not like to remember my having been involved in the changes.

Angie and I lived in a flat in Wilton Crescent. It would have been impossible not to be happy with her, because her enjoyment of life was infectious. I remember a time of frivolity and parties and endless activity, the only shadows being perpetual worries about money, for Angie was extravagant and extravagance, too, can be infectious.

Every room in the flat was hung with expensive curtains and the walls covered with expensive papers, but she managed always to convince herself that each piece of material or paper amounted to an economy, because there had been in the shops others that she had liked quite as well, if not better, and which had cost far more.

Her cupboards swelled with new clothes, each item representing in

166

her mind some sort of saving, no matter what its price and the fact that she had no need of it.

The final card in any discussion was to ask if I was saying that I did not like whatever it might be. I always had to say that I did like it, as her taste was faultless. The flat looked perfect and she was beautifully dressed.

'Then whatever is all the fuss about?'

My children ask me what it was like in the Sixties. When one is living at a time that later is given a label, one does not think anything of it. It was just life. It happened that Angie and I were involved in those fields that later observers chose to decide made the period wild and permissive.

Through what are afterwards seen as turning points of history, the majority of people continue with their normal existence. Even in the French Revolution many aristocrats sat tight in their country estates without much happening to them. Jane Austen apparently paid no attention to the Napoleonic Wars. Certainly most of the population in the Sixties were unaware of a slight shift in customs. Possibly more to the point, the only real change was that people did more openly what they had always done before with caution. The increase in so-called illegitimate births, for instance, was due not to a sudden upsurge in the number of pregnant girls, but to the fact that no one now insisted that the boys who were responsible should automatically marry them. The British capacity for humbug was mildly diminished.

There was a heavy dividing line between those who had had some adult life before the war and those like myself who had merely heard about it or seen it with a child's eye. Our elders talked of 'sherry parties' and of people they had known when young as 'old dancing partners'. They wore hats and gloves and carried umbrellas. They frowned at what they called correspondent shoes and were much upset by any transgression of their sumptuary laws. They used to roll back the carpet in the drawing room, put a record on the gramophone and dance cheek to cheek. We knew their rules and would abide by them in their homes, but saw no reason to follow them in our own.

An aunt coming for dinner said, by way of encouragement to Angie, who had made an egg mousse: 'How amusing to have a luncheon dish at dinner.' It was on a par with Randolph Churchill's observation that 'only jumped-up people have soup for lunch'.

There was nothing startlingly different about our lives, merely an emphasis on informality and an abandonment of many social barriers.

167

British Society, contrary to received ideas, has always been the most mobile in Europe. On the continent, the upper classes demanded sixteen quarterings in the coat of arms of any prospective bride; in Britain, the aristocracy married as often as not for love. It was, by comparison, easy to move up the social scale and, as a result of primogeniture, far more usual to move down it. Moreover, the British Establishment has always embraced dissenters, drawing them into the system. In this way our revolutions have been bloodless.

Against that, the British, especially the English, have always been snobs at every level, which is quite a different matter. Few could equal the tones of contempt I heard once in the voice of the Bermondsey widow of a coalheaver, speaking of 'those fish people' – the workers at Billingsgate. Those unpleasant aspects of snobbery faded as the war receded. Nancy Mitford's pronouncements on U and non-U were seen as a game rather than anything to be taken seriously.

Divorcing and marrying again means not exactly changing one's friends, but something more like shaking a kaleidoscope so that new patterns appear. Some unseen chips now shine bright in the middle and some old ones slide dimmer to the edge.

Angie's working at the *Sunday Express* on the fashion pages and my brief venture into the realm of films and then the Charles Greville column produced many new friends and acquaintances. It became our habit to give parties after dinner, for which the large sitting room in Wilton Crescent was well suited. In my memory, they all slide into one.

Dudley Moore sometimes played the piano. George Melly may have sung or, on more than one occasion, have performed his perennial joke of coming into the room stark naked first as a man, then as a woman and finally backwards as a bulldog. His wife, Diana, would sigh and say: 'I do wish you wouldn't do that, Georgie, your father did it so much better.'

Sandie Shaw, who had just won the Eurovision Song Contest, sat on the floor with Bill Wyman and Keith Richards. I had met her because someone had told me that she had never eaten spinach and I thought it would be interesting to take her to the smartest restaurant at the time – the Mirabelle.

Sandie was a marvel. Her agent had become excited about the idea of her protégée's going to so chic a place. She wanted her to dress up in a satin cocktail frock and to wear a bow in her hair. Sandie, barefoot as always, arrived in a red knitted dress, understated in exactly the right way for a beautiful girl in a fasionable restaurant.

She explained that spinach was a posh vegetable, in those days never eaten in Dagenham where she came from. Everything about Sandie was delightful. She was happy to try any dish and wanted to learn why some things were so expensive and others neglected. She looked at the serious businessmen's faces and made me laugh with her wonder that people so rich could be so gloomy.

Some of the parties produced bemused or indignant juxtapositions such as Peter Sellers with Arthur Koestler, or Jocelyn Stevens becoming purple with rage in discussion with Bernard Levin about Karl Marx and even more so with Kenneth Tynan about Cuba, offering to send him there to see for himself what sort of hell it was.

It was interesting that even in supposedly relaxed and liberal circles very few managed to behave quite normally with royalty. Princess Margaret always maintained that she never allowed herself to form an opinion of anyone until after at least two meetings, because their initial response was so often out of character. When she and Tony first came to our parties, it was entertaining to watch the reaction of other guests. Some, like Dr Johnson meeting Queen Anne, would bow so low that they could see back between their legs. Others would say aggressively: 'I'm not going to call you Ma'am, you know.'

Evenings in other people's houses come back. Ken Tynan had such a peculiar mixture of intelligence and puerility. His endless campaigning for the use of four-letter words and nudity on the stage was plainly dictated by a disturbed sexuality (although according to David Carritt, who lived above him at one time, it was quite as likely to disturb the sleep of others) rather than by a wish to strike a blow for freedom. His white-suited urbanity could suddenly switch to the prurience of a schoolboy. Edna O'Brien sat on a sofa at his house, chatting to Paul McCartney. Ken, in his role as host, worried that the young Beatle might not know how to extricate himself if he wanted to, and asked me if I thought he should rescue him. My view was that he looked happy and that, if he had achieved the sophistication of being invited to one of Ken's parties, I should have thought he could look after himself. At that moment, Edna and McCartney stood up and left the house together. Ken was transformed, weaving fantasies about a romance. What actually happened was that Edna took McCartney home to Putney where he innocently made up songs for her children.

Ken was differently confused one evening at Kensington Palace when Princess Margaret had invited us to watch Bryan Forbes's film *Seance on a Wet Afternoon*. While the film was showing, Ken felt in the dark for an ashtray on the table beside him. There was a small one that he filled with his chainsmoking. When the lights came on, he found it was not an ashtray, but a now-charred miniature of Charles I. Princess Margaret, with admirable tact, laughed it off as a matter of no importance.

It was soon after this that the subject of seances came up at dinner with Peter Sellers. Michael Bentine, who happened to be there, having informed us at length about Egyptian scarabs, having tripped lightly through the quantum theory and given a lively dissertation on the best varnishes for boats, told us that he had investigated the matter of ectoplasm and that it was not only real, but so substantial that it was difficult to cut through it even with a saw. He had plucked some from the mouth of a medium and knew what he was talking about.

I asked Peter later whether one could believe any of this. 'Never doubt the word of Bentine,' he said with what I thought was a measure of bitterness. He went on to describe one of the tours the Goons had made round the country. On the second day, Bentine was reading the paper at breakfast.

'Good God,' he said, in that strange nasal accent. 'I see old Ponte's skipped it.'

The headline said that an important atom scientist called Pontecorvo had defected to the Russians.

'What do you mean, "old Ponte"?' the other Goons demanded.

It turned out that Bentine had been a serious student of physics at one time and had shared a work bench with Pontecorvo.

A few days later, they were in Nottingham. Bentine said:

'I think we should go out into Sherwood Forest and shoot an arrow in memory of Robin, don't you?'

Bentine led them to an archery shop, where he tried out several bows, most of which Peter said he could not even draw, so strong were they. Bentine bought the biggest, flexing it like a whip. They went to Robin Hood's oak.

'I think that branch up there,' said Bentine, pointing to the top of the tree.

He drew the bow with casual ease. The arrow flew straight to the branch.

When they reached Cleethorpes, where they were to entertain at an RAF camp, they hit on a plan to catch Bentine out. Peter had run into a Polish officer stationed in the camp, his face nicked with duelling scars. He had been fencing champion of the Polish air force.

'Ever done any fencing, Bentine?'

'Epée, foil or sabre?'

They fixed up a match in the camp gym. It was no contest. Bentine won every bout, pinning the Pole to the wall.

In Cardiff, their lodgings were grim, the railway passed a few feet from their window. It was hard to sleep, so they all got drunk and thought it funny to stand naked in the window as the trains went past.

'And who do you think had the biggest wedding furniture?' asked Peter. 'No, never doubt the word of Bentine.'

It was an ordinary July weekend in Hampshire. Philippa and Jane Wallop's house was a large cottage on their father's estate. We had taken with us Grant, my young South African driver, because Angie's first baby was due in a couple of months and she could not help me in the way that she normally did. Grant was excited. 'I've seen some helluva big buck out there. Where's the gun and I'll shoot them?' He would not believe that anyone kept deer in a park just for the pleasure of looking at them. It was a comic start to the weekend.

Angie was in pain. We rang the local doctor in the morning, but he would not come to see her. She went to him. Without looking at her, he told her that it was just the baby pressing on a nerve, to take an aspirin and to put a brick under the foot of her bed. These remedies did nothing for her that night. Angie always had an amazing courage. Her control was such that I could not think that there was anything serious to worry about. Rather than cause any inconvenience, she insisted on going out to a lunch that had been arranged with Robin Douglas-Home. His wife, too, was having a baby, but he could not bear any mention of such things. Angie writhed in silence until we went back to the cottage.

We had to ring the doctor three times before he would agree to come. When he did, he looked at Angie and said: 'We should be able to get to the hospital in time, if not I can always deliver it in the ditch.'

Memory's choice seems tilted towards the better things. I would never recognize that wretched man, but the kind face of Dr Mitchell, the gynaecologist at Winchester Hospital, I can conjure up with ease. An hour or so of wonder, at the calm dedication of the hospital staff on a summer Sunday, at Angie's bravery, but most of all at nature – the thrill and beauty of a birth, the shimmering cord as the baby was lifted up, the selfless smile of pleasure from the nurse.

Caspar lived four days. Angie said that he looked like me, but he had her broader face. I do not believe that a month has passed since then when I have not thought of him.

After leaving the *Daily Mail*, I was undecided as to what to do. The idea of writing books tempted me and I made a long journey round Europe to do research for an architectural book, and I had plans for a book on monarchy, but little came of these projects.

I lunched again with Lord Rothermere, who had rapidly tired of his new editor but said that he must give him a chance. This proved wise in that Randall soon won the Newspaper of the Year award for him, although the circulation did not mount. I asked him why his newspaper was so gloomy. Enoch Powell and Iain Macleod had that day refused to serve under Sir Alec Douglas-Home. The *Daily Mail*'s headline read: 'Home loses two.' The triumph I would have thought, from the point of view of a Tory newspaper, was that Sir Alec had managed to form a government at all. Why not: 'Home gains forty'?

'My father,' said Rothermere, 'was a gloomy man. I think that's the reason.'

It never seemed to occur to him that the responsibility for the tone of the paper was his. It was this attitude of detachment that led to a breach with him. Early in June 1964, the *Daily Sketch*, another of Rothermere's papers, published two articles entitled 'My Marriage by Mrs Jeremy Fry', which purported to be the result of an interview with Camilla Fry, who was trying to decide whether or not to divorce her husband Jeremy. She had given no such interview.

I wrote a long letter to Rothermere, detailing the inaccuracies and inventions contained in the articles. I ended:

All in all two loathsome, ludicrous and inaccurate articles. Indeed I can think of no journalistic ethic that they do not flout.

Now what should Mrs Fry do? She could sue the *Sketch*. She realizes, however, that this would merely prolong the publicity . . . Here is a woman who is undergoing great misery. But your newspapers add to it a hundredfold. It is a misery you have been through. Would you have cared to have had added to it the attentions of the *Sketch* reporters? No, you are safe. I have had cut out of my articles for the *Mail* innocent references to Ann, to preserve your sensibilities . . .

How can you publish such stuff? How can you claim respect if such gutter journalism can still appear in your newspapers? When you saw the story why did you not protest to your Editor? You cannot believe that a decent woman would have poured out her heart to the scum you employ on the *Sketch*. Would you have done when Ann left you? . . .

So what are you going to do? Above all I hope you will not take the course, which has been taken before, of sacking the reporters concerned. I have called them scum. They are scum only because they are driven to be so by the demands of their editor and employers. The responsibility, as you well know, lies with those at the top.

Will you have the courage to print an apology, denying each point in detail, admitting that your Editor published a story that was completely fictitious? Will you do that without the threat of legal action? Mrs Fry won't sue as I have said. But you could still do this for Mrs Fry. I hope you will.

He didn't. In fact, he did absolutely nothing. A week later, I wrote again to say that as he had not printed any apology, nor even bothered to answer my letter, I had told Granada Television the facts in case they wanted to correct any false impressions given by the *Daily Sketch*.

This time Rothermere replied by return, saying that it seemed to him that if I had reason to believe that my allegations were correct, I should have advised Mrs Fry to present her objections to the Press Council, which had been established for this purpose.

Meanwhile, Randolph Churchill had become interested in the story. He wrote an excoriating article in the *Spectator*, full of his brand of humour.

Some people refer to him as 'poor Esmond.' I always say: 'you mean rich Esmond.' I suppose they mean poor in spirit.

The result of Randolph's article was a writ from the reporter who had written the original story. I replied to Lord Rothermere's absurd note:

Mr dear Esmond,

Come now, are you seriously suggesting that I should have advised Mrs Fry to go to the Press Council, without a word to you whom I have known for twenty years and worked for for three?

I told Mrs Fry that you were an honourable man and that, as soon as you had heard that she had been maltreated by your newspaper, you would wish to make amends. In view of this she stayed her hand.

I naturally assumed that you would hasten to put your house in order, and be capable of doing so, without promptings from outside. Now you tell me otherwise. I find this odd, for it would not have occurred to me to do anything without first having put the facts before you.

However Mr Churchill has, as you know, already done what you suggest . . . A little courage and no outside body would have been needed. You did not reply, so I acted as I told you. Now writs are flying.

Let me ask you this. If you did not believe Mrs Fry, why have you not issued a writ, instead of cowering behind your reporter? The reporter has a career at stake. You have nothing but your vanity. He is doubtless a poor man. You are a rich one. Why let him carry the can, unless of course you believe Mrs Fry.

If you do believe Mrs Fry, do just summon up that ounce of bravery and admit you were wrong, and put a stop to all this . . .

Yours ever,
Quentin

Once more he did not answer. As Randolph put it, trying to argue with Esmond was 'like trying to flog a jellyfish'. Mrs Fry decided that, as there had now been so much publicity, she would sue the *Daily Sketch* after all.

As is the way with legal affiars, the thing dragged on for a long time, during which I saw a lot of Randolph. When one had become accustomed to various awkward characteristics, he was one of the most endearing people one could hope to know. It was tedious to be rung up at two in the morning with the question, 'What's the news?' or with some snippet that could well have waited until we next met. Staying with him in Suffolk, it was sometimes difficult to remember that one was not expected to be offended by anything said after half past ten in the evening.

He had a boyish eagerness and trust that led him even into snares laid for him by his father, in a mood of mischief. My brother Colin was staying with Sir Winston on the weekend that Randolph got from his publishers the first copy of his book on Anthony Eden. He gave it to Sir Winston, who took it up to bed.

In the morning, Randolph hovered about anxiously until Sir Winston at last came down, just before lunch.

'Have you looked at my book, Father?'

'I've just finished the last page.'

174

'Oh good, then tell me what you think of my analysis of his attitude to Nasser.'

'I couldn't say anything about that. I've only read the last page.'

Randolph enjoyed his battles with the press as if they were a military campaign.

'We'll say nothing about that for the moment,' he would announce. 'Always keep masked batteries for the enemy to run into.'

He knew what he was about. Rather to his disappointment, the *Daily Sketch*'s case was withdrawn. Much to Mrs Fry's relief, her case was settled out of court with an apology and an award of £5,000.

CHAPTER FOURTEEN

A COLUMN IN THE SIXTIES

Michael Christiansen, the editor of the *Sunday Mirror*, said that the paper was going to go up-market. He wanted a column that could be about anything from politics to butterflies. It could be light-hearted or sombre. It must be readable, but equally must not talk down to anyone. It was an interesting challenge and it provided me with more fun than any other job I have ever had. My first column appeared in September 1964.

Mike's father, Arthur Christiansen, had been the editor for many years of the *Daily Express*, a dapper, small man of colourless obedience but considerable tenacity. Mike was quite the reverse – huge, round-faced, and somewhat disorganized in appearance. On his nose was what looked like a giant blackhead that Robin Douglas-Home said he longed to squeeze.

A weekly newspaper, with its smaller staff and time for reflection, is a more intimate affair than a daily. The editor can be directly involved in each operation. Mike ran his in what was in some ways a playful manner. He loved games and toys of all sorts. He would arrange cricket matches, pressing the most unlikely members of the staff into a hopeless team to play on one of their two free days against the village team of anyone who lived in the country. In the pub, one was expected to play spoof, and he was often to be found practising his putting on the carpet of his large office. He was always encouraging me to write about some gadget he had discovered. I introduced him to hot air balloons and we made larger and larger ones, once nearly causing a forest fire near Henley. On Saturday nights, when the paper was churning out but there was still a chance to change the last edition if

176

some dramatic news came from those parts of the world that were awake, we would play poker in Mike's office.

While all that might appear frivolous, I never worked for a more honourable editor. He never tried to force upon me anything I did not like. He would argue, sometimes convincing me that I was wrong, but he never asked me to temper an opinion if I were determined on it. If I look back at the cuttings I have of my column, which lasted for seven years, I am astonished, comparing it with what appears in today's *Sunday Mirror*, by the latitude he allowed me.

He was perfectly happy with pieces about astronomy, the habits of elvers, aspects of the French Revolution, speculations on the nature of pithecanthropus or whatever. I even wrote the first interview in a British paper with Marshall McLuhan, who in the Sixties was compared to Socrates, Newton and Einstein. (He was in reality something of a humbug and not quite as original in his thinking as he would have had us believe.) Of course, there was plenty of other material to balance such improbable stuff for a tabloid with a circulation of three million.

I do not think that Mike's superiors, in particular Hugh Cudlipp, much liked my column, but he never let that influence his opinion and never made me aware of any displeasure. Not suprisingly, I grew to be very fond of him.

The column had many unexpected consequences. Somehow I met a French scientist, Alexandre Korganoff, who worked on underwater weaponry for the French Navy. He told me a tale of Spanish treasure.

In 1641, the Spaniards in Mexico broke one of their strictest rules. Usually, they disposed the workings of their gold and silver mines and the loot that they stole from the Indians among several ships, expecting to lose one or two on the journey home. In that year, they put the whole treasure onto only two ships – *Nuestra Señora de la Concepción* and *Santissimo Sacramento* – one hundred tons on each.

The *Sacramento* went down at the entrance to the Spanish harbour of Cadiz, in seas where it is impossible to recover anything. The *Concepción* sank earlier, having been driven on to one of the myriad reefs sixty miles north of what is now the Republic of Dominica, in the West Indies. This staggering loss was still much talked of forty years later. Although there were 194 survivors from the wreck of the *Concepción*, the Spaniards had never been able to find the galleon.

In 1681, William Phips, a young boat-builder from New England, went to Dominica and met one of the survivors, who gave him some clues. With the backing of a group of Englishmen, calling themselves the Gentlemen Adventurers, Phips eventually brought up twenty-six tons of bullion and jewels, valued even then at £300,000.

There were several more attempts to get at the gold, but without diving equipment no one could have time to hack through the coral that had grown over the sunken ship. By the time the equipment had been invented the location of the wreck was forgotten.

Korganoff had an obsession about the *Concepción*. For years he had worked through the records of the Spanish treasure fleets in Seville and Phips' papers in the British Museum. With the Dominican playboy diplomat, Porfirio Rubirosa, he made an expedition. He located the wreck, but their crew mutinied, hoping to take the gold for themselves. He got out of that predicament and made another couple of journeys, but he was always defeated.

He wanted to mount a more serious expedition, with better equipment and a reliable crew. I was convinced by his story, partly because Phips had found some of the treasure, which meant that it existed, and partly because of the documents he produced to prove what had originally been on the ship. In Paris, he showed me a film of what he said was the reef. It had a curious rock that jutted out of the water at a peculiar and easily recognizable angle.

I wrote about Korganoff's hopes of finding a possible fifty tons of gold and silver, worth anything up to 200 million pounds. The result was a cascade of letters from young men all over the country who wanted to join the crew. More surprising, I had within a week pledges amounting to £15,000 from various friends who wanted to back the search.

We decided to form a modern version of the Gentlemen Adventurers, and with no difficulty raised £50,000. The subscribers were a disparate group including a former Minister of Public Works, Lord Glendevon, a gaggle of other peers, Lords Bath, Hopetoun, Scarborough, Hambleden, Lichfield, and O'Neill, a Hollywood screen writer, Ivan Moffat, an arms dealer, Geoffrey Edwards, and the chairman of an advertising agency, Antony Snow. The founder of the SAS, Colonel David Stirling, was to look after security if we found the treasure.

Korganoff set about preparing his boat but, as the months passed, and then even a year or more, it was not clear that he was making much progress and the subscribers became rather impatient at the delays. We were introduced to a Captain Bill Sutton, a forceful sailor who we thought might stir Korganoff's rather dreamy Russian character to a little more activity.

There were meetings of the Gentlemen Adventurers from time to time. Sutton attended one or two of these and inspired us with his confidence. He claimed to have learned from Korganoff all that he needed to know to mount the expedition and find the treasure even without Korganoff, who in any case virtually resigned.

Sutton was quick to equip his boat and, at the end of 1970, set off for the Caribbean. A month or so later, Antony Snow flew out and joined him for a spell, and later still, Colin went. They dived a few times, with little hope of finding anything. Sutton and his crew complained of the concourse of sharks that surrounded the site and both Snow and Colin came back with gloomy reports.

When we next heard news of Sutton, it was to say that his boat had been impounded in Florida, a writ nailed to its mast. The fun was over. It had been fun, rather expensive fun perhaps, but it was enjoyable learning about Spanish colonialism, about diving techniques and above all about gold. The whole history of the *Concepción* and her treasure was enriched by stories of human greed, of treachery and skulduggery. I do not suppose that many of us really believed that we were all going to end up as millionaires, but it was pleasant to dream of what we would do with the six-ton, pure gold Madonna that legend held was part of the cargo.

That our dreams were not so fanciful was proved much later when an American consortium raised a great deal more of the gold and silver and jewellery. There is some on display in the museum in Santo Domingo in Dominica. I went to see it about five years ago and was not much impressed. I could not but wonder whether much more had been found and not declared, but shared in secret between the treasure hunters and some corrupt Dominican officials.

A day or two after I saw the treasure, I sat on the north shore of the island gazing out towards the Silver Shoals, as the reefs are known, reflecting happily on what might have been had we been cleverer. By one of those odd coincidences that are so perplexing, I went back to my hotel a few miles down the coast and turned on the radio to listen to the BBC World Service. One item stood out. Captain William Sutton had been arrested in Bordeaux that morning and was being held in jail while the authorities investigated the large collection of arms discovered in the captain's boat.

My column produced a mixed correspondence. I was surprised by how many people wrote to me for advice. The heading at the top of the page used words like 'provocative', 'controversial' and 'original' – not adjectives, I would have thought, to prompt mothers to write to ask for my suggestions as to how to stop little Kevin from playing truant. I still feel twinges of guilt about the case of a Welsh miner who wrote to me about his pregnant daughter. The circumstances were so grisly and so destructive of what was plainly a happy, thoroughly affectionate family that, contrary to my usual beliefs and I suppose, at some risk to my job, I arranged an abortion for the girl.

More comical was the case of Florence Marsden, who wrote from Chingford about her agoraphobia. She had not dared to venture out of her house for fifteen years. I always answered all my post, even from manifest loonies whose letters were, for some reason, usually written in green ink on lined paper. So I wrote Florence an encouraging line. She wrote again, saying that my letter had cheered and emboldened her to such an extent that she had opened the front door and peered out at the world. I replied and a regular correspondence sprang up. Florence told me how much braver she felt as a result of my sympathy. Slowly she gathered the strength of will to go out – first on to the front door step, then twenty yards to the garden gate. After a while she got to the letter box at the corner to post her letter to me herself and, at last, half a mile to the nearest shop.

I was rather proud of what my compassion had done for the poor woman. Dining with Bernard Levin, I told him of my success with Florence Marsden. He laughed. 'Ah yes, and how far has she walked for *you* then?'

Oh well, perhaps we both did something for her loneliness.

Bernard Levin was responsible for a far sadder story in my column. He rang me one day to say that he had been approached by a Mr Eric Hatry for some help. It was not a situation about which he thought he could do much, so he had suggested to Hatry that he should get in touch with me. He left it to me to judge what to make of it.

Eric Hatry asked me to lunch. Everyone knew about his brother, Clarence, who was jailed for fourteen years in the Twenties for an immense financial fraud, but I knew nothing of Eric. This is how I described him.

As soon as I saw him, I recognized a bizarre species quite common in the 1920s.

A slightly flamboyant character, snobbish, beautifully dressed, a little too clever and cross, but imbued with a rigid sense of honour. A clubman and a name-dropper, but entertaining and infinitely courteous.

Together we had a lavish lunch at which he wanted two wines and port. It was almost Woosterish, and the waiters loved him.

Eric gave me a picture of his life. A barrister. Being wounded in the war – 'God, I was glad when I was wounded' – the Stock Exchange. And a moment of explanation of how he worked to pay back money his clients had lost in his brother's crash. No fuss about this, just a matter of honour.

He had explained why he needed help. One night he was walking home after dinner at the Guards Club. Just after he passed a shop that sold glass, he heard a loud crash. He went back round the corner. The shop was one he knew well; he bought his wedding presents there.

'You can get things that look good for about £6. My present for Angus Ogilvy and Princess Alexandra cost, I think, £25.' (Hatry often said things one wished he had not said.)

The shop window was broken. A brick lay on the ground, and near the hole, inside the window, was a fine glass jug. He picked up both and, so he told me, was going to ring the police. Round the corner came a policeman who arrested him. He was tried and found guilty of stealing the jug. He was fined £200, but it was not the sentence that was important. It was the disgrace.

He wanted something written in a newspaper, some public denial of his guilt or, at least, doubt cast on it. He said he wanted this for the sake of his brother Clarence's grandchildren.

'First their grandfather, now their great-uncle. Think of their shame.'

He continued to say that it did not matter to him, as he would not be around. He had resigned from his clubs and spoke of tidying things up. It was plain that he was planning to commit suicide.

Although I did not find Hatry in any way an endearing man, I felt that I must do something to prevent his killing himself. Usually when someone is contemplating suicide it is their unhappiness that one finds unbearable but that was not the case with Hatry, if only because he showed no kind of fear. I think I was moved in part by the outdated code by which he lived, something that belonged to my childhood that I had once found admirable, but now rejected. It was a muddled emotion. But more important was that simple feeling that one must save a life that is in danger.

I was surprised by how little there was that anyone could do in such circumstances. The police said that they could do nothing until a crime had been committed or a disturbance caused. The Samaritans told me that they could not approach anyone, but must wait to be asked for help. They could not interfere. I wondered a lot about the rights and wrongs of that.

One of the clubs he belonged to was Pratt's, which is owned by the Duke of Devonshire. I rang the Duke, explained what was happening and asked him whether he could refuse to accept Hatry's resignation.

'Oh Lord, I thought we'd got rid of him,' Devonshire said, but with his usual consideration wrote at once to tell Hatry that the club would ignore his resignation.

The vicar at the fashionable church where Hatry worshipped was grudging in his agreement to go to see him and not surprisingly failed to make an impression – the consequence of choosing one's church for the wrong reason. I believe his doctor made a firmer attempt, but Hatry was immovable. A week passed after our lunch. On Saturday, perfectly composed, he went to a party. On Sunday, we chatted on the telephone, but he would not come to the country for the day. On Monday, he wrote letters all day. That night Hatry lay down and killed himself with an overdose of pills.

I wrote his story, as nearly as possible as he would have wished, casting doubt on his guilt. Why should a man with an adequate income throw a brick through a window to steal a jug worth £48?

A furious woman wrote to me. How could I defend a man who was cruel to animals? Look in the files, she said. I did. There I found a headline from 1936. 'Hatry on Cat Cruelty Charge.' He had lived in Soho with a pair of Jack Russells. For their evening walk, he used to take them through the streets on cat hunts. In my notes of our lunch, I found he had said; 'Don't go away with the idea that I am a good man or anything.' I hadn't. He was just an old-fashioned cad, with an old-fashioned sense of honour.

Angie did not like abroad, unless it was supremely comfortable and preferably in Italy. I had discovered this on our honeymoon. She had asked me to choose somewhere as a surprise. I was not to tell her where it was until we arrived. Rhodes proved to be definitely not what she wanted. She had bought ten – or was it twelve? – bikinis and at least seven different things for the evening.

There was no one in the hotel to compete with at dinner, and on the pretty, lost beach that Antonio, our regular taxi-driver, took us to, there were only two or three tourists to see the bikinis. I used at that

I married Angie in 1961 at St Bride's Church in Fleet Street.

(Below left) Angie's grandmother, displaying the largest pearl in the world.

Edgy with the Pekingese I gave her to console her for the loss of her cat.

(Below) Princess
Margaret and Tony
Snowdon at Wootton.

(Above) Angie and I on
holiday with Peter Sellers
in Ischia where he and
Britt Ekland were filming
After the Fox.

(Right) Ken Tynan, with
his wife Kathleen and
daughter at Wootton.

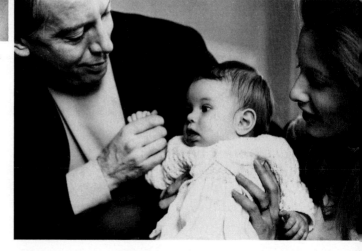

Myself in the 60s.

This page

(Left) Wilfred Thesiger, who has been source of much encouragement to me *Copyright Popperfoto.*

(Below) In Jeddah with, in the background, some of the old Arab buildings still remaining and now, I believe, lost. *Reproduced by kind permission of the photographer, Robert Fréson.*

Opposite

(Above) Huamel, one of the guides, showering me with hot water from a deep well in the Empty Quarter of Saudi Arabia. *Reproduced by kind permission of the photographer, Robert Fréson.*

(Below) My guides bring Abdullah back across the sands just after he had cut his throat. *Reproduced by kind permission of the photographer, Robert Fréson.*

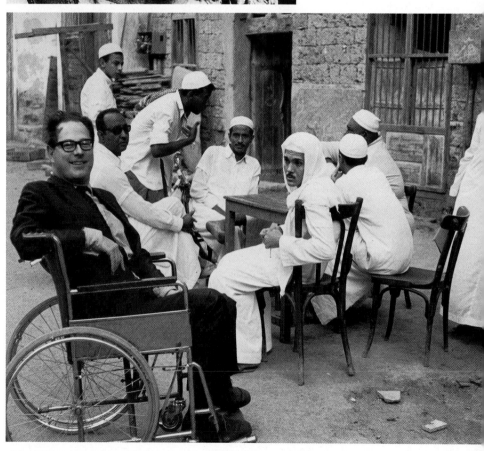

(Above) On safari in Kenya with Jock and Betty Leslie Melville. *Copyright John Seymour.*

(Right) With the Butler family of Gipsies in the Forest of Dean near Cinderford. Katie sits in the tub with one of her brothers. *Copyright John Seymour.*

(Above) Sue in the dining-room at Netherset Hey, with Nat and Charity. Her ancestor Nell Gwynne hangs on the left.

...ing round the farm on my golf buggy, with ...e's sister Harriet in the background.

...ncess Margaret with Charity at Netherset ...y.

(Right) Planning our ideal village at Leycett. The slag heap in the background was to be removed. Permission was refused as Leycett was in the Green Belt.

(Below) Nat feeding a Rothschild Giraffe at Giraffe Manor near Nairobi.

(Below) From left: Sabrina, Charity, Sue, Sebastian, Nat (on floor), Candida, Angie and her daughter Eugenie Howard-Johnston.

time to enjoy swimming, but I have never been interested in sunbathing; fifteen minutes is the longest that I can bear to lie on a beach. Angie liked to roast for hours.

Fortunately, the taxi-driver was an amusing fellow who had had a tiny part in *The Guns of Navarone*. He was also a backgammon enthusiast, so he and I could sit in the shade and while away many pleasant hours with some ouzo, film talk and fierce battles on the board. Angie found this less satisfactory. Nor was the visit to Antonio's house a success. Angie had a phobia about dolls. Until one has met someone with a real phobia, one is inclined to think that such things are nonsense and that all that is needed is a little common sense and a bit of pulling yourself together. I had quickly learned that Angie's phobia was hideously real. Any simulacrum of the human form disturbed her. The more realistic it was, the more it terrified her – she had to pick her way carefully through shops in case she came face to face with a tailor's dummy. Sabrina once brought a doll to the flat. Angie fled, sobbing, and did not come back for three hours.

When we had settled down for tea in Antonio's house, he told his eight-year-old daughter to go to fetch something to show us. The child came, full of pride, with a doll as big as herself. Angie screamed, buried her head in my lap and lay rigid, breathing in desperate gasps. 'Phobia' may be a Greek word but to try to explain such a reaction to a Greek island family was impossible.

Over our honeymoon, too, hung the threat of the Cuban missile crisis. It really seemed that the world might be blown to pieces. I toyed with the idea of buying a Rolls-Royce, on the grounds that I would almost certainly never have to pay for it.

Angie was unable to come on much of my three-month journey of research round Europe, because she was working, but she agreed to meet me in Salzburg for an opera. I had made no hotel booking and was anyhow economizing as the trip was expensive. The only reasonable hotel I could find was one where you could have a bath only between certain hours and then had to pay extra for it.

I was filthy, having driven a long way with the roof down, and wanted to bathe before meeting Angie at the airport. With difficulty I persuaded the hotel owner to break the rules and let me into the bathroom outside permitted times. 'I know it is a mistake,' she said. It was.

Mark, the young man who was travelling with me, was tired and asked if I could manage on my own. I was certain I could. He went to rest. The bath was big. I sat on the edge, still dressed, while it filled up. When it was ready, I reached across to turn off the taps – and fell in.

I had had an aged uncle who had died in the bath because he could not reach the hot tap to turn it off, so that he was scalded to death. I had often wondered why he had not pulled out the plug, so, when I could not reach the taps, I knew what to do. Instead of a plug on a chain, this Austrian bath had one of those silly continental devices operated from beyond the taps. I could not pull the plug out with my toes. I shouted and screamed for Mark, who slept heavily on. The water rose, but somehow I was wedged and did not float up with it. My head at least was above the rim over which the water flowed inexorably.

Experience had taught me not to lock doors, for I had more than once fallen in a lavatory and the door had had to be broken down to get me out. I decided that that was more embarrassing than being discovered by strangers in the bath. So when the porter came to find out why water was pouring through the foyer ceiling, he turned off the tap and woke Mark.

The owner was out, but when we got back from the airport her lively abuse did not encourage Angie to add Austria to Italy.

Even Italy could have hazards, as I discovered when we drove from Salzburg to Venice. I was confident that this would go well, as we were to stay with the Contessa Cicogna in the house she had built just off the Grand Canal. I had slightly underestimated the grandeur and I had also managed to dissuade Angie from travelling always with her whole wardrobe. As we stepped out of the launch, a smart woman in a Chanel dress, her arms clinking with bangles, greeted us in a gale of expensive scent. It was the housekeeper, but Angie took her for our hostess. This confusion over, the housekeeper deftly unpacked Angie's cases, holding up each piece for inspection.

'What will you wear for dinner tonight?'

Angie had brought only one evening dress, a not very grand one at that.

'Would that be suitable?' she asked.

'Yes, perhaps,' said the housekeeper, 'there's only Sir John Gielgud tonight, so it should be all right, but what about tomorrow night?'

It was all my fault, of course, for restricting her luggage, but Angie was equal to the occasion. Anna-Maria Cicogna had one of the last three private gondolas in Venice (the other two belonged to Peggy

184

Guggenheim and to the art dealer Arthur Jeffress). Angie set off in it and soon remedied any deficiences with a morning's shopping.

When Angie became pregnant again, the doctor made her stay in bed for six months. The bedroom in Wilton Crescent was in the basement and, despite Angie's gift for decoration, it was dark and dismal, so that it was difficult to make life interesting for her. Princess Margaret was also having a baby, so she was more in London than usual. She and Tony used, most weekends, to bring a projector and set up a screen at the end of Angie's bed and we would watch films. If we had no one to cook, Princess Margaret would send round a complete dinner on trays for all of us.

The cliché about remembering where one was when one heard that President Kennedy was assassinated was certainly true in our case, for it was in that bedroom, apart from when I was at work, that we spent half a year.

Candida was born in June 1964. Her room, too, was in the basement and we decided that it would be more agreeable to live in the country.

Wootton House stood five miles west of Bedford. It was at that time my ideal house – built in 1685, with a large stone-flagged hall and a broad staircase lit by a Palladian window. The hall, staircase and a few of the rooms had a dado of plain oak panelling. None of the rooms was too large and there were enough of them for Angie and myself each to have a study.

The front of the house looked out over a lily pond and, to one side, the church. Behind there was a walled garden of nearly two acres. The immediate country round us was not very beautiful, and an unfriendly wind sometimes brought a sulphurous stench from the brickworks whose tall chimneys we could see in the distance, but we were protected on all sides by fine trees and a fifty-acre wood.

On our first weekend in the house Princess Margaret, Tony, Jocelyn and Jane Stevens arrived as a surprise, landing on the lawn in Tommy Sopwith's helicopter, and Princess Margaret spent the afternoon with Angie tearing the old wallpaper off the drawing-room wall.

Angie, of course, long before we moved in had planned every curtain, carpet and bathroom tile. She would not hear of doing the place up slowly.

'There is nothing that isn't cotton,' she said in defence of her insistence that everything must be done at once, as if all would normally have been in Japanese silk and Flemish tapestry-work. As always, it looked superb.

185

Our life at Wootton was luxurious. Angie was working for television as an interviewer and I was working not only for the *Sunday Mirror* and *Queen* but also, later, for the *Evening Standard* as well.

My chauffeur at the time, Chris Eaton, had suggested that his wife should come and work for us as housekeeper. Edgy, as she was called, was a quite exceptional person. Her life had been hard. She was born in Dulwich, but when she was thirteen she won a Newcombe Foundation scholarship. These were established in 1674 to teach a craft to six boys and six girls. There she learned the fundamentals of domestic science, ranging from how to make soap to the care of furniture, as well as cooking, sewing and cleaning. She started work at the age of sixteen as a kitchenmaid with the Bishop of Southwark, who was later promoted to Winchester. Edgy went too. When she was nineteen, there was an important lunch for twelve people. About an hour before lunch, the cook fell dead on the kitchen floor. No one wanted to tell the Bishop's wife. Edgy took over and lunch continued – hosts and guests in perfect ignorance of any mishap. It was Shrove Tuesday and Edgy conjured up a dozen perfect pancakes. At the end of the month there was an extra ten shillings in her pay packet.

Edgy had been married to a man who had treated her badly and finally deserted her, leaving behind his son, whom she cared for as if he were her child, but who rewarded her with treatment not much different from his father's. Edgy appeared always to be savaged by the people to whom she gave so much.

It was not easy to persuade her to come to the country, for she protested that she was a Londoner and quite unable to live without the noise of buses and, above all, without Sainsbury's. Furthermore, Joey, her cat, might not like the country any more than she did. She was working at the time for an ageing alcoholic whom she used to have to carry to bed more and more often. Edgy agreed, at last, that we offered a greater security.

I cannot think of anyone I have ever known who worked harder than Edgy. During the four years that we lived at Wootton, she took only two days off and she always refused to have a holiday. The furniture sparkled, the house ran smoothly, and above all, Edgy was a superb cook. While she took pride in everything, her kitchen was what mattered most. One evening she came to announce dinner:

'One of the outhouses is on fire, but the soufflé is ready. Shall I call the fire brigade first or can I serve it now and call them after?'

Edgy demanded as high a standard from others as she set for herself.

186

She had great respect for Doris Hutchings, who came in the mornings from the village to help in the house as she had done for twenty-seven years, since the days when the Ormsby-Gore family had owned the house. Doris had the same kind of dedication to her work. Edgy cared less for the various girls who looked after Candida, who she thought were lazy, inefficient and spoilt.

There was no doubt that Edgy was unlucky. When we had been at Wootton about a month, Joey disappeared. He was, indeed a London cat. In the garden there was a water tank, covered with a green film of algae. Joey must have thought it was grass, for he was found drowned in the tank – he had been unable to climb out.

More serious in a way, but less evidently distressing to Edgy, her husband Chris walked out one Christmas Eve. We had a dozen people staying, but as with the death of the Bishop's cook, Edgy never faltered, although she did resent having given Chris a handsome bag of golf clubs for a Christmas present.

Nonetheless, she stayed on and she made what became more difficult years for Angie and myself easier than they might have been, for she was never so happy as when the house was full of visitors for the weekend.

For the most part the visitors were our families, but Edgy kept an autograph book which she asked any guests that she particularly liked to sign. Her favourites were my nephew Bamber Gascoigne, Reggie Bosanquet the newsreader, and Nigel Ryan, who was the editor of Independent Television News. The page in her book of which she was most proud was the one on which John Betjeman wrote a short poem and Osbert Lancaster drew a picture.

The weekend that they came, Collins had just published the two-volume guide to English parish churches that John had edited and he had brought us a copy. Nothing pleased him more than driving round looking at villages, so we decided to see how well it covered Bedfordshire. John was insatiable and we visited about twenty churches in a morning while John kept up a running commentary. We were coming back through, I think, Keysoe.

'Not especially interesting, but we might as well look now we're here. Prominent spire, it says, and fourteenth-century font. We'll find that easily then, look out for the spire.'

We looked and looked but could see nothing. At last I saw a small sign saying: To the Church. We drove up to find that the spire had fallen down four days before.

John missed nothing, particularly the curious names that people gave to their houses. He chanted them as we drove along a row of what looked like retirement bungalows: 'Mon Repos, Bide-a-wee, Dunroamin, Petrolia . . .'

'Nonsense, John, you're making it up, no one could call his house Petrolia.'

He made me back the car to see for myself. There it was – in marvellously inappropriate Gothic lettering.

'I can see them now,' said John. 'They gave up the filling station at the end of the summer, when all the caravans had gone home. They have put the Hillman up on chocks for the winter . . .' He went on to weave a whole fantasy about the lives of the people who lived in Petrolia.

In so many ways, nothing could have been more agreeable than our life at Wootton. We were close enough to London not to feel cut off from our friends or from the stimulus of variety that I needed in order to write my column. All the same, Bedfordshire was unexpectedly rural and unsophisticated. We used to have the village fête on our lawn each year and a tea party for the elderly. At the local village dances, the boys and girls were too shy to make any approaches to the opposite sex and the girls danced mostly with each other. I became a Member of the Parish Council and spent many evenings discussing drains and lampposts. It was all immensely English and did not belong in any new, permissive age.

At the time it suited me to perfection; I enjoyed the entertaining and the feeling of being part of a community. I would not like it today. I no longer want to live in that way, with the relics of an old-fashioned formality. It would also be impossible, for the equivalents of Edgy and Doris do not exist. It seems to me that so many stages and moods of my life have coincided with the ending of an era. And with each new beginning I have been happier.

CHAPTER FIFTEEN

PUSHERS AND SHOVERS

As my ability to walk declined, so my dependence on other people increased. This had several side effects. The first was that I learned more of how complicated almost everyone's life is. No man may be a hero to his valet, but, equally, few valets are heroes to their masters.

I first had a chauffeur after Martha and I came back from Japan. I could drive perfectly well with hand controls, but parking was impossible when I went to work. My first driver was called Parker. It was still usual to call him by his surname and for him to wear a uniform and a peaked cap. He was rather splendid to look at, bearded and handsome. With the roof down in the yellow-and-white convertible. I felt a little like somebody in a Hollywood B-movie when Parker was at the wheel. I cannot remember where in London he came from, but it must have been north of the river because he was absolutely honest. Over the years, I came to believe that people, or at any rate chauffeurs, who lived south of the river were more shifty and inclined to steal than northerners.

Parker was very dignified and an excellent driver, but there came a week when he was driving so badly that I asked him what the matter was.

'I'm very tired, sir. I'm sorry.'

'Why are you so tired?'

'I'm not getting much sleep, am I?' he said with that Londoner's slightly reproachful trick of turning a statement into a rhetorical question.

'Why not?'

'Because I'm sleeping on the couch.'

189

'And why are you sleeping on the couch?'

'Because the wife's got her lover in the bed, hasn't she?'

For the sake of their five-year-old son, Parker was prepared to put up with this drab arrangement.

Thorne's matrimonial problems were even more muddled. Thorne was a miner from Durham who had come to London to seek a fortune. He was a kind man of amazing strength, although he was quite short. By the time he came to work for me, I was living in Wilton Crescent with Angie. I could stand, but could walk only a very short distance. To save time and trouble (for me, that is) he used to carry me on his back to and from the car. In this way, too, he would take me to the cinema or into a restaurant. We had great friends, Willy and Angela Landels, who lived in a fifth-floor flat with no lift. Thorne would carry me all the way without a rest.

Thorne's wife was pretty, several years younger than he was. He telephoned for help one Sunday morning when he was not working. His wife had disappeared. She had gone down to Essex on Saturday to see an aunt and she had not come back. The aunt said that she had left at about ten in the evening. Thorne had rung all the hospitals but their records departments were shut.

We were just leaving for lunch near Windsor. I told him to ring the police and that I would call him as soon as lunch was over. When I rang he had no news, except that the police were being unhelpful and would make no enquiries. I drove back to London, picked up Thorne and went to the police station, thinking in vanity that they might listen more to me.

A policewoman asked if she could help me, her expression making it plain that she was not going to.

'Only a spouse or near relative may report a missing person,' she said.

'It is Mr Thorne's wife who is missing.'

'I cannot be sure they are married unless I see their marriage certificate.'

I said that Thorne had worked for me for a year and that of course they were married. How did I know? Well, if you know someone, you get a feeling for these things. Had I seen the marriage certificate? No. Well, then?

I asked Thorne where it was. When he said it was at his flat, I told him to get it. He was gone for a long time. The policewoman and I gazed at the wall, our eyes meeting awkwardly from time to time. At last Thorne came.

'The wife's back,' he said.

'Wife,' the policewoman said. 'This I must see.'

We all went to Thorne's flat where we found Mrs Thorne, her mother and her mother's current lover. Then this tale unfolded:

Mrs Thorne's father had died some years before leaving £40,000 to his widow and £20,000 in trust for his daughter, which she would get when she was twenty-five or on marriage. Her mother had spent her share and now wanted her daughter's money.

The daughter and Thorne were not married. (I refused to meet the policewoman's eye.) The mother had found someone in Birmingham who would marry the girl for £500. She had forced her daughter to agree to this, knowing that Thorne, had he married her, would never have let her part with her money. Had the plan succeeded, mother and daughter would have split the proceeds. Mrs Thorne had not been to Essex at all, but to the Midlands to see whether she was prepared to marry the man her mother had found. On the journey, she had debated with herself and now she could not do it. Indeed, she had decided that her mother was a cheat. She loved Thorne.

As we left, I asked the policewoman how she had known.

'You get a feeling for these things, you know.'

Thorne married the girl and, with her father's money as a deposit, bought three Austin Princess limousines to run a grand taxi service. The business, so I heard, went bust.

Brand's marital upset was of a different kind. He was a tall, unimaginative man. When he got a blister on his heel from wearing too loose a shoe, he said: 'It hurts something awful if I bend my leg like this,' and then bent it like that and fell to the floor with the pain.

He married, in October, a rangy girl as tall as himself and large in every particular except one. By February the marriage had still not been consummated. They lived in the basement of the house of a friend of mine called Dick.

Dick worried about them and judged it to be a psychological problem. He devised a cure for their troubles.

'Go and buy a small bottle of olive oil, light a fire in the sitting room and run a deep, warm bath. Pour the olive oil into the bath and then lie in it together. When you are warm and happy, get out and go and lie in front of the fire and everything will be wonderful.'

In the morning, Dick met them. Mrs Brand's arm was in a sling. Brand had a bleeding gash over one eye.

'You see, sir, what happened was this. We did as you said, poured

191

the olive oil in and all, and when we was all warm we let the water out and we both stood up . . .'

The corollary of my becoming involved with the lives of my drivers was their becoming involved in mine. While it was a relief to Angie that she did not have to park the car if we went to the theatre or to carry the luggage if we went away for the weekend, it meant that we were rarely alone; moreover, the driver was almost bound to know more about our business than we might have wanted.

When later our marriage became strained, it was inevitable that whoever was looking after me should be aware of the tension. I had an Irish driver, Michael. As he and I drove away from the house after a painful parting, he started to philosophize:

'Oh, Mrs Crewe was crying, I believe she was. I never like to see a woman crying, you know. It saddens me. My mother, the poor soul, sometimes her eyes flow enough for two broad rivers and I . . .'

'Shut up, Michael, for God's sake. I don't give a damn about your mother . . .'

'Insult my mother, will you? Holy Mary, I'll kill you.'

He put his foot down and we hurtled through the lanes of Bedfordshire at terrifying speeds. It was twenty miles before I could calm him down. He left soon after.

Memory here seems to select the bizarre. There was a bearded terror who threatened to push me down a lift-shaft, a paedophile who smuggled young boys into a later flat. Dismissing them could be a risky business; one left with a gold cigarette case, another poured brake fluid over my newly resprayed car, a third broke in and stole a Hockney, a Graham Sutherland and a small drawing by Lawrence. On the whole, though, my opinion of human nature has always been encouraged by the kindness of those who have looked after me.

The world of chauffeurs was somewhat precarious and emergencies were common. In reserve, as it were, was an organization called Chauffeur Services. They would send someone at short notice when my driver was ill, had left in a rage or had been wounded by his wife.

One morning came Mr Cargill. His suit and cap were grey instead of the usual blue. His air of superiority was inspiring rather than offensive. He looked at the car and gave a trace of a sigh.

'Might I take the car for twenty minutes or so? It could benefit, I think, from a little attention.' He reappeared with the car looking cleaner than I had ever seen it and the engine ran with a soothed murmur. I have no idea where or how Mr Cargill got cars cleaned.

I feel sure that he never lifted a duster himself, but he knew everything.

I might say to him that we were going to a dance in Gloucestershire and would stay at the Swan in Bibury.

'Excuse me, sir, but I would discounsel that plan. The Swan of late has had some problems. The Snooty Fox at Tetbury, however, is now run by Mrs Maxwell Joseph herself and has been renovated in good taste. The rooms would be more commodious and convenient. Should you wish it, I will make the necessary arrangements.'

Mr Cargill had qualities that Jeeves would have envied. The introduction he gave me to an Arabian prince later helped me to save a man's life.

For several years, whenever I was stuck, I would find Mr Cargill. In a way, he personified the change that took place in the kind of people whom I came to depend upon more and more.

Gradually, Mr Cargill became Ted and grew to be a friend rather than an employee. He shed his peaked cap and grey uniform when looking after me and, when I was once again living alone, joined in much of my social life.

As I came to need more help – getting out of bed, in and out of the bath, dressing and undressing – so the disturbance to our private life became more irritating to whoever I was living with. Originally, the intrusion was, in estate agent's terms, only in the public rooms. Gradually the bedroom and bathroom were invaded – something intolerable to most women.

What one can grow accustomed to on one's own behalf is one thing, on someone else's it is much more difficult. I do have strong preferences, some quite unreasonable, about helpers. I can get used to almost any kind of person but, given a choice, he should be young. For some reason, I am less embarrassed taking off my clothes in front of young people, although common sense tells me that someone young is more likely to be revolted by an older person's body. For practical reasons I need him to be tall and strong and I would wish for him to be good-looking, on the indefensible grounds that I find ugly people depressing. Intelligence is obviously useful, but too much intelligence is exhausting because, whoever he is, he will have an opinion on every subject and opinions are provocative. I used to think that a homosexual would be the best bet, but experience has disproved that. Heterosexuals are calmer, if less amusing.

Even with the person who fulfils all my criteria it is a tricky relationship. I am always in the position of asking. It is ignominious enough without being naked on the loo, which is the circumstance in which I have several times met a helper for the first time. I like to think that I have overcome most inhibitions and all resentment, but sometimes I wonder whether a little residue of bitterness does not smoulder somewhere within me. If it is hard for me, who has had a gradual lifetime to come to terms with these aspects of disability, it is not surprising that a young wife may feel frustration at the rupturing of her privacy.

Latterly, alone again, peaked caps long since forgotten, and with no inclination to inflict my problems on any more generous-hearted girls, I have a different way of solving them. There are innumerable young men who find themselves at a crossroads, uncertain which route to take. It is in fact one of the paradoxes of our time that greater choice has made life more difficult for young people. They find it useful to have a job that gives them time to consider, especially as, at best, it also often means a journey to somewhere that they might otherwise never have seen and, at worst, six months in the most sun-filled part of France.

CHAPTER SIXTEEN

ACROSS THE EMPTY QUARTER

The feminist complaint that men have two lives rather than one is something with which I have always sympathized. We can and do escape into our jobs and are in consequence more detached and, if you like, privileged. Far from my doing something to improve this, I have compounded it by having a third life into which I have from time to time disappeared, thereby probably giving an impression of even greater detachment. It is not that I feel any less deeply, nor that I want to get away from responsibility or from anything else. It is more a positive search for a quality of sparseness, a special kind of freedom.

Two men with less in common than Wilfred Thesiger and Geoffrey Edwards would be hard to imagine, but in their different ways they were responsible for my first desert journey.

Wilfred's book, *Arabian Sands*, had fascinated me. It was not so much the adventure of it, but the picture he painted of a freedom unlike any that I had ever contemplated, but that I recognized at once as ideal, although probably impossible for me to achieve. It was not a freedom from rules or even custom, but a freedom from the inessential, the freedom of the nomad.

His account of crossing the Empty Quarter of Saudi Arabia was not only inspiring, it also warned me how little time was left for the people of the desert to live their life without interference. I was determined to see the tribes that he had written about while their pattern of living was still unchanged.

Jeremy Fry and I decided to make an expedition in 1966. Already at that time, it was difficult to get permission to visit Saudi Arabia,

195

except on business. For Jeremy this was not an impediment, because the valve that he had invented was used on practically every pipeline in the world. For myself and Robert Fréson, the photographer who was to come with us to record the last of the tribes, it was a worry.

By good fortune, I had written a piece about Geoffrey Edwards and his treatment by successive British governments. Geoffrey was an uncommon character of ebullient charm. He was a compulsive salesman. Once, sitting in the Tivoli Gardens in Copenhagen with his brother, he got fed up waiting for lunch to arrive and went for a stroll. Somehow he wandered into the Danish Ministry of Agriculture. An hour later he rejoined his brother.

'We must hurry back to England, I have just sold six hundred tractors so we had better go and find some.'

In the early Sixties, he was wandering around Saudi Arabia with a vague notion of selling the Saudi's some pyjamas. He heard that they were really more interested in arms than in pyjamas. Britain had no diplomatic relations with Saudi Arabia at the time, but Geoffrey made friends with the Emir Sultan, who was in charge of buying armaments. When diplomatic relations were restored under the Tories, one of the first acts of the Foreign Office was to try to deter Emir Sultan from dealing with Geoffrey. Nonetheless, he kept going. Two years later Labour came to power. They were a bit more encouraging and, after seventy-one trips to Saudi Arabia and spending £84,000 of his own money, Geoffrey won a contract to supply £100 million worth of arms to the Saudis. It was John Stonehouse, the disappearing MP, who announced the deal in Parliament, never mentioning Geoffrey and blithely accepting the congratulations of the House himself. With Geoffrey's help, Robert Fréson and I got visas with great ease.

Before going, Jeremy and I lunched with Wilfred Thesiger, who gave us a lot of useful advice. He recommended that we take with us soup, Marmite and tomato paste to enliven the food, lemon crystals to take away the taste of the water, and various medicines especially Epsom salts. More bizarrely he suggested a circumcision kit. Circumcision was an operation that often caused death in the desert.

I was full of old-fashioned ideas. My father had often spoken of special provisions being put up by Fortnum and Mason. An elderly assistant was miserable: 'I am sorry sir. Before the war we could have fitted you with everything, but there are no more real safaris these days.' No lemon crystals, no desert food packs – just foreign soups in packets.

At John Bell and Croyden, the chemist in Wigmore Street, older ways still obtained. I bought surgical needles, already threaded in neat tubes of alcohol, to stitch a serious wound.

'And may I propose some injections of morphine, sir, in case of a painful accident far from help?' Why not? But these and various other drugs, since banned altogether, had to be delivered to my aeroplane.

Jeremy made me a collapsible loo out of a card table that lasted fifteen years, until I lost it in the Sahara.

When we arrived in Riyadh, a Palestinian friend of Geoffrey's, Hussein Amin, looked after us, helping us to hire two trucks and drivers and a couple of lads to help. We bought quantities of rice and sugar, two sacks of flour and a haunch of meat, as well as drums to hold two hundred gallons of petrol and one hundred gallons of water.

Ted Cargill, my Jeeves-like driver, had given me an introduction to the King's brother, Prince Salman bin Abdul Aziz, the Governor of Riyadh, whom he had chauffeured in London. Salman provided me with a letter to show to anyone if we were in trouble or needed help.

In our innocence, we thought we would set off across the Empty Quarter when we had found a local guide at one of the oases that lie on the fringes of this great desert – the largest continuous tract of sand in the world, covering an area bigger than France.

This first attempt was not perhaps a complete failure, because we learned a certain amount about the land and the Arabs and desert travel. We learned the unimportance of time, we learned how to eat with one hand, how to clean our teeth with a stick and our bodies with sand. We accustomed ourselves to temperatures that rose to 120°F by day and dropped to 40°F by night. We acquired a knowledge of the sands, to know the hard from the soft, and how to get the trucks out when they sank up to the axle. But we got nowhere near the Empty Quarter.

The Rub al Khali, as it is called in Arabic, is almost a symbol for horror – mentioned in the Koran as a place of evil spirits and monsters. Whenever we spoke of our intentions, everyone froze. Even the Emir of Sulaiyil, quite a big oasis, assured me that it was full of lions and bears.

The further we got from Riyadh, the more suspicious people were of these strangers. The Emir of Laila gave us a splendid meal. I sat at a small table, while everyone else sat on the concrete floor round a sheep that had been killed for the occasion, cut up and spread, together with huge amounts of rice, over a sheet of American cloth. The Emir put the whole head on to my plate, tearing off an ear for himself. I asked him if it was true that the eye was a special delicacy. 'Not really,' he said, gouging one out and popping it into his own mouth. I was afraid that he was going to give me the other one and, in a moment of inspiration, said eyes were forbidden by my religion – an excuse I have often used since for things I don't think I want to eat.

The Emir said we might lose the way to the next oasis and offered us a guide. We said it was kind but unnecessary and that we were happy on our own. He insisted in a manner that I realized was an order rather than normal Arab hospitality.

Sayid was a policeman and the most dreadful bore. He argued about everything and chanted verses from the Koran whenever he was not talking. It was intolerable to be in the same truck with him.

At the furthest oasis, Wadi Dawasir, it became plain that we were never going to get anyone to take us into the Empty Quarter. Jeremy needed to get on with his business and managed to get a ride in a plane back to Riyadh.

Bob and I turned back the way we had come. At Laila we were to drop Sayid off at his house in a back street. When he had joined us, he had had with him a small bundle. Getting off, he had a large roll, done up in his prayer mat. Bob, braver than I, asked him what was in it. When he demurred, Bob ordered him to open it up. Inside were many of our possessions – sleeping bags, binoculars, compass and some clothes.

Bob remembered that he was missing a sweater. He asked for it. Sayid parted the front of his shirt. Under it he wore Bob's sweater. Bob told him to take it off. Sayid's hand strayed towards his gun.

'Oh, never mind,' said Bob, 'the sweater's a present.'

Depressed, we drove back to Riyadh as quickly as possible. We had not before sought any official help, in case the request resulted in official prohibition. Now there seemed to be no other way. I asked for an audience with King Faisal.

His court was traditional in that the King was, in principle, accessible to any of his subjects and, in consequence, there was an air, if not of informality, of greater equality than I had expected. There was none of the cringing that one would have found in an old or even a modern European court. The solemnity was provided by the dignity of the King.

When my turn came, the King said: 'I am afraid that you have had an unhappy journey through our country.'

'Oh no, sir, it was an extremely interesting journey. I learned much and enjoyed much and was received with kindness.'

Geoffrey had told me that one should be flowery.

'I think, though,' said the King with emphasis, 'that there were unfortunate incidents on your travels which I regret.'

I realized that somehow he knew about Sayid's having tried to steal our belongings.

'If there were any such incidents, sir, I have entirely forgotten them.'

'And what do you want to do now?'

'I would like to go across the Rub al Khali.'

There was a long pause. Then: 'That should surely be an interesting journey. Talk to the Minister of the Interior tomorrow morning.'

The setting up of the expedition took many days. Regularly we would go down to the Ministry to ask how things were going. '*Boukra*' was the equally regular reply, but 'tomorrow' was a long time in coming. To show our gratitude, we spent the days visiting the things that the officials would have preferred us to take an interest in – industrial projects, agricultural endeavours, the new television station. On Friday everything shut. What should we do, we asked our guide, who was going with his family for a picnic in the desert.

'You could go to the executions,' he said, as if suggesting the movies. Bob and I debated the rights and wrongs of this. We wondered whether it was pure ghoulishness that made us want to go. We did not deceive ourselves into thinking it was our duty as journalists. At the same time, our not going would not in any way change what was to happen.

I had always disapproved vaguely of my great-grandfather Richard Monckton Milnes, who went with Thackeray in 1840 to see the public hanging at Newgate of a young Frenchman, Courvoisier, the murderer of Lord William Russell. Monckton Milnes, an MP at the time, was a campaigner for the abolition of capital punishment. Thackeray was horrified by the experience, writing that he felt ashamed at the 'brutal curiosity which took me to that brutal sight'.

Monckton Milnes had obviously not been so affected, as he afterwards collected autographs and woodcuts of Courvoiser, of Calcraft the common hangman and other notorieties connected with crime and its punishment. Perhaps I shared with him the feeling that one should have almost any experience, with the obvious provisos of excluding cruelty, criminality and the corruption of others. In any event we went.

There was so much about that morning that was odd as well as ghastly. The executions, dismemberments, lashings, stoning of adulteresses and any other punishments decreed by the *Shari'a* took place on Fridays outside the Governor's palace. The penalties were not always quite according to Koranic precepts. In the Koran, the stoning of adulterers was meant to apply to both men and women and the restrictions were specific. The sinner was to be blindfold or put in a sack and the stoners were to stand in a circle, leaving a gap through which the guilty person could escape. The stones were to be no bigger than a pigeon's egg, and were to be thrown with the right arm, under which a copy of the Koran was to be held at the same time. It was never the intention that the adulterer should die. The object was humiliation. Similarly, the beatings were meant to be performed by a man holding a copy of the Koran under the arm that wielded the lash or the cane. Murder and rape were the only secular crimes to be punished by death. The rules were often exceeded.

The crowd gathered early, milling all over the square, pushing and shouting – although they must have known, as we did not, that the police would clear half of the square, pressing the crowd back. A boy took Bob up to a rooftop so that he could take photographs. I sat, rather apprehensive, in my chair as the crowd swayed around me. I felt that they might resent a foreigner who had come to gawp. The firing squad arrived. The officer in charge spotted me and said that I would see nothing, and asked me if he could move me to the top of a short flight of steps on the front of the palace wall against which the prisoners were to be shot.

The crowd had thinned when the muezzin called the people to prayer and the devout had filed into the mosque at the far end of the square. Now it was noon and they rushed from the mosque to get near the front. A great scuffling followed as the police pushed them all back, leaving a clear space littered with lost sandals.

Three brightly painted trucks swept up – two blue, one red. In the back of each was a chained man. With hobbled steps they were brought to the wall. The two further men were in black, with red head-covering. The nearest one, not ten paces away from me, was all in white. His face was set, his eyes dull with a resigned fear. Then he looked up and saw me. Probably he had never seen a wheelchair before. For an instant our eyes met and I saw in his wild surprise.

Then he remembered and his eyes glazed again. At that moment, I did not care what he had done. All I wanted was that he should live. In fact, the three of them had raped and killed a fifteen-year-old girl. That was, in a sense, irrelevant. I just knew that no one had the right to kill him, any more than he had had the right to kill her.

In our society, if we are to be shot, we stand and face the firing squad – blindfold as a rule, for whose greater comfort I am not sure. This was different. The three men crouched down facing the wall, their backs to the three firing squads. The order snapped. The two further men fell first. The man in white just began to turn his head to see what had happened, then he too fell. They threw the bodies on to the trucks like rubbish and drove away.

There were other differences from how it used to be in Europe. There were hardly any women, no equivalents of the *tricoteuses*, but little boys wriggled through to the front of the crowd with no one thinking it not a sight for a child. There was no sense of theatre, in that the lesser punishments followed the executions whereas, surely, had this taken place at Tyburn, we would have started with the comparatively gentle beatings and built up to the deaths.

They believed that the public executions were a real deterrent and they were puzzled when I asked how it was, in that case, that they happened every Friday.

At last nearly everything was ready. Two brand-new pick-up trucks – a Chevrolet and a Ford. Eight men – two guides, two drivers, two cooks, Huamel the chief and Abed, whose qualification seemed to be that he had killed five men. I liked them at once. The trucks were loaded with everything we could need – a huge tent, drums of water and petrol, quantities of food, some rifles and a machine gun. The only hitch was the matter of an interpreter. There was one available but, they said, he was not the best. The best would definitely come tomorrow – *boukra insh'allah*. The idea of allowing all these people, whom it had taken a week to assemble, to disperse and relying on God's being willing that they and the interpreter should all turn up the following day, seemed risky. I said that I was sure that we would be perfectly happy with the available interpreter, and that we might as well leave right away.

Abdullah was brought. He was a pudgy fellow, a civil servant, nervous, but very friendly and anxious to please. He came, not with the rough mat roll that the others, all desert tribesmen, had brought,

201

but with a fancy bundle and a satin pillow edged with lace. I heard later that they had had a lot of difficulty finding any interpreter who was prepared to go into the dreaded Rub al Khali.

We drove only a short distance that day, but far enough to be sure that we were really under way.

At Haradh, the last oasis on the fringe of the great desert, the Emir came for dinner with us, also a young man from a local agricultural project, who had been educated at a university in Oklahoma.

The Emir, after the usual pleasantries, gave a disconcerting verdict on our equipment: 'You have the wrong kind of vehicles, you should have four-wheel drive. If you had the right vehicles, you have the wrong tyres. If you had the right tyres, you are too heavily laden. If you were less heavily laden, you have too little petrol and not enough water. You will die.'

Abdullah translated little of this, but the young agriculturalist, with a pretty echo of the Emir's poetic style, relayed it in detail. He added that the oil companies who had explored the northern part of the Empty Quarter, never ventured into it with fewer than sixteen vehicles, two of them tracked. The guides were respectful to the Emir, but were plainly not put out. I asked if we could buy a little petrol. The only possible source of supply was the agricultural project. Huamel asked the young man to sell him some. He refused.

Thinking that it would be harder for him to refuse a foreigner, I tried to persuade him and he said: 'How can I give you any? You are Ministry of Interior and I am Ministry of Agriculture.' But in the end he agreed to part with a little. Huamel refused to take it. He told the young man to keep it and hoped he would drown in it. 'If this is education, we want nothing to do with it.'

I did not envy the young man his task, which was to settle three thousand proud nomads on the ten thousand acres of desert that he was hoping to reclaim.

Whilst on the unsuccessful journey I had learned a lot, I had been a little disappointed. The romance of the desert, the spirit that had informed Doughty, Burton, Lawrence and Thesiger, was missing. My eyes were trained to landscapes busy with incident and splashed with colour. Presented with vast expanses, bleached and robbed of shape by the high sun, they saw nothing. The desert looked like a gigantic vacant lot, scrubby and dirty, lifeless and abandoned, miles and miles of drab sameness.

After a few days with the Bedouin guides, I could not imagine how I had ever felt like that. The desert in their care became a place of infinite change and subtlety, alive and powerful. What had seemed repetitive was now exciting in its delicate permutations.

Nowhere in the world does the time of day make so great a difference to the landscape. In the early morning, the sands are red and vibrant, instantly awake as soon as the sun gives shape to the dunes. The great crescents and domes of sand look highest in the morning. The air is cold, crisping the knife-edge of the dune crests, and the colours are sharper than you remember them from yesterday.

By ten o'clock, it is hot and the sun takes everything out of the desert. There are no shapes, no shadows – only the shimmering streaks of the mirages. The sun grips the desert until about four o'clock, when the white glare slants away from your eyes, revealing an almost glacial beauty. The shapes of the dunes return, somehow more rounded, perhaps blurred by the heat. Strangely, while the sands glowed in the chill morning, now in the hot evening they look cold, reflecting the light.

Then it is dark, suddenly and conclusively, and the desert ceases to exist. There are only stars – more vivid and real than you have ever seen them.

This is a far cry from the apparently drab wastes of the first day. But perhaps more important than the new meaning held by the vast spaces is the recognition of the abundance of interest that lies within a hand's reach. At a glance, you can tell who or what has passed that way – men and their camels, gazelles, scorpions, lizards, chameleons. So skilled at this are the tribesmen that often they can name the person who has left a track – he must be coming from Jabrin, for his camel droppings are a certain colour. Passing here, he must be going to Haradh. His camel is very light. That can only be Ahmed bin Hussein.

Having first had to absorb spaces greater than before, the eye then has to see the land more minutely than was ever necessary.

When we had not gone very far, two hundred miles or so, we were looking for a meteorite, the size of a small house, that I knew lay somewhere in the region. The guides could not find it. We were crossing a deep depression in the dunes, when suddenly the sand snatched at our wheels and both trucks sank deep. We were used to getting stuck about six times a day, but we had never sunk so low. The sides of the depression looked very steep. I wondered how we could get out; I wondered a bit if the guides really knew where they were. Abdul Hadi, the best guide, had argued with Hamed about which way to go. They had even listened to what I had to say, impressed by my maps and compass. It was midday and beatingly hot in this hollow. I asked for a drink. We had two drums of water left; we had been a bit extravagant.

Dafr brought me a bowl of water. I took a draught, and choked. It was turpentine – not pure turpentine, but so badly contaminated as to be undrinkable. We broached the last drum. It was horrible, not as bad as the first drum, but very nasty. I thought we might be able to drink it *in extremis*. Then it dawned on me that we were *in extremis* – stuck, lost and with only turpentine to drink.

There is a cliché that claims that it is only people with no imagination who feel no fear. For the first time, I recognized the dangers. A few hours ago the desert had felt so friendly. That is the way of it, in the cool months. The sun rarely shines so fiercely as to be unbearable. Usually there is a light breeze, so that, except for a few hours in the middle of the day, it is the most perfect climate. There is nothing to alarm you.

Then you are lost and stuck fast in the sand and you remember you are in a vast waste, hundreds of miles from the nearest habitation. You can only walk. (Well, I couldn't, but some of the others could.) But how far?

I remembered that no one would start to look for us for at least three or four weeks. They would not know where to look in this space larger than France. They would not know that we had nothing to drink but turpentine. We had no radio, not even any flares.

For the first time in my life, I pondered on death. The desert still looked the gentle, soothing place that I had come to know and in which I had felt inexplicably happy. Then I thought of the white bones and the skin shells of animals I had seen on the way, of the human arm bone one of the men had picked up by a burnt-out hut in an oasis where there had been a tribal battle. Those bones had been so bleached and innocent that I had given no thought to their original vitality. I sat and wished and wished.

It is a dreadful moment when you think you are going to die in this way. It is so much worse than a gun pointing at you or a car rushing at you. These are recognizable dangers, known evils. The desert claims you with a smile. I had never been so afraid.

We got out of the sand after several hours with surprising ease, but the fear lingered. Abdul Hadi came back from a long, trotting hunt for clues and said he had decided where we were. He had found a marker left by the Arabian American Oil Company. Its number was missing, but it could correspond with one on my map. We camped and I wrote in my diary: 'It is reasonable to hope. Pointless to worry. Bed at 8.45.'

Half an hour's drive in the morning brought us to the well that Abdul Hadi said we would find in half an hour. We fell on his neck and embraced him. It was the most exhilarating moment.

The fact that the well was dry and that we still had only our polluted water did not matter. We were all eager to plunge on deeper into the Rub al Khali, forgetful of dangers and fears. All of us except for Abdullah, who wanted to go back to Riyadh. He could not forget what the Emir of Haradh had said and it preyed on him more and more heavily.

For the rest of us it was our day. At noon we came to a real well, drilled ten years before by Aramco at the southernmost point of their oil explorations. The water from it spouted up from some thousands of feet below, too hot to hold one's hand under and smelling of sulphur.

Bob and I insisted on bathing, and everyone joined in the game of squirting us with the water that spurted from the hosepipes attached to the well-head. Suddenly, everyone vanished behind the trucks and I heard the click of rifles being loaded. Bob rushed for his cameras. I was left sitting, drying off on a small camp-stool, and it was two minutes before I saw what the guides had all seen while larking about playing games by the well. A man on a camel was coming over the rim of the saucer of land in which the well lay. We waited tensely. I was glad that Arab modesty had dictated that I keep on my underpants.

After some minutes Abdul Hadi ran out and up towards the rider, who dismounted. The two rose slightly on their toes and kissed, bumping their noses three times. It was Abdul Hadi's uncle – a chance meeting in 250,000 square miles of emptiness.

For two hours we watched the most beautiful spectacle, a sight unchanged for thousands of years, of nomads arriving at a well. Slowly and gracefully, the camels came. At first a handful, then in scores – white camels, black camels, laden camels, ridden camels. The people came in family clumps, in all about forty, and as each man came Abdul Hadi greeted him with three kisses.

They all worked, even the small children, to water the camels which had not drunk for four days; they tended the animals before they fed themselves. Camels took on a new dignity in my eyes. I had always thought them unattractive with their barrel bodies and heads like furry snakes. Now I saw them as creatures of beauty and dependability. To the Bedu camels are his life. He rides them, milks them, eats them, sells them. His world is centred round them, and in Arabic there are at least eight thousand words devoted to all aspects of the camel.

The work done, it was time to eat. There was a momentary flurry in one part of the camp. Abdul Hadi's uncle was holding down a baby camel, about to slit its throat – a feast in our honour. Our men were trying to prevent this expensive gesture of hospitality. A wonderfully technical argument followed.

'We were here at the well first, so you are our guests,' said our side.

'That may be, but this is our country. We are the hosts, for none but the Murra tribe come here.'

'But we are not stopping here. We are leaving now, just passers-by.'

'You are bound to stay the night for it is soon dark, so you will spend the night in our company as our guests.'

'But we shall not raise our tent, so we are not true visitors.'

'You swear it? You swear you will not raise your tent?'

'We swear it.'

The camel was reprieved on this curious point, puzzling to me as we had only once put up the tent, all of us preferring to sleep under the open sky. I was doubly delighted because we could now give them the sheep we would otherwise have had to eat – killed five days before, the remaining meat was green with putrefaction. It proved, as it happened, a short reprieve for the camel, because on our return journey we found them again. By then, we were old friends and no argument would prevail.

As we went on my respect for my companions mounted. The drivers were amazingly skilful. When Bob moved one of the trucks, when neither of them was near, he got stuck at once. Their judgement of the sand was extraordinary. When the sun is high and a man's shadow no longer than his shoes, there is no perspective, making it hard to judge the size of dunes and their steepness. Sometimes we would race up the curved back of a dune and just in time, realize that the far side of it was a precipice with an eighty-foot drop. It was astonishing what they could drive down. The worst was a dune with a forty-foot drop, the last fifteen being sheer.

We hesitated at the top, but Nasr said he would tackle it. Bob got out to photograph our descent. He called up to me: 'I am dreadfully sorry to have to mention it, but you're not going to make this one.'

We did. I thanked Bob and as a mark of favour got Hussein, our Yemeni cook, to give him the sheep's gizzard for dinner that night.

If the drivers were remarkable, the guides were incredible. We met a small band of camels and a few men. Huamel, after the usual exchange of greeting and reply – 'What is the news?' 'The news is good, thanks be to Allah' – made some wary enquiries. It was not clear what these people were doing.

One of the strangers brought over a baby gazelle, which he offered to sell to me. I was tempted for a moment, but what could I have done with it? Then I saw money change hands and thought that perhaps the guides had bought the fawn for me, as they saw that I liked it.

Abdullah was still sulking from the day when we could not find the meteorite and would translate nothing. With my poor Arabic, I asked Huamel what had been bought. His answer seemed so ludicrous that I though I must have misunderstood.

We drove for three hours through the rough rolling land, weaving among the unending dunes, indistinguishable one from the other. There were no tracks, no footprints. We had covered, I suppose, twenty-five blank miles when Abdul Hadi gave a cry: 'There it is.'

'There what is?'

'The benzine we bought from those men.'

Under a bush were three drums full of petrol. We had bought two of them.

'However did you find them?'

'He told me where they were.'

I was so astounded by this feat that I forgot to wonder why a man on a camel came to hide petrol where no truck might pass for countless years. Nor how we would have managed for fuel had we not had this chance encounter.

This instinct for the way is unshakeable. Later I took Abdul Hadi's brother back to Riyadh. He had never seen a city. He was goggle-eyed in our modern hotel, falling about with laughter at the sight of Western women in short skirts, their heads uncovered. I tried to confuse him, leading him this way and that through the hotel where all the blinds were drawn against the midday sun, up in the lift, down more passages, into my room.

'Where is Naifa?' I asked. He pointed in the right direction. It was a game they had played with us in the evenings by the fire. Where is such and such a place, they would ask me. And I would point. They were delighted when I got it wrong and laughed. Gradually, I got a little better. Like much else it is partly a question of paying attention. They laughed, too, when I got it right, taking pleasure in my learning.

It was not just their skills, it was above all their fortitude and their contentment with their life that I found admirable and enviable. Abdul Hadi was my particular hero. When the sand was really tricky, he would trot ahead of the trucks, picking out the best route. He might jog like this for an hour, even in the heat of the day, yet when he got back into the truck he would not even be out of breath. When Bob wanted once to photograph a particularly high dune, he hurried off downhill for some four hundred yards. As he came back in the full sun, I saw that his eyes were closed with effort and he was counting each dragged step in the soft sand. During a rest, I noticed one of the men asleep on the ground. I could not make out who it was: he looked so small, a mere bundle of sleeping bones. When he woke and stood up, I saw that it was Abdul Hadi, who I had always thought was a tall man, such was his presence.

The perfect happiness of the days before we were lost had soon returned; I felt wonderfully detached. One morning I found an ostrich egg in the sand. How long had it lain there? The Arabian ostrich has long been extinct. I picked it up and I thought of Browning's poem:

> Yet but a hand's-breadth of it shines alone
> 'Mid the blank miles round about . . .

Abed drove a splinter of wood under his thumbnail the whole length of the nail. I had a scalpel but no tweezers. I cut away a bit of the nail, exposing the end of the splinter, but I could not draw it out. I had to cut to the end of the nail and further before I could get hold of it. Abed went on chatting about a rabbit he had plucked out of a bush that day and telling a story about hunting, as if nothing were happening.

The code of the desert was rigid and appealing. No matter what happened, the trust between travelling companions was inviolable. I knew that if Abdul Hadi's brother were to attack us, Abdul Hadi would kill his brother in order to defend us. It was wonderful to be in a situation where, for once, the human element was the only infallible one.

I asked Huamel what he would do if the trucks got irretrievably stuck or broke down completely.

'I would walk.'

'How far could you walk?' We were then six hundred miles from the nearest habitation and had been travelling for more than two weeks.

'It happened once. I walked fifty miles on the first day, though that was in an easy desert.'

I liked also the ambience of a working religion. In Riyadh and in the villages, the strictness of Islam seemed perverse, even hypocritical. In the desert, it was a natural part of life. Quite soon I learned not to be pained when a man to whom I gave something regarded it as Allah's bounty and not mine, for I knew that he would without thought give me anything I asked for. It was perfectly reasonable, if one behaved today exactly as one had behaved yesterday, that a misfortune or a piece of luck should be attributed to the will of Allah. Fatalism, when indeed the tiniest event, such as a ten-minute shower of rain, may change your destiny, seems not to be so feeble a concept.

These tribesmen were, however simple or even primitive their lives, totally civilized. Their belief in Allah was unfanatical, but it guided everything. They killed easily, but they abhorred torture. Their treatment of me was a perfect example of their uncomplicated approach to difficulties. My disability was the will of Allah; it made no difference to their attitude. I had never encountered strangers with whom I felt so much at ease on this score. The contrast with, for example, the Japanese was surprising to me.

They judged me as a person, not as a cripple. When they had weighed me up, they gave me a nickname that they told Bob carried some connotation of courage.

I spent much time wondering about the children of the group we met at the well. They had little time to play, though they were plainly mischievous. I watched one little boy, in the early dawn, creep into a huge water-skin on a camel's back, hoping by hiding to be able to ride instead of walk for the first few hours of the day. His father found him, walloped him, and they both laughed.

But what of the boy's future? All he could look forward to was a life of tending camels, eating the same food every day, hunting occasionally, telling stories round the fire, perhaps a visit to the city – an acceptance of the will of Allah.

His only education would be in the lore of the desert. He might never read or write; even be unable, like his father, to understand a photograph, turning it this way and that, seeing only a meaningless black and white pattern, his eye incapable of making the transference from two dimensions to three.

I believed and still believe in equal opportunity, but I could not help doubting the certainty of my belief. The adults of the group were I felt sufficiently aware of other ways of life for them to have made a deliberate choice. Abdul Hadi's uncle, for instance, had worked for an oil company. He could easily have acquired a transistor or some other symbol of modernity, but he had not. He preferred the traditional, precarious way of life to be undisturbed.

So did I and, with hardly any shame, early on in the journey snipped a wire in Abdullah's radio to preserve the glorious peace of the desert from its eternal wailing.

Abdullah was another argument in favour of leaving the Bedouin alone, instead of settling them on the land, forcing them, as one put it, 'to exchange the whole world for a garden'.

From the day when we were supposedly lost, although I came to realize that that had meant that they were not quite sure to within ten miles where we were, Abdullah had been behaving oddly.

When I was trying to get the splinter out of Abed's thumb, Abdullah suddenly rushed over and started fossicking about in my lap. I asked what the hell he was doing.

'There is a snake,' he said. I told him it was nonsense, and anyhow if there was one I did not want it alarmed, especially just there. He went on grabbing at me until I had to abuse him.

He went away, but came back in a few minutes and tried to snatch the small bottle of iodine out of my hand. I let him have it, and asked why he wanted it.

'I have lost my keys and I thought maybe they have fallen in the bottle when I speak to you about the snake.'

I realized that he had gone mad. At first, the guides were unsympathetic. Huamel gave him a severe lecture and Abdullah locked himself into one of the trucks. As we travelled on, the others were inclined to tease him, talking of bandits and suddenly letting the machine gun off, but when we explained that fear had sent him mad they stopped, for they were kind by nature.

The further we went, the worse Abdullah became. By day, he would do wild things such as drink his bottle of eau-de-cologne; by night he retched and moaned.

We reached Naifa, a well beside an enormous dune that rose sheer to about six hundred feet. This had been, as it were, our El Dorado, the point from which a short journey would bring us to the border of what was then the East Aden Protectorate, though no one could say exactly where the border lay. This part was marked on my War Office map as Unexplored Desert. Not even Thomas or Philby or Thesiger had been across that bit.

Our journey had been long and I was disturbed about Abdullah. I decided that we would make a proper camp and leave him with Abed and the two cooks while the rest of us drove off, our trucks empty of everything so that we could go faster. He watched while we made the preparations. He thought we were going to leave him there to die. I explained that he would be safe, with a guard to protect him.

We made to leave. He ran up, sobbing, begging me not to leave him. He was so pitiful that after a while I gave in. His weight would make little difference. He got in. When we had gone only a hundred yards, Abdullah attacked us. The cabin of a pick-up truck is not an easy place in which to fight. By the time we had got Abdullah out and subdued him, Bob had a deep bite in his arm and the rest of us had cuts or bruises. We drove away, leaving him tied up in Abed's care.

Unexplored desert, I have to admit, looks very much like other desert, but there was an absurd private pleasure in bumping across land that no other Westerner had ever seen. We went on until we were sure that we had crossed that undefined border, and then turned back. We were all happy – the Bedouin because they had given me what I wanted and I, not for the achievement, because reaching summits, crossing deserts, travelling the length of rivers are silly objectives in themselves, but rather for what I had learned and for the understanding that had grown up between the Arabs and myself. It had, during our dash to the border, struck me that it had never crossed my mind that the tribesmen might take Abdullah's side and insist on our returning to Riyadh. They did not take a narrow view.

On the morning after our ecstatic return to Naifa, we started the journey back. I hoped that the prospect of going home would cheer Abdullah, but it was impossible to get it through to him. I tried to talk to him about his family, but found no response of any kind.

The guides kept him tied up in case he should attack us again. I thought this sensible at night, but I could not bear by day to see him bound, looking like a picture of Barabbas in a children's Bible. He seemed harmless and all was well for a day or two.

We were stuck in the sand, as happened several times a day. Abdullah wandered away from the trucks. Then he ran. A mad flight to be free, I thought. Cries from the men – '*Sikkim*, a knife.' They ran. A flash of steel. Abdullah slashed and ripped at his throat.

'Let him run,' said Abed, fed up.

The younger men dragged him down. He lay on the sand. We waited in suspense. They stood him up and led him back. There were four deep cuts in each side of his neck. Through one I could see his windpipe, below all was blood.

'We must kill him,' said Huamel. 'He is a danger to us all.' It was true; he could set fire to the trucks, he might do anything – and we were six hundred miles from help. The code was clear.

Abed drew out his knife and the others mimed different ways of killing Abdullah. I talked to Huamel. Abdullah was a present from the King. I was responsible for him and must take him back to the King.

'But the King will only cut his head off. We might as well do it now.'

It was a desperate situation. They were right. I had come to admire their code, and according to the code Abdullah must die. But then my code said he must not.

'May I try something? Do you think we can make Abdullah laugh?'

'Abdullah will never laugh again.'

'If he laughs, can he live?'

They laughed at that.

We got out the morphine. I gave Abdullah a huge dose. I had little idea of quantities. I wanted to calm him and even elate him, but I didn't want to put him to sleep. I was lucky. In a short time, a sort of idiot peace spread across his face. I told him a joke I knew he would like and he made some sort of choking noise that I claimed was a laugh.

The men, in any case, were now interested. We were not far from Al Juhaysh where there was the deep well with the hot, clean water. I said that if we could go there we would show them something else.

The wind was blowing and the sand, mingled with dried camel dung, scudded in a constant stream above the ground, but with hot water Bob managed to wash Abdullah's wounds. He filled the cleaned cuts with half a bottle of antibiotic powder and, with our sterilized needles and thread, he stitched. The skin on Abdullah's neck was thick and hard to sew. The first shot of morphine was wearing off and Abdullah thought Bob was trying to kill him. I gave him another shot. Bob managed to close each cut. The men and I watched with different kinds of amazement and Abdullah slept. In the morning, he was no worse. Bob had saved his life.

For the rest of the journey back I kept Abdullah quiet with morphine, but I was afraid that I was turning him into an addict, so I only gave him small doses. As we drove into Riyadh, he waved his bound hands above his head, shouting to passers-by to come and rescue him.

I went to thank Prince Salman, who had selected our guides, and to beg him to spare Abdullah's life.

Some months after I got back to England, Hussein Amin, the Palestinian who had helped us at the beginning, came to London. He told me that Abdullah had been sent to a clinic in Switzerland. Sayid, the policeman who had tried to steal our belongings, had had his hand cut off.

Today, Wilfred Thesiger tells me, there are no nomads left in the Empty Quarter. They did succumb to the lure of modernity. They race around in Land-Rovers, their skills and their lore forgotten. I cannot help feeling that just as Abdullah, whose parents and grandparents were surely nomads, had found nothing with which to replace the traditional strengths of the desert, a singular notion of liberty has been lost to us and little if anything has been gained.

Curiously enough, Hussein provided a ludicrous example of the distortion of Arab dignity in the modern world. He invited me to come to meet a fellow Palestinian, who lived in New York and kept a permanent suite in London, at Claridge's. The purpose was to get me to write something in support of the Palestinian cause, with which he knew I felt great sympathy.

The man was offensive, rude and stupid in his arguments, hardly a sensible way to enlist someone's help. The talk dragged on until eleven o'clock. I would have walked out long before, but I liked Hussein and his brother, who was there also. Nevertheless, I was hungry and asked if we were going to have any dinner. The only place they thought worth eating at was the nightclub Annabel's.

It was incongruous to sit eating caviar by candlelight in a fashionable restaurant, while discussing the plight and poverty of the Palestinians. Eventually, the Palestinian became so unpleasant that it was not I who left (I couldn't as I had sent my driver away for an hour or two) but Hussein's brother. He stood up and flung £200 down on the table. The Palestinian picked up the bundle of notes, told Hussein's brother that he did not need his money and then burnt it in the candleholder.

When I got back I noticed a change in Angie. I realized that while I had been away, something had happened. I worked out that she had become involved, to a greater or lesser degree, with someone else. It was, I thought, perhaps a revenge for my third life or a need for a release from the constraints of being married to someone in a wheelchair. I had come to see jealousy for the repulsive emotion that it is and, quite apart from that, to think that physical infidelity was not something of very great importance, so I forgot about it. Although I did decide that what was true for one was true for both.

CHAPTER SEVENTEEN

CONFRONTING APARTHEID

Politics did not figure very largely in my *Sunday Mirror* column, except for comments and jokes about the absurdities of politicians. Later, when those repulsive Ulster Orangemen betrayed my half-brother Terence O'Neill, who, as the first decent Prime Minister they had ever had, introduced 'one man one vote' to the Province, I did express some views, but it was a rare event for me to take politicians seriously. However, in 1968, Mike Christiansen suggested that I should go to South Africa to see in what way, as Sir Alec Douglas-Home had suggested, the treatment of black people was improving.

Apart from Morocco, I had never been to Africa, so I made a journey of it, travelling up the Nile, visiting Sudan, Ethiopia, Kenya, Malawi and what was then still Rhodesia before reaching Johannesburg.

In Ethiopia, I telephoned the Emperor's granddaughter Mary Abebe, on the rather slender pretext that Haile Selassie was my brother Colin's godfather. I spoke rather slowly in careful English, hoping she would understand. Back down the line came a shriek: 'Oh, how simply lovely. You must come to tea at once.' She had been at school in England, at Heathfield.

Mary, although her husband had recently been made a senior Minister, lived in a modest house that would not have been out of place in Purley. At tea there were her three half-sisters – Molly, Colly and Woinab Messai-Andargatchew – and Sarah Abraham, an exquisitely beautiful girl married to the Emperor's grandson Iskander Desta. Sarah was surprisingly not of the same tribe but an Oromo, usually a rather underprivileged tribe, and her father was a leading

215

member of the Lutheran Church and Minister of Communications. They all chattered away in English and were fun. While I was there, they took it in turns to look after me.

There was nothing grand about the girls' lives, although once a week they had to have lunch with the Emperor. They nearly all had jobs; Molly worked for the United Nations, but I cannot remember what the others did. Their interests were broad and I learned much about Ethiopian culture from them.

Addis Ababa was fascinating; there were still a few of the old, rusty red mansions, built entirely of corrugated iron, even with onion domes of sheets of iron at the corners. The modern architecture was exciting and imaginative. I liked especially one building built in the shape of a drum.

There was an intriguing ambivalence in the relics of the medieval society that my father had often described to me and the advances of the twentieth century. There was always present the feeling that the whole scene might suddenly turn back a thousand years. One of the girls' great friends was an artist called Afawork Teklé, who had designed the stained-glass window in Africa Hall, the headquarters of the Organization of African Unity. Afawork was a willowy figure with rather a precious manner. One felt he would not have been out of place in a camp New York gathering. He wore always an exaggeratedly high-necked tunic, but one could just see the tip of a scar below his Adam's apple. The girls told me that Afawork had been captured by the Danakil when he was a youth. They had, according to their usual custom, slit him from the neck down, castrating him to add his testicles to their necklaces of such trophies. I no longer thought of him as willowy.

They sent me to see the Crown Prince, at one time the playmate of my half-brother Terence, who knew him as Mamou, but whose Amharic name was Asfa Wossen. My mother once asked the Emperor what the name meant.

'*Elargissez les frontières,*' said the Emperor.

Asfa Wossen had none of his father's strength. His younger brother, the Duke of Harar, might have been able to change Ethiopian history, but he died in a car crash. The Crown Prince, amiable enough but weak and unwell, would never extend any frontiers. When I was there, he was in the remnants of disgrace. While the Emperor was abroad, he had allowed himself to be drawn into a plot to get his father to abdicate.

The plot failed. To show his people who was in charge, the Emperor made a progress round his country. At each stop, the Crown Prince was made to sit at the Emperor's feet. It was a typical punishment from the man who has been unjustly accused of so much cruelty. Implicated on the fringes of the same plot was a boyhood friend of the Emperor, Ras Imeru, who happened also to be a friend of my father. He was nearly eighty and he hated travelling. Haile Selassie's penalty for him was to say that, whenever he went abroad, the Ras must go too.

Nevertheless, for the Ras to be involved in dissent against the Emperor must have meant that much was amiss, and so it seemed to me when I had an audience with the Emperor.

Johnny, my companion, and I sat alone in a cramped antechamber. The palaver of getting there had been great – being stared at, checked, questioned. On a sofa was the Emperor's chihuahua. For a mad moment, I thought that the way to an Emperor's heart might be through his lapdog. If I made friends with it he might be impressed. I put out my hand. The dog looked at me with more malice than I would have thought could fit into such a small creature. I abandoned that plan.

A man led us through another antechamber, then into a room where the Emperor sat on a throne – a small, still figure in a fawn uniform, his chest covered in medal ribbons. I bowed. Then the Emperor stood up and took my hand and looked deep into my eyes for a long time. Standing, he was hardly any taller than I was in my chair. The attendants and ministers and courtiers studied me. Then he sat down and continued to look at me in silence.

Disconcerted, I reeled off in English, all in one go, the questions I had planned about topics of the day, a journey he was soon to make and whether he had achieved all his ambitions. When I stopped, he sat for a moment, quiet and in thought. Then he started to speak in Amharic. The Minister of the Pen sat on the floor by the throne. He wrote in huge writing in a shorthand notebook, fewer than ten words to a page. When the Emperor stopped, the Minister of Information read what he had said in translation. The Emperor had answered all my questions, in order, forgetting nothing.

It was an achievement for a man of seventy-five, but I was saddened by the formality. I asked if he would prefer to speak in French. From that point, we managed far better.

'Do you know who he is?' the Emperor asked me, pointing to the

Minister of the Pen who, lacking French, had given up his furious scribbling. 'He was your father's office boy.'

He seemed to enjoy the questions that his courtiers thought impertinent. He would give a little smile and answer with perfect candour, while they fidgeted. He did not even mind my asking what he thought would happen when he died, a question that produced a horrified gasp from the court. The Emperor laughed but, for the first time, gave an answer that was, if not mendacious, certainly not a forthright response.

'There is a perfectly good constitution, why should I dictate the future? Ethiopia, you know, was not created just for me.'

It was too late. Old Ras Imeru had said to me: 'Whenever I see His Majesty, I try to persuade him to introduce a more constitutional monarchy. He listens, but nothing much happens.'

Haile Selassie had held power for more than half a century; it had become a habit. It was perhaps inevitable, as he grew weak with age, that it should be taken from him by force, and even more inevitable that the ruler who came after him should rule worse and with greater brutality than he ever had.

The girls all came to see me off at the airport. Mary gave me a fifteenth-century Ethiopian cross, and the others a gold puzzle-ring with the Lion of Judah on it.

Mary committed suicide in prison after the Emperor died also in prison, probably murdered. The others survived, but all now live abroad. I have never wanted to go back.

Kenya was different. Jock Leslie Melville was really a friend of Angie's, and had come several times to stay with us in England. He was tall, with a long, lean face and a marvellously sensuous head of hair. When smartly dressed, his good looks held an invigorating hint of the moors or the plains; while when he was untidy, his hair blown in the wind, they lent him an air of unfailing elegance. His romantic appearance was somehow enhanced by an arm withered by polio that he supported with a leather strap.

Jock's father had emigrated to Kenya before the war and Jock, apart from his being educated in Britain, had been brought up there and lived there ever since. When independence came to Kenya, he saw himself as a Kenyan and took Kenyan citizenship and was, for a while, involved to a mild extent in politics.

When he had last stayed with us, he had talked a lot of an American woman, who had comforted him when he had recently been ill. He asked if we thought he should marry her. Almost everything he told us about her sounded unpromising. She had had two husbands; she had three children and Jock did not much like children; she was older than he was. However, he so plainly wanted to be encouraged that we advised him to go ahead.

They had married and I went to stay with them in a ridiculous suburban house, with pretentious classical mutterings, of the kind that the whites were inclined to build on the outskirts of Nairobi – in fact in Karen, called after Isaak Dinesen, whose farm, immortalized in *Out of Africa*, was half a mile away; a house by the way, with multiple associations, for it was here that Sir Henry Delves Broughton was living when accused of the murder of Lord Erroll.

Jock and Betty were in love in the most attractive way and almost at once I became as fond of her as I was of him. Jock's placid warmth, his particular form of good manners, his thoughtfulness and easy, simple humour had always been endearing, but there had also been a slight ineffectiveness about him. He was the Nairobi agent for Hilti Power Tools and a more inappropriate job could not be imagined. Doubtless he charmed customers into buying his wares, but he had no engineering knowledge or skills. Betty recognized his real talents and knew precisely how to foster them, without ever appearing, in his eyes, to direct him.

Jock spoke perfect Swahili and he had played as a child with Kikuyu and Masai children. He knew all that there was to know of tribal customs, of wild-life and of the political situation in East Africa.

It was the time when the safari business was burgeoning. The horrors of Mau-Mau were nearly forgotten, though not so far behind as not to produce some chilling stories to tingle the imagination of tourists. The animals still roamed in their thousands. Betty had an instinct for what would sell safaris in America – not least a handsome, aristocratic Scotsman.

In a sense, Betty fashioned Jock into what she wanted, so that occasionally I was surprised at his compliance with what my idea of a handsome, aristocratic Scot would have found unbearably vulgar, but that was to overlook several things.

First, he loved her and even if he had disliked some of the things she landed him in, he would have done anything to please her; secondly, whatever gimmicky enterprises they embraced, he had never before had such stature, for all depended on his knowledge. It overlooked, too, her love for him and the care with which she built up his self-respect. Together they wrote books, appeared on endless American television shows, went on lecture tours of the States and received thousands of tourists a year in Kenya. They became personalities.

Betty had a tigress quality. She would fight harder than any woman I have known for her family, for security. She was born, if not on the wrong side of the tracks, into comfortless poverty. She worked, not greedily, but with a determination informed by that memory.

This picture of Betty leaves out most of the point of her. Once security was set aside, she was entertaining and often outrageous. She had the most unexpected collection of friends. There was Victor, in New York, who inexplicably developed leprosy and, when his nose decayed, found it difficult to seduce girls. He joined the Samaritans, answering calls from the despairing, whom he comforted so well that he sometimes managed to coax them into bed. There was Helen, a perfectly pious nun, who saw nothing wrong in watching a porno-graphic movie that somebody had given to Betty.

Betty had an appealing honesty about herself. She would admit happily to being tiresome or noisy or whatever in order to get her way, particularly in places like airports, where I would hide when Betty went into action to achieve whatever it was.

'Don't be so silly,' she would say to me. 'Do you want to get on this plane or don't you? If you do, make a fuss. It's an obvious principle – the squeaky door is the one that gets to be oiled first.'

She was always direct: 'What do you think of my face-lift. Do you think they did a good job?' And she would do whatever amused her and, with luck, other people. She always made me laugh. In the right mood, she would leap on a table and dance the black bottom. When travelling in the car on the long journey to the coast, where they had a house on the beach, Betty would sit in the back, typing letters while Jock drove. Suddenly she would lean forward and clap her hands over Jock's eyes and say: 'Do you know the way, Jocky darling?' It was never dull with Betty.

On that first visit, they taught me to love Africa. It was still possible at that time to rent a hunting block. For some risible amount, you could book ten thousand square miles of the plains, which were yours for a few days, shared with only a few Masai and countless animals. With two of their friends, Miles and Esther Burton, we wandered over this untouched chunk of Africa, not with the idea of killing anything, although our lease included the right to shoot an antelope for the pot,

220

but just looking and, in my case, learning – learning to see what Jock saw without looking, learning why the elephants were red and how to tell if they were about to charge, how to know where the lions might lie in the day, how to know in the night the noise of a leopard, learning how to make friends with the Masai.

It was very different from the desert, but it affected me in much the same way. There was no deprivation, for we had brought everything, but there was that intense relationship with a landscape and, in this case, an essential knowledge of the wild-life without which it would be quite easy to die.

In the evenings at our camp, we ate under the stars, and Miles and Esther would play their guitars and sing. And, in the dawn, we would wake to the sight of the magical mountain of Kilimanjaro, its snowcap hanging in the sky, glowing fourteen thousand feet above us, and I would reflect on the impertinence of Queen Victoria. How could anyone dare to think that they had the right to own so great a wonder, let alone give it to someone as a birthday present, above all the Kaiser?

I thought also how lucky I was in my capacity for enjoyment. So many of my friends, I knew, would have found these entrancing days unspeakably dull. One group of impala would be to them just like the next, the Masai would not fill them as they filled me with that satisfying spark of envy for their nomadic freedom, and how they would have loathed to sit by a camp fire while people sang to a guitar.

Then I wondered, and have often done so since, what it may be that I have missed that means so much to others. Sport I had to teach myself not to crave for, and after all much of the pleasure of it can be had vicariously as a spectator. Music was for years of my life a matter of annoyance for me. There was this enormous source of pleasure from which I appeared to be excluded – I could enjoy a concert or an opera, but I could see that those around me were getting so much more than I was from the experience, and I resented it. Somehow, this gradually seems to have remedied itself, perhaps by more careful, less impatient listening, and whereas before I would not have missed it much, to hear no music now would be a grievous misery.

I was to go back and back to Kenya, for love of the country and of Jock and Betty.

It did not take long to discover that far from being better the plight of the blacks in South Africa was becoming worse. Sir Alec Douglas-Home had evidently not noticed that the previous few years had seen more and more oppressive new laws, passed in the vain hope of giving substance to the preposterous and inhumane fantasy that was apartheid. The manifest injustice of three million white people ruling fourteen million black people, who had no say of any sort in their affairs, and of the three million keeping for themselves more than four-fifths of all the land, led naturally to the need for restrictions and controls and self-deceptions that would often have been funny had they not been so monstrous.

Colin's young brother-in-law, Johnny Seymour, was helping me and combining that task with taking photographs. For both of us, our journey round the country was a harrowing experience. So many images come back of the two extremes of human nature, for never have I seen good and evil so simply counterpoised, nor so clearly personified.

Nana Sita, a frail wrinkled Indian in his seventies, had lived in the Pretoria suburb of Hercules, in the same road for forty-five years, in the same house for thirty-seven. When he was a boy, he had sat at Gandhi's feet and listened to his teaching of non-violent resistance to oppression. Under the Group Areas Act, Nana Sita was ordered to leave Hercules, which lay in an area that had been pronounced white.

He did not move. The judge sentenced him to three months in prison. When he came out, he went back to his house in Hercules. After a while they came again for the old man, and this time it was six months. Then another six months, hard labour that is, for in prison they made him carry sand and cut wood. He had just come out.

'And, what will you do now?'

'My wife is a little tired. I will take her for a holiday. Then I will go back to prison. They say it will be two years this time.'

It was an Indian doctor who took me round Soweto on more than one occasion. We had done the official tour and listened to the Afrikaner guide telling half-truths – pointing out the schools, but not mentioning that, while education was free to whites, blacks had to pay. The doctor was risking arrest, possibly his life, in taking us round.

I noticed that he never asked anyone for anything until a sort of relationship had been established. We had a puncture and he needed a spanner. The doctor went over to a man who was working outside his house. They chatted, spoke of the year's crops, the Boeing air crash, then the man asked: 'Can I help you?' It was always like that, a soft contrast to Western ways, and it applies all over black Africa.

The doctor brought us to Jimmy's house. I never wrote down his name in case my notebooks were confiscated. We talked of the dry season, of the flowers he was trying to grow. Then: 'Can I help you?' The doctor told him what we were doing and asked if we could see his house.

It bore no resemblance to the houses we had seen on the official tour. Rough-cast walls, no ceilings, no bathroom, no electricity.

'To hell with a ceiling, I wouldn't care if it had no roof if I could only own my house and know that I could never be kicked out.'

Jimmy went on to list all the hideous restrictions on his freedom, the journeys he could not make, the jobs he could never aspire to, but for some reason what sticks in my mind was the look on his face when he said: 'In the centre of Johannesburg, where I work, there is nowhere I am allowed to sit down and eat my lunch, which is why you see us all eating our lunch on the pavement.'

We found Abel and Pamela Ford in Strand, outside Capetown. They were living in the disused premises of a garage. Oily bits of machinery lay about. We clustered round a shaky workbench, for it was late and the place was lit only by three candles.

Abel was coloured, perhaps a quarter white. Pamela was pure African. They had been married for ten years and had four children. Under the Group Areas Act, there was nowhere they were allowed to live together even though their marriage was legally binding under South African law. He must live in a coloured area, she in a black one. No one was sure where the children should live. Pamela had been arrested twice and Abel had been advised by the police 'to stop screwing this Kaffir woman and producing kids'.

Their courage was magnificent. They insisted on being photographed. They said that they wanted the world to know their story. While Pamela went to get the children ready for the picture, Abel said: 'I love Pam. I did not marry her because her skin was black. I married her because she has all the qualities I admire in a woman.'

It was a long time before Pamela came back from the other half of their makeshift quarters. I saw why. The children were now dressed in spotless clothes, the girls in frilly organza, the boys with little bow ties. It was madness. This couple represented everything that decent people strive after the world over – a true marriage, fidelity, loving parenthood – but they were forbidden to live together.

That same quality of love I saw in a more educated African couple. I knew them as Tom and Jane, their real names again lost to memory.

223

They lived in Soweto. I asked what they would do about their children's education.

'When they are old enough,' said Tom, 'I shall send them abroad, even if it means that I will never see them again. As for me, I will be all right – I have my girl and I love her.'

How often the Africans spoke of love, I thought. But would he have his girl, his wife? She had only a visitor's permit to be in Soweto. She could be turned out under one wretched Act or another at any time.

While the good shone with one, clear face, the evil took so many forms. Johnny and I saw children of ten working on farms from sunrise to sunset for ten pence a day.

We saw, at a mine in the Transvaal, the living quarters of the miners, twenty to a room, twenty feet by twenty-two, tiers of concrete bunks, no blankets, just a piece of felt. And it can snow in the Transvaal. Their pay was £5 a month.

'Sometimes,' said the white superintendent, 'when they come back for a second contract after a spell in the homelands, we don't recognize them, they are so thin. But after a week or two they are fat and shiny again.'

We found camps no journalist had ever written about, with ironic names like Sada ('At last we have found a home') or Illinge ('Welcome Valley'), where unwanted people who could not be said to have a homeland, people of no certain tribe, were dumped like worn-out machinery, thousands of them, mostly women and children. There was no work. Row upon row of minute huts. No trees. The people were hungry, the children's bellies swollen with malnutrition. The doctor called once a week. If someone was seriously ill, an ambulance would come.

'It calls almost every day,' said this white superintendent appreciatively. They never seemed to realize what they were saying.

The cruelty, too, was perhaps unconscious. At Limehill, near Ladysmith, we found people frantically building pathetic houses on plots fifty yards square. Two thousand of them had lived at Meran, twenty-five miles away, in pretty mud houses, painted with traditional patterns. They owned their land and they tended their cattle with pride. On a Friday, the children came home from school with a message for their parents. They must be ready to move on Monday. On Monday lorries came to take them to Limehill, a bleak hillside with only brackish water to be had from any well. The bulldozers

224

came too, that morning, and knocked down the pretty mud huts at Meran, for Meran now was white.

It was typical of Michael Christiansen that, when I came back with a report that was the exact opposite of the brief he had given me, he accepted my version with equal enthusiasm and gave me all the space I needed for what I was burning to say.

The articles that I wrote for the *Sunday Mirror* about South Africa in 1968 ran for four weeks. I like to think that they were the most worthwhile pieces of journalism I ever wrote. Until then, most of what had been written on the subject of apartheid was, as you might say, technical. Political writers gave informative explanations of what each ghastly new law meant, but it was dry stuff for the popular press. There was nothing that most readers could identify with. I wrote about everyday people like Abel and Pamela. I was also lucky enough to find the dumping camps that not even South African journalists had found.

I felt that I had succeeded when the attacks launched on me by South Africans became personally vicious. 'Crippled in body means crippled in mind,' wrote one man in another of those self-revealing phrases they were given to.

The South African Government wrote to say that I was no longer exempt, as other British passport holders were, from the need to get a visa should I want to go again. This was their normal response to any press criticism.

Their other reply was less usual and more comical. Two men arrived unannounced at the *Sunday Mirror*. They had a good story for me, they said. It took me a few minutes to work out what was odd about them, until I realized that everything that each of them was wearing was brand-new. Suits, ties, shoes – all of it. It was somehow suspicious. They told me that they were English and had been working in South Africa, but had become disgusted with the place. Their accents were a little odd, but a few years abroad changes some people's voices. Then one of them said: 'I have a Bantu wife.'

I knew then for certain that they were phoney. 'Bantu' was the official term for blacks. No black person, nor anyone married to a black person, would ever have used it.

The story they had come to tell me was that they had proof that in the family history of every member of the South African cabinet there was black blood. They were bewildered when I told them that I

225

wanted nothing to do with any such story, because it was based on everything that I was opposed to – judgement according to somebody's race.

When they left I asked a reporter to follow them. They went straight to South Africa House. I was rather affronted that they should think I would be so stupid as to fall for such obvious nonsense and thereby be at once discredited.

These articles were also the cause of my leaving *Queen*. Jocelyn Stevens had by this time sold it to a Mr Michael Lewis, whose interests lay in the clothing trade. The editor was Hugh Johnson, whose useful books on wine later became famous. I discovered that they planned to produce a twenty-page supplement on South Africa, backed by advertising. I protested that I could not, when people in South Africa had risked their lives to help me uncover the truth, work for a magazine which was encouraging people to go there for their holidays, thereby bolstering the lies. They persisted.

Admittedly to stir things up, I wrote to *The Times* saying:

> . . . I argued for two months with the editor at *Queen* that no British publication should give comfort to such a regime. Last week it became plain that nothing would alter his decision to publish this supplement. I therefore resigned.
>
> That is a matter of no great interest. However, it has been suggested that it is not the business of journalists to try to influence the publications they work for. But at what point does it become impossible for a journalist to ignore the policies of his newspaper?

The results were surprising. Many people cancelled their subscriptions to *Queen* and I received a flood of letters of approval from an immense number of distinguished people. Many also came from journalists, including Cyril Ray, who had refused to take over my job.

The Afrikaner who had written to say that I was sick in body and therefore in mind was of the opinion that disabled people should be put down – 'humanely destroyed' as he put it, 'we have mistakenly preserved too many of you'. I wondered how he knew I was in a wheelchair. Until that time, I had nearly always avoided mentioning in my journalism that I was disabled. I took the view that it was irrelevant to the job that I was doing.

When I presented a not very successful television programme

about politics, Associated Rediffusion built a high desk to conceal my chair, and I am amazed now to think that I acquiesced in this, but then I had been turned down for the possible job of doing *What the Papers Say* because, according to the Australian producer, someone at Granada had seen my screen test and said: 'What's the matter with that guy, he looks as if he's falling to bits.' I think I excused what I now regard as feebleness by telling myself that readers and viewers might be distracted from what I wanted to say.

Several things changed. I became more confident, the public's attitude to disability was shifting and Tony Snowdon made me a wheelchair. Tony and I both served on the committee of the charity which started as the Polio Research Fund and is today Action Research, funding medical research into disability. One section concentrates on the engineering side of medicine. Over the years the Fund had given money for many projects to rethink wheelchairs, but no real advance had been made.

Tony is by nature impatient and he decided to make me a powered chair. He rejected everything that was conventional and came up with what was really a motorized platform on to which one could put any smallish chair. The first one was driven by a motor pinched from a mechanical toy of his four-year-old son. It had many advantages. I no longer had to sit in a thing that looked like a bit of plumbing. I could put a high stool on it and be the same height as other people. I could vary the chair, instead of sitting always in the same rigid thing of metal.

Of course, Michael Christiansen took to it – it was fun and it was new, almost a gadget. Tony persuaded Sir Alfred Owen, the head of the engineering firm Rubery Owen, to manufacture the platform. Mike persuaded the Mirror Group to buy 2,500 of them for £250,000 to sell at a discounted price to *Mirror* readers.

It was a wonderful little machine and it served me well for fifteen years. But it served an additional purpose. In having to promote the chair by writing about it and even publishing pictures of myself using it, I learned that my inhibitions about mentioning my disability were absurd. My disability was as much a part of me as, say, being Jewish was a part of Bernard Levin or stuttering was a part of Patrick Campbell. It was no longer a thing to be hidden; it might even be a benefit rather than a handicap.

Our lives, Angie's and mine, were perhaps too frantic for us to pay

227

CHAPTER EIGHTEEN

ROMANY ROADS

According to a Swiss saying, marriage is a covered dish. Whether this means that no one can ever know what really is the relationship between two married people, or whether it means that it is better not to look under the lid of marriage, has never been clear to me. Either way it makes sense.

The whole subject hardly bears discussion, because marriage has no definable rules or shape. What is true, or approximately true, in one country or in one age is by no means true in another society or moment in history. Arranged marriages are said by some to work far better than marriages for what we see as love, as they are made for practical reasons that endure, while love may fade. Was the virtually inescapable marriage of the nineteenth century better because they had to make it work? But, when it was hell, the hell of it must have been worse.

The stuff of romantic novels is not romance; it is a brand of fantasy that women use as an escape from reality, as their lives are, and their natures are at bottom, practical. Men cannot read them, because we are truly romantic. We like a life in which our loves are unsullied by the practical. It may be idiotic, but for most of us it is the case and it colours so many masculine failings.

One of men's commonest inadequacies – immaturities might be more precise – is getting bored with girls whom they have yearned for as soon as they surrender and declare their love in return. This is usually explained by the idea that it is the chase that gives a man the real pleasure. It is more likely, I believe, that he is disappointed at his paragon's loss of virtue; a feeling comparable to Groucho Marx's

229

view that he would not want to join a club that would have him as a member.

I had a friend, Lionel Birch, who at that time edited *Picture Post*. He was married eight times, as often as not to other friends of mine. There was nothing disagreeable about him, but each time he got married he believed that it was to be perfect. At the first minor disagreement, his romantic faith was shattered. He thought it was all over and his search for perfection would start again. I never knew his eighth wife, but I believe they were happy; I presume that they never quarrelled.

There was something of this in my make-up. It would be hard to analyze what the search was for in my case, but it was in my mind always romantic rather than any simpler motive of loneliness or sex. As always seems to have been the way in my life, there was no common denominator linking the girls that I fell for, no colouring, no line of interest, no similarity of background. In the years about now, I loved two or three or four, maybe, with deep affection – but one, above all, tore at the heart of me. The folly of love in this case would have led me anywhere, but there were other impediments.

It is there that injustice lies for wives. What hope has a wife against a girl who has no responsibilities, who does not see the irritating habits, the little meannesses, the sandpaper side of intimacy?

People used to wonder, perhaps, how it was that a man in a wheelchair could manage to have any physical success with girls. I had no intention of enlightening them, then or now. Patrick Lindsay, an acquaintance of long standing, soon to be a cousin by marriage, had a theory that on the stroke of midnight I could leap from my chair priapic and triumphant. It seems as good a theory as any.

But they came and they went, these loves. And when Angie, too, was gone and I was alone, it was peaceful.

At a party I met Sue Cavendish. She was animated and challenging in some way, and conversation with her had the quality of swordplay. I was entranced and puzzled by her. When she admired a ring I was wearing, I gave it to her and she took it with no mock protest. But she would not come out to dinner.

A Gipsy wrote to complain that I was always writing about oppressed minorities abroad – South Africans, South American Indians and Australian aborigines. Why did I not write about the Gipsies, who were an oppressed minority in my own country?

I had never given much thought to Gipsies. I had read Eleanor

Smith when I was a boy and a little later started, but then abandoned, Borrow. I thought that the man who wrote to me was putting it too strongly, but set about researching the question.

The cliché, and I suppose I had always accepted it without thinking, was that the real Gipsies, the Romanies, were slightly mysterious, romantic people but the ones in caravans on highway verges, with their washing hanging in trees, were dirty, thieving, lazy, immoral nuisances, who were not real Gipsies at all, but probably Irish tinkers.

A little reading soon revealed that the romantic picture was silly. The Gipsies started to move westwards from India six or seven hundred years ago. When they reached Europe most of them settled in the Balkans but, driven on, the others came further, reaching Spain, England and Ireland. On the way they married and mixed, adapting themselves to whatever country they ended up in, keeping only traces of their original culture.

In Britain, they speak among themselves a garbled Romany, they have a few customs that have survived the centuries and their clothes distinguish them a little from other people – but not much else is immediately obvious. Many are fair-haired and blue-eyed, looking as if they owed more to the Norsemen than to the East.

The Gipsies are made up of a very few fairly pure-bred Romanies, a lot of Poshrats or Didecois (of mixed Romany and British origins), some nineteenth-century squatters who adopted the Gipsy way of life, some refugees from Hitler's purges, some Irish tinkers and a number of drop-outs of all kinds.

One of the most famous Gipsy families is the Price Clan, who stretch in a crescent across England from Exeter to York. The original Price was an eighteenth-century cobbler who married a Gipsy girl. Presumably they would not qualify in the romantic mind as 'proper' Gipsies, so I soon dismissed that half of the cliché.

I think it was the wording of the 1968 Caravan Sites Act that decided me to investigate the other half. It placed a duty on local councils to provide sites for Gipsies, although the sites were small and the escape clauses very broad. The corollary was an enhanced power to move people on. The act made it an offence for anyone 'being a gipsy' to stay anywhere for any time, other than on private land with the owner's consent – where he might stay only twenty-eight days. It was 'being a gipsy' that struck me as being legalized discrimination. What would have happened if any Act prohibited something to someone 'being a Jew' or 'being a black man', or come to that wrote jew instead of Jew?

I rented a caravan and, once again with Johnny Seymour, set off on a journey round England and Wales. I had not realized how much I was going to enjoy it, but the moment we were on the road I felt, even in the familiar landscape and within reach of telephones, a flicker of that appealing freedom of the nomad.

On our first afternoon, we found a group of Travellers, as they generally called themselves, parked on a wide verge near Kidlington in Oxfordshire. We asked if we might stay with them. I had been nervous as to how we would be received, but during the whole journey of several weeks no one ever turned us away.

Freedom took a knock when the police came at two in the morning, angry in their shame, to thump on the roof of each caravan telling us to move, waking the babies and frightening the old. There was a moment of farce when I protested and the police were startled by the unexpected accent, but the Connors family in the next caravan told me not to make a fuss. They were used to it, and I was to become so. At nearly every Gipsy camp we visited, the police came for one reason or another. It was like everything else – pain, unhappiness, in this case insecurity – miseries of all kinds breed an acceptance.

Fred Connors had a bandaged head from an earlier visit from the police, when they had come asking about some stolen copper and had bashed Fred's head against the window of his caravan, breaking the glass. Two days later, they had come back and said they were sorry; they had found the real thief.

The Connors had shrugged and bought a new window. There was no point in making a fuss. They made none now and we moved on in the night.

As we went west, I came to understand the Gipsies better and gradually to realize that they were an oppressed minority. Having decided that they were not a race of people in any strict sense, I concluded that what separated them from the rest of us and bound them together was a cast of mind, a traditional attitude that divides them from most of us far more than racial differences. It is stalwart independence and a determination to maintain the way of life that they have chosen, no matter how much it affronts the set rules of our society and brings down on them the hatred and contempt of half the population.

The other half of the cliché soon seemed as silly as the first half. The first Gipsy caravan I went into, before I even started on the journey, belonged to Johnny Brazil, who lived on a council site at Hainault in

Essex, a fenced-off space of concrete with eight sinks and eight loos, for sixteen families. Each family paid the present-day equivalent of £25 a week in rent for some concrete, forty feet by forty feet, and half a sink and half a loo.

From the outside, Johnny Brazil's caravan looked large but perfectly ordinary. To go inside was a breathtaking surprise. I might have been wafted to a Balkans parlour – a shining world of splashing purples and reds, satin cushions plumped up full in their lace covers, polished woods and bright-painted shelves. Most surprising of all was the collection of china and cut glass, many of the pieces fine Crown Derby – the favourite of all Gipsies – the least practical of all things in the caravan and so the most treasured, taken down and wrapped with care before each journey.

Everything was wonderfully clean, and so it was in nearly every Gipsy caravan I saw, yet Mrs Brazil that week had been refused service in a restaurant because she was a Gipsy.

The charge of dirtiness was not a just one, nor I came to see was that of idleness. Of course, they did not have regular jobs, for the whole point of their life was that it was not sedentary. Their traditional trades of making clothes pegs and artificial flowers had been finished by the coming of plastics. Automation had reduced the seasonal need for them in the hop gardens, and in many other agricultural jobs. Cars had replaced their beloved horses, although they all tried to keep a few, which of course was forbidden on local council sites.

With copybook ingenuity, the Gipsies adapted themselves to work that was compatible with their itinerant habits. They took to dealing in scrap metal and in laying Tarmac for people's driveways. Because it was casual labour Gorgios, as they called the rest of us, did not think it was work.

As for their honesty, they did go in for a bit of stealing. 'Not like the Gorgios do,' one of them said to me, 'breaking into houses and stealing valuables. We may take something nobody will miss much, a chicken or an old bicycle no one has bothered to mend for two years.' Even the police agreed that the crime rate among Gipsies is below the average, and for a Gipsy to be charged with murder is almost unheard of.

The further I went, the more I liked them. Being a Gipsy is rather like belonging to a club, or perhaps to the aristocracy who intermarry and have cousins all over the country with whom they can stay and save the price of a hotel. The Gipsy family names recur in every county – Fletcher, Butler, Lee, Boswell, Hughes, Stanley, Brazil, Nicholas,

Cooper, Smith, Price. The cousinships are all worked out. It is as if they all carried in their heads a Gipsy *Debrett*, remembering who has whom for a wench and who bides where.

They would pass us on from one group to another, telling us for instance to find Chris Richards over by Bridgwater. Chris was part Boswell and part Lee. 'The English Gipsy Rose Lee was my great-aunt and she was sister to John Lee, the man they could not hang. Three times the trap didn't work.'

All Gipsy reminiscence had a mythic quality, perhaps because their rate of illiteracy was then about ninety per cent. Statements were not necessarily true, but conveyed the essence of a situation carried to an extreme conclusion, so that a rich woman would be said to keep 'a tin tub in her van, filled to the brimming with gold sovereigns'.

Chris was a good story-teller, but no one could equal Albert Butler to whom he sent us. When we arrived at the camp at the edge of the Forest of Dean, Albert warned us not to mix with the people further up the hill, they were not proper Gipsies. This was a common device that the Travellers often used, oddly echoing the Gorgio cliché. In the North, Johnny Seymour had been beaten up by a youth who thought that we were working for television and wanted to take out on us his rage about a recent programme about Gipsies that he thought was unfair. Our neighbours, a particularly pleasant couple in a horse-drawn caravan, said they were sorry, but of course the youth was not a proper Gipsy. He turned out to be their nephew. Often it was a further expression of individuality, but Albert Butler, I suspect, wanted merely to keep us to himself to regale us with his stories. Naturally, when the police turned up, everybody always banded together in perfect unity.

For many nights we sat round the fire while Albert talked. His wife, Georgina, gave an occasional snort of disagreement if the story concerned them.

'You'll have heard of Iron Price, never beaten in a fight he were. He was from hereabouts but would go anywhere he would for a fight. He heard of a man over by York, so he rode through the night and he arrived there and he went to the pub where he knew the man would be. And he stood by him and said not a word, but he dropped his kerchief and, the man, he knew the meaning of it. And they went outside and when the man lay in the dust, Iron Price, he mounted his horse and he rode back through the night and he never said a word of it to nobody.'

I never asked Albert questions like how, in that case, anybody knew that Iron Price had done this feat.

Both the words and the rhythms of his speech belonged in a different time and I loved listening to them. Talking of the importance of marital fidelity among the Gipsies, he told me of his uncle who had come home on leave during the First World War to find his wife 'in the wicked arms of another man. He turned on his heel and went straight back to the front and no one ever had a leaf from him from that day to this.'

Albert's own adventures, however recent, had the same legendary ring about them. Their elder daughter, Eileen, a year or so before, when she was twelve, had been taken to hospital.

'She got no better. Those drugs, I say to them, are no good. You're doing her more harm. And I took her home, pale and thin as a broom handle. "Beware" they says, "we'll be watching you". And I was afraid. Eileen grew worse. One night I said to the wife, "Tomorrow, I'll walk the river." "What for," says she, "to drown yourself?" "No," says I, "for her." Come the morning, I went down the river. All day I walked the river and I came back with what I knew – the yellow flower of the water bitney and some eldenbloom. I mixed them in a brew. "You'll kill her," says the wife. "You hush yourself and wait," says I. Three days and three nights I gave it her. And she was well.

'Then came the doctor. All round he looks, his eyes a-glitter. "Where's Eileen?" he asks. "Out playing," says I. "She's not," says he, murder in his thinking. Just then comes Eileen, laughing and playing. The doctor stares amazed. "What did you give her?" he asks. "You tell me now." "Never," says I, "else you'd be as wise a man as me, Doctor." '

No Gipsy herbs could cure their other daughter, Kate. She was about four. Her head was large with what I supposed was hydrocephaly; she was deaf and dumb and could not walk properly. Most of the day, she sat in a large tub near the fire for safety, because she would otherwise crawl towards the brook that ran near the camp. She just sat rocking herself and making strange sounds. Every so often, her mother would pick her up and hug her and kiss her, calling her 'my Queen'. It was only after two or three days that Albert mentioned anything about Kate. 'I don't know if you've noticed our Katie, a little touched she is.'

Her affliction made no difference to her parents nor to her brothers and sister. She was a lot of trouble, needing to be watched all the time, but her condition was just a part of the cycle of things. She was a member of the family and their love for her was not thought out or measured or by way of compensation. No one would ever have thought of parting with her, putting her in a home, any more than they would have parted with an old grandmother who grumbled away in a caravan not far from ours as only someone who has had eighty years to accumulate grumbles can complain. There was and surely still is a quality of loving among the Gipsies that Gorgios have lost.

The further I went, the more involved I became. I found that there were customs that had come from some foreign past, some things such as that the kettle must never sit on the ground, a plate licked by a dog is broken at once, the bowl for washing dishes must never be used for washing clothes. Death, above all, had its special rules. It, too, is accepted easily as a part of the cycle, something to be talked of freely. When someone is dying he is taken from his caravan and put in a tent, for any important event should take place out of doors. His family do anything to prolong his life even by a few minutes, some believing that if they hold on to something that the dying person is holding some of their energy will pass to him.

When he dies he stays out of doors, lying in an open coffin lined with bright material. He will have tried to die somewhere near where he was born and will always be taken there to be buried. Until he is buried none of his family will sleep. They no longer burn a dead person's caravan, it is economically impossible when they cost many thousands of pounds, but often they do destroy all his possessions, a symbolic recognition of the individuality of every man and woman.

During our tour, I had seen prejudice and cruelty that made me ashamed that it could happen in Britain, but I had also been excited by the courage, simplicity and the camaraderie of Gipsy life.

In my notebooks, after being moved on one night, I wrote:

Are we so precarious, so unsure of ourselves that we dare not allow freedom to a tiny group? For in the end it is we who are the losers. This freedom – a mood rather than something that can be tabulated with facts, a spirit of freedom communicated rather than a positive happening.

When they moved us, reluctant and cursing good oaths, somehow we felt we were the masters. They could tell us to go, but could not tell us which way to go. In the starlight we could pick our way, soothe the babies and choose where to stop, at least for a while.

We knew what they did not know. We knew where the wind would blow, where the pheasant might be to make our supper. We knew how to lie warm in the cold, dry in the rain. For them it was late, but what were hours to us who had so many of them?

It takes more than a bigoted councillor to break six hundred years of independence.

That was all very well, but was it realistic? It was, in a way, the same conundrum that had troubled me in Saudi Arabia. This liking for simplicity that accorded so ill with my perpetual excitement about the future. It was perhaps the problem of being born in the first quarter of the century – the illusion of the unchanging past feels so much closer and is tempting. The next ten years were not to provide a solution.

On this journey I had driven through what was still North Lancashire. I had thought of Sue, the girl to whom I had given the ring. I knew that she lived almost on our route and toyed with the idea of calling on her, but I thought that the sight of Johnny and myself, having just left some grimy urban Gipsy site (somehow we never managed to keep our caravan looking like theirs), would not be the right way to approach her.

Two days after I got back to London, she rang. She was rather short of money, she thought of selling the ring, was it really a present, did I mind? This time, she said she would come to lunch.

CHAPTER NINETEEN

HOME FARM

A joke of the scientist Lord Rayleigh comes to me from childhood: 'Caesar and Pompey were very alike, especially Pompey.' Similarly we are all singular, but there are some who are more singular than others. Sue is one of the most singular people I know; she is simply not like anyone else. It took many years before I could begin to predict what she would do in any situation, and now, after twenty years, I cannot be at all certain how she may react to something. It is not that there is anything strange about her. It is just that she is singular.

Her beauty, of which her large eyes of variable green are the supreme feature, was surely designed to be calm and still, but it certainly is not. Her tempestuous nature ruffles it into the kind of enchantment one sees in a mountain stream – here a pool of smooth water, there a rill of pretty bubbles, sometimes a noisy waterfall, but there are places where the rapids can be painful.

She lives her life in the superlatives of emotion, consuming love, furious hate, wild elation, with fortunately only an occasional deep depression. When I met her she was nineteen – her character unformed, but exciting. I came back from the Gipsies in October 1969. We were married in March 1970.

While there was much about Sue that was unpredictable, there was also much that was familiar. She was, by one of those slips in generation, a second cousin of Sarah Macmillan, her father Richard Cavendish being a first cousin of Lady Dorothy, who had often talked to me about Holker Hall, the house in North Lancashire where Sue was born and brought up, and where Lady Dorothy had spent many

238

childhood holidays.

Sue's potential had not been realized in any of the jobs she had so far had. Besides the potential, I detected, I thought, a recognition comparable to mine at that age that there was a more interesting and better world than had been so far opened up to her. The indoctrination in her case had been far stronger and far more absurd than in mine and the outside influences negligible, apart from a girls' school more inclined to reinforce than correct the unrealities of her home life.

Holker was a paradise, reminding me in many ways of the Shanes Castle of my childhood. The estate had come into the family of the Dukes of Devonshire in the eighteenth century. The early part of the house dated from the seventeenth century, but half of it had been burnt down and a large Victorian red-sandstone wing built to replace the part that was lost. In Victorian and Edwardian times, it was used by the family mostly as a holiday house until the eighth Duke gave it to his younger son, Richard's father.

The deer parks and the woods beyond stretched down to the sea where the River Leven flowed into Morecambe Bay. The shallow tides raced in and out over the wide sands at such a pace that, jumping in, one could be carried a mile or more by the water's flow in a matter of minutes. The sands were treacherous, but the fishermen with their horses and carts, or, more recently, their tractors, picked their way with cautious skill to stake their nets in the ephemeral streams to catch the shrimps. Yet, sometimes, a cart or even a man would sink with heaven knows what ghastly gurgle under the quick, sucking sands.

There was everything a child or a young girl could wish for. There were horses to ride, there were farms to visit, there was even a racecourse on the estate at Cartmel where, twice a year, there was the excitement of some of the most unlikely racing in the calendar. There was no need ever to leave the estate unless for a picnic in the Lakes or on the wild fells for a change.

By that slip of generation, Sue's father was stuck in an age that was over. He was hospitable, mischievous and often funny, but his attitudes were seigneurial and would have been quite untenable had they not been backed by the cushion of seven thousand acres. It was impossible to dislike him, because he bore no ill-will, but he was emotionally and physically indolent. In Sue's seven years of boarding school, for instance, he very seldom visited her.

Richard's whole existence centred on his inheritance. When he came into it, the estate was in debt. He managed to preserve it, modernizing a good deal, improving the farming, opening the house to the public, developing some slate quarries, but his mind remained that of an eighteenth-century landowner.

Sue's mother had an almost comical admiration for the ways of the upper classes. A duke to her was an object for reverence and her father-in-law was the son of one and her mother-in-law the daughter of another. She got carried away with the rituals of country-house life. She instilled all kinds of nonsense into Sue and her brothers and sisters so that, when they were young, they used to count how many people would have to die, in the style of *Kind Hearts and Coronets*, before Richard became the Duke of Devonshire and they little lords and ladies.

Sue was by far the most intelligent of her family so that, while early indoctrination is hard to shake off, she was ill at ease in the unreality of her parents' supposititious world.

When my step-grandmother died in 1968, Colin and I inherited some land at Madeley, where we had lived during the war, on the borders of Staffordshire and Cheshire. The house and most of what remained of the Crewe estates had gone to our nephew Raymond O'Neill. We had three tenanted farms and some odd acres here and there.

The tenant of Netherset Hey, Mr Benyon, was a widower of well over eighty. He had had no son, and one of his two daughters had been killed on the small coal railway that ran across the lane that led to the farm. He lived with his surviving daughter in a hugger-mugger fashion in the farmhouse. He stayed mostly in the kitchen, where they avoided the need for cutting wood by putting the end of a small tree into the fire and suspending the other end from the ceiling so that, as the top burned, more pushed in.

Chickens pecked round his feet and sat on the furniture. When one went to see him, he would say: 'Move that fowl from the chair and set you down.' And, when one did lift up the hen, there might well be an egg under it.

The farming that he did amounted to little more than ranching, but even that had become too much and he was glad to surrender his tenancy in return for something to help him in his retirement.

Sue and I decided to live at Netherset Hey. The house was built sometime in the eighteenth century in the vernacular, of a burnt red Staffordshire brick. The local farmhouses were often big, not only to accommodate the larger families and often some of the farm workers, but also to provide warm rooms where the round orange Cheshire cheeses could be dried. We knocked two of the three living rooms into one. Mr Benyon's kitchen we made into a dining room, and fashioned a new one for ourselves from a warren of sculleries and storerooms. We ended upstairs with eight bedrooms, five bathrooms and a playroom. The levels were odd, but we fitted a lift that came out opposite our bathroom with the result that it was impossible, on the first floor, to get from one side of the house to the other without going through the bathroom.

It was a friendly house that made no demands on one – being far less grand than Wootton had been and so better suited to a less feverish decade.

The house and its attendant red-brick buildings sat in a space protected, one way and another, on all sides. To the west, the fields sloped down three or four hundred yards to where the main line ran from London to the North, through Crewe nine miles away. Beyond the railway the land rose again to where, half a mile away, one could see the cottage belonging to one of our other farms, the only house to be seen from ours, unless you counted the neat new cottage we built for our head cowman.

Behind the house, the fields were steep, the crest forming a boundary between us and the next farm, and the hill itself making a sound barrier against the roar of the M6 motorway which ran through our neighbour's fields.

To the south there was a small valley. A stream, lined with alders, flowed through marshy fields spiked with rushes, the spongy land a reminder of boyhood struggles when I had followed my father as we went in pursuit of jinking snipe that I could never raise my gun quickly enough to shoot. The snipe had gone, as had the woodcock we used to see, again swerving too deftly for me through the hundred-acre wood on the far side, so bizarrely named Hey Sprink. Instead, there was now a small herd of fallow deer. We dammed the stream and made a lake, not two acres in size but big enough to fill with trout and to hold a minute island where Canada geese nested, safe from foxes.

To the north, our lane ran nearly a mile to the village and, turning the corner of the farm buildings, we could see the church tower and, in the far distance above the village, the white stucco of our old house.

Nothing could ever encroach on us behind the barriers of the railway, the motorway and Hey Sprink wood. As with everything else, we soon got used to the noise of the railway and were half-surprised

241

when people asked if it was a nuisance. The prevailing wind carried away the noise of the motorway, but even when that failed its roar behind the hill sounded like distant sea.

Colin and I had come to an arrangement with Stanley Furnival, the tenant of the farm on the other side of the railway, to form a partnership. We would put in the three hundred acres of land, the old buildings, and the new cottage; he would provide the capital to buy cows, to instal milking and other machinery, and to build a place for the silage – and he would do the work.

I had spent nearly twenty years of my life living a day at a time; nothing is so dead as yesterday's newspaper. It was wonderful to drive up to Madeley on Friday nights and to sink, as if into a warm bath, into a world where one talked of what we might do in two or three year's time. I had to learn a new patience, quite apart from learning about milk yields and varieties of wheat and all manner of disasters that I never knew existed, like leather-jackets and aphids, mastitis and warble flies. The sheer scope of my ignorance I found intriguing and the excitement of learning was stimulating.

Some kind friends gave me a three-wheeled American golf-buggy. My Snowdon Chairmobile was splendid indoors, but had never been meant for use out of doors, so the golf-buggy added another whole dimension to my life. The land, because it had not been properly farmed for many years, was much smoother than it might otherwise have been, undisturbed by ploughing and not poached by the hooves of a large herd. I raced around the fields, able to go out into the country for the first time for fifteen years entirely by myself. In the spring, I could wander through Hey Sprink among the sheets of bluebells, crushing clusters of wild garlic under the fat tyres of the buggy. I could sit alone by the lake and watch the geese launch into the water, their goslings in obedient Indian file, while a heron stood hoping for one of my trout, their firm flesh a proud pink from the freshwater shrimps, and in the evening the deer came, their every sense alert, to drink.

As always, though, it was the people who gave me the greatest pleasure. The name of Furnival was more associated with the village of Mucklestone about eight miles away on another part of the original estate, where it had appeared in the rent rolls over the centuries. Fred Furnival, Stanley's father, was a distinguished man, the very epitome of hard work and sound judgement. When young in the 1920s, he had been given the lease of a two-hundred acre farm; then the next-door farm of nearly four hundred fell vacant. It was a rule of the estate never to give two farms to one tenant, but farming was at a low ebb and Fred was such a reliable and enterprising tenant that he was given Manor Farm, so called because in one of the fields was a sandstone arch, the last remnant of the original Madeley Manor.

With his wife, Louie, Fred brought up four sons and a beautiful daughter with whom in youth I exchanged chaste if ardent kisses. By the time Fred died, Bill was farming fifteen hundred acres in Kent, John and young Fred each had substantial farms and Stanley was now working seven hundred acres. As a family, they represented everything that nostalgia would have us believe made Britain great. They worked hard and long. They were tough but fair employers, never asking anyone to do anything that they were not prepared to do. They were scrupulously honest, although not in a hurry to point out when they were getting the best of any deal.

Stanley had married the most attractive girl for miles around and it was a delight to work with them, Stanley making me laugh and Elaine helping Sue get accustomed to the ways and, not least, the language of Staffordshire.

Finding people to help me, now from Stoke-on-Trent rather than London, I again learned that people's lives do not vary from one part of the country to another as much as I had imagined. Politeness, hospitality, eating habits, vocabulary, small quirks of behaviour like keeping letters behind the clock on the mantlepiece may be different, but within England attitudes do not alter much from place to place. Southerners may think themselves more sophisticated, but matrimonial tussles, wife-swapping, homosexuality and all forms of permissiveness were as common in Staffordshire and Cheshire as they were in the South.

There were contradictions in the concrete facts of life at Madeley running parallel with those in my feelings, brought about by life on the farm. So much was different from my childhood when, both at Manor Farm and at Netherset Hey, horses had played a large part in the working of the farms. Stooks had stood in the harvest fields, convenient hides for shooting pigeon, and there had been haystacks to romp in. Now, with Stanley and his brother Fred, we bought a great red Martian of a combine-harvester that gobbled a thirty-acre field in a short day. What little hay we made was scooped up and spat out by another machine in shoe-box parcels, compact and hard and uninviting, while yet another engine squirted runny manure over the

243

fields in a fashion that reminded me of the way a hippopotamus whirls its tail to chop its faeces into scattered fragments to pollute the river less.

But Geoff Lafford, one of the cowmen, could have belonged in any age. Unmoved by cold or heat, he walked from his cottage in the village at six every morning, carrying his 'snappings' ready for midday. He loved the 'beasts', as he called them, though treating them roughly, yet if a cow had trouble calving or a calf was struggling to survive, Geoff would often be in the yard at midnight. And, when milking was over, while everyone else drove the cows out into the fields, Geoff led them and they followed him.

His Blarney-tongued father was an old rogue, who used to steal up the lane and pick all the mushrooms before we could get to them. I don't know how far the Laffords stretched back, but I loved the feeling of continuity that they engendered, a link, in fancy at any rate, to those who dug the abrupt bank, traces of which ran down our fields and beyond the railway round Stanley's land, once the confines of the seventeenth-century deer parks of Madeley Manor, or even further in time to those responsible for the rising and falling waves in the surface of the old pastures that one could see in certain lights, and I could feel in my buggy – evidence of Saxon ploughing.

At the same time, I did not feel happy that I could never persuade Stanley to call me by my Christian name, and it was only with a visible effort that Elaine could force herself to call Sue by hers.

This paradox far outreached the farm. The village had changed so much in twenty years. The population had risen from something like two thousand at the end of the war to about seven thousand, and the standard of living had risen immeasurably. Whereas, when I was young, there had been very few cars, it had become almost unusual for a family not to have one, except on the poorer housing estates.

My nephew had sold our old house and it had been turned into flats. Sam Davies, whose Ayrshire cows used to graze the park, had been murdered and a teachers' training college had been built there. In gross contempt of any respect for the countryside, the wood behind the house, that my father had laboured so hard to clear, had been filled with the ugliest villas imaginable, each one incorporating a different insult to taste, architectural sense and practicality – picture windows looking out onto dark copses, shutters which could not cover the windows they were meant to decorate, multi-coloured crazy-paving, carriage lamps and every other horror.

But there was much that was the same. The pubs, forbidden to me by my mother's particular sense of fitness, had not yet forsaken cut glass and benches in favour of carpets and pleated lampshades. The houses lining the Holborn, so named by the Offley family, who were London merchants and owned Holborn in London (so that in my lifetime we still had chief-rents from the Prudential building in High Holborn), were undisturbed. The Old Hall, a fine half-timbered house built round a central chimney, looked unmoved by change. Inevitably, given so large a place of concealment, King Charles was supposed to have hidden in the chimney, which was said to account for the odd inscription running across the front of the house: WALLK KNAVE WHAT LOOKEST AT.

Nathaniel, our son, was born in London shortly before we moved to Madeley and his christening was one of the first events after our arrival. Among the people in the village it was evidently an occasion of some interest. The vicar told me that the bellringers would like to ring a peal to celebrate and many people came to look.

What they saw did not please some of the old ladies. Penelope Tree, then a well-known model, was one of Nat's godparents and she was living at the time with the photographer David Bailey. Penelope's summery dress was transparent and David wore a catsuit made of leather. Several of the villagers turned round and went home.

We managed to overcome this setback and established a happy relationship with the community, but it was in some ways always clouded for me by the paradox of the old and the new order of things. I cringed when one old woman said to me that she was glad that someone was 'back at the helm'; yet I was conscious of the links with the past.

Sir Thomas Offley, the merchant who was Lord Mayor of London, bought Madeley in 1547 for £1,000 and lived in the old Manor House on Stanley's farm. His grandson, Sir John, built the village school, so that it was noticeable that documents to do with the natives of Madeley in the seventeenth and later centuries were signed not with a cross but with confident handwriting. Sir John's son, another John, whose portrait as a boy hung in our dining room, had been a friend of Isaak Walton and it was to him that *The Compleat Angler* was dedicated. The third John in succession married the heiress of Crewe and, as was to become a habit in my family, changed his name to hers.

The absurdity of attaching any importance to the 'age' of the family was emphasized for me when I came across a copy of a conveyance of a piece of land that my great-great-uncle had sold in the 1870s. He usually never parted with an acre, but he had made an exception in this case for some compassionate reason. The wrench was so great that he had reserved for the Crewe family the right to ride across the land for the next three thousand years.

Yet I was much touched by the village wheelwright, Tom Philips (the third Tom, by the way, of those known as Old Tom, Young Tom and young Tom's son), who made Nat a wheelbarrow because, fifty years before, his father had made one in mahogany for the Earl of Madeley, my mother's half-brother, who had died when still at school.

There were really three aspects to this question, which I may be labouring too much. The first is an almost primitive feeling for the ownership of land, so deeply instinct that it is impossible to judge it good or bad. I used to think it comparable to the passion of a collector for whatever it may be that he loves to possess, but it is not that. It is a fundamental love of the source of nourishment, common not only to sedentary farmers but to nomads who roam over pastures that they see collectively as theirs and to hunter-gatherers like the forest dwellers of the Amazon. That aspect, then, was neutral.

The second aspect, I was not ashamed to enjoy because often I could feel that I was able to do something worthwhile. Colin and I had inherited the right to nominate, under the Church of England's curious system of patronage, the vicar or rector in six parishes.

The most important of these was Nantwich, which was exceptional in having only one church for a town of its size; and St Mary's was known as the cathedral of south Cheshire. Although the salaries of all incumbents of parish churches had been made equal, a rich Parochial Church Council could augment the rector's stipend considerably by paying for his telephone, heating, car expenses and other items. In this way, Nantwich was regarded as a plum living, and bishops often use such livings as a kind of reward for clergymen who have served a diocese well.

Canon Southwell had been at Nantwich for nearly quarter of a century. He was a bluff, contented priest, who liked to discuss the merits of various years of vintage port. He was the butt of many Trollopian jokes on the lines of:

'Has the Bishop talked to you about retiring, Canon?'

'No, I had no idea he was thinking of leaving so soon.'

His church on Sundays was not very full.

The Bishop, as is the custom, suggested various names to me and numbers of men in late middle age came to tea. In the study, we had over the fireplace a glorious painting by Tony Fry of a nude lying with her back to the artist. The aspiring vicars on seeing the picture could rarely repress a little cough or embarrassed comment, whereat Sue would worry them even more by announcing that it was a portrait of her. With the exception of one who told me that he had worked in Africa and that the natives were not much different from monkeys, they were worthy people, but none of them was, in my view, the kind of person to revive the sleeping parish of Nantwich.

The Parochial Church Councillors whom I had, as is usual, consulted had expressed their preference, as Parochial Church Councillors always do, for a married man in his forties with young children. I felt that someone younger, less conventional was needed and found, in quite another diocese, an energetic man of barely thirty.

Jim Richardson infused Nantwich with new life. He was a showman and go-getter. The music in the church became first-class, the ladies of Nantwich stitched away at a magnificent new curtain, funds poured in from an appeal we mounted, a young curate arrived to help and, above all, the church was full. By the time Jim left to become Vicar of Leeds, St Mary's had become once more the centre of Nantwich and we could look for an incumbent of a different timbre.

It was not always such a success. In one case, in another parish, we chose a vicar more committed than I had realized, or he had revealed, to the new patterns of churchmanship. He belonged with those who like to take out the pews, to kiss whoever is next to you in church, to pray with the flat words of modernity. Some old parishioners in his village were so troubled by his innovations that after seventy years of unfailing worship every Sunday, they could not bear to set foot in the church. Nonetheless this church again was full. The new ways may not have suited the elderly, but they appealed apparently to those who chose to live in new and hideous housing, like that in the wood round Madeley Manor, so perhaps it was right after all.

I loved Nantwich, one of the old salt towns of Cheshire, with its fine half-timbered houses. It was from a house that still stands in Hospital Street that Randulph Crewe set out on a legal career and rose to be James I's Lord Chief Justice, earning enough money to build Crewe Hall and buy back the estates that his ancestors had owned and lost.

His descendant John Crewe, a staunch Whig and friend of such figures as Charles James Fox, Horace Walpole, Sheridan and George Canning, and a member of the Holland House set, built in Nantwich some almshouses. These had fallen into disrepair, as had some earlier almshouses founded by a Lord Mayor called Wright in another part of the town. The trustees of both sets got together and planned to amalgamate them and asked me to join them in the enterprise. They were remarkable people, modest, hard-working, and selfless, reminding me of figures from Arnold Bennett. The most enlightened of all, perhaps, was an architect, Jim Edleston. There were ten Crewe houses and six of the Wright ones, set about a mile from each other. There was no space to improve the seventeenth-century ones, but a good plot of land adjoined ours.

Jim conceived the bold idea of removing the older ones completely and rebuilding them beside the later ones. He got grants and we raised money and the trustees achieved their object. They restored both sets to modern requirements and preserved in perfect harmony two historic buildings – interestingly enough at £1,000 less per person housed than in the Council's old people's housing then building on the opposite side of the street.

On a smaller scale at Madeley, we refurbished the almshouses built by Sir John Offley, the founder of the village school. Oddly enough one of the people who came to live there was Arthur, Bob Boothby's old manservant.

This aspect of my paradox was immensely English and I could enjoy it, but even the enjoyment had in it an element of a third and to me detestable aspect. What had inheritance to do with anything? When people accorded me respect simply on the grounds that my family had owned land for some centuries, it saddened me as somehow demeaning them, and if I accepted it and even sometimes took some pleasure in it, I should have found myself despicable. But most of us, St Augustine for one, like many things we disapprove of.

Curiously, there was a corollary of sorts in my muscular dystrophy. As a child, I had wondered so often why it was I who could not walk properly. What had I done? Was it a punishment? 'Why me?' is a question nearly everyone has asked at times of misfortune. But I realized one day that no one ever asks 'Why me?' when they fall in love, win the football pools or have any other piece of luck. I never thought 'Why me?' again.

This contented, somewhat bucolic life ambled pleasantly along, so that the years passed easily. At weekends friends came from London, giving sometimes Chekhovian shocks to our placidity, but I was sure that this was to be the lasting shape of my existence.

What happened in those years? Our daughter Charity was born in the hospital in Stoke-on-Trent. Sue shared my fondness for games, and we played cards together in the evenings and talked endlessly in a way that had not quite been the case in my other marriages.

Not long after we moved, Michael Christiansen told me that he no longer needed my column. I was so surprised that I sat and stared at him, which he found confusing. I could see no point in arguing, so I just waited. This prompted him to be more open than he might have meant to be. He floundered a bit and explained that the board had decided that the *Mirror* newspapers should go down-market and that I was therefore not wanted. I took it as a compliment.

Slowly the farm took on a new appearance. Sue built a terrace and created a small garden; roses and honeysuckles climbed up the house. The awkward-looking cows we had bought at the beginning were replaced by the better and better ones we bred from them. It was fascinating to plot the progress of the herd and to see the various effects of the bulls that Stanley chose to sire the calves, and to watch the milk yields rise.

At length we became more confident. Our partnership with Stanley worked well, but we each felt some constraints. We decided that both sides would be happier with independence. We sold Stanley the freehold of Manor Farm and bought from him his half-share in Netherset Hey.

The fields acquired a different look from being worked and I had to take more care, for the ground was now bumpy and I had overturned my buggy fracturing my shoulder.

The first head cowman had left and, in the new cottage, there was Trevor Williams and his wife, Cathy.

An old friend, Michael Butterwick, became our farm adviser. He was an eccentric agricultural expert whom it was hard at times to take seriously, for he kept his light well hidden under several bushels. Just occasionally, one would get an inkling of his expertise when it would come out that he had been helping the Labour government with its agricultural policy in Europe. When Colin rather hesitantly asked Con O'Neill, one of our EEC Commissioners, if he had ever heard of Mickey, he said:

'The only man who understands what the hell it's all about.'

I struggled with figures and VAT returns and with advisers from the Ministry of Agriculture, so we muddled along very agreeably, but none too well financially. I never learned to accept as Stanley did the disasters of farming. When there was a plague of aphids I would, in panic (and partly for the fun of it), summon an aeroplane to spray the wheat at enormous cost, while Stanley waited for the swarms of ladybirds which would surely come to eat up the aphids. Sue, when the children started school, had not enough to do. She decided to take a course in dairy farming at a college at the edge of Nantwich so that she could help Trevor. She triumphed, winning a prize for being the most promising pupil as well as her diploma.

She and Trevor achieved an excellent relationship, she deferring to his years of practical experience, he listening with intelligence to her tactful exposition of the latest theories.

There was no reason to think that this happy existence would ever end. Sue's family lived a hundred miles to the north and there was constant coming and going between Holker and Netherset, which was a natural stopping place for any of them driving to or from London. We made many friends in the neighbourhood and we were well occupied and amused.

Sue and I took my elder children to Kenya for a holiday and my wanderlust was assuaged by Mickey Butterwick, who twice invited me to India, where he was the director of several companies that owned tea gardens in Assam and the Douars. I was to go back much later to write a book in India, but at that time I enjoyed it really because of its improbability and challenging impenetrability.

Travelling in India is not like travelling anywhere else. Other continents have their astonishments – waterfalls, cathedrals, wild creatures, festivals, cave dwellers or whatever – but no other country has quite the same element of surprise and slipped reality.

'India is not so much a place,' said an old Calcutta hand, 'as a state of mind.'

We were sitting under an awning looking out over a cricket field, behind which rose the foothills of the Himalayas, with the peaks of Kangchenjunga sharply white above them.

From the group around us came cries of 'Played, sir' and, 'I say, good stroke.' Every so often a goat would stroll among the fielders, and, when the sun dipped and Kangchenjunga shone pink, a herd of cows wandered home across the pitch. It was perhaps the most beautiful cricket ground in the world and the spirit of play was as eager and sporting as a village match in England eighty years ago.

The players were tea-garden managers from the two areas where

Mickey's gardens were. They were all Indian, apart from one Scot. 'It may seem like that to you, but you are seeing only outward behaviour. Underneath it is very different. So much of Indian life is lived in the mind.'

The occasion was a centenary of one of the tea gardens. There were sports for the tea-garden workers too. Running and tug-of-war for both men and women; a bicycle race for the men, who rode furiously round on ancient boneshakers; musical chairs and a race with water pots on their heads for the women. Pretty girls put garlands round my neck, with flirting laughter. It was innocent and happy as a vicarage fête, I thought.

But the cricket-playing managers had not let any of the English company directors attend these labour sports. 'There might have been indiscipline,' they said.

It doesn't much matter whether they or I had misjudged the mood. Every aspect of Indian life is a compromise of some sort. Part of the art of living is understanding which aspect has the upper hand at any moment and judging just when the balance will change. It is the balancing act which creates the surprises.

The wife of an Indian Navy commander once said to me: 'My husband is always complaining about our inefficiency. He asks why we cannot be more like the British. Why can't people answer letters, trains be on time, the services work? I tell him it would never do. If 750 million people, living in poor conditions, dreadfully over-crowded, with too little to do, all started to mind about such things it would be intolerable. We would all murder one another.'

Western standards have little relevance to the intractable problems of poverty, disease, overpopulation and natural disasters. Indians approach them quite differently.

A friend in the Calcutta police took me to see the Karwal Nats, a tribe of hereditary criminals. We drove some forty miles out of Calcutta to Kanchrapara, a village much like any other, thronged with ox-carts. There was a cluster of newish brick dwellings set a little apart.

I thought there might be some hesitation when the people were told that a journalist had come to see them. There was none. At once fifty people appeared. They set chairs in the lane and brought tea. My friend introduced each family.

'These are the Muckerjees, who do shoplifting. These are the Guptas, who steal suitcases from trains. These are the Battacharyas, who are first-class pickpockets, absolutely.'

251

The British used to keep the Karwal Nats in an enclave at Saidpur (now in Bangladesh), where they were made to spin and weave. Some of the older tribesmen could remember Saidpur, where the fun was to climb out in the night and pursue their true professions.

The Indians deal with the criminal tribes less predictably, settling them in villages where the pretence is that they are reformed. Many duly told me that they had given up their old ways and liked to send their children to school, 'to get gentle'.

Krishna, a lively young man, drew me aside. 'It is all nonsense. What is the point of sending the children to school? They can't get jobs with our reputation. My little boy is doing very well. He can get through a hole that big.'

He pointed to a drain which I would have thought only a small cat could get down.

'We all teach the children. Especially, they are good at distracting people so that we can rob them. I always take my son with me on any job. He is seven now.'

As we drove away, the detective said: 'There, you see they are good people. They would never commit crimes round here and give us trouble. They go to Lucknow or somewhere like that and are no inconvenience to Bengal.'

In Calcutta, one of my favourite places was the Marble Palace, built by Raja Mullick in 1835. It is a fantasy of a house, standing in a back street. Inside, it is filled with grand European paintings by, according to the guidebook, Reynolds, Gainsborough, Rubens and even Leonardo da Vinci. They are all fakes, though one could hold out a little hope for one of the Rubens. But the collection of Chinese ceramics looks superb.

What it was all for is hard to imagine, this meaningless yet timeless building. It is said that the Raja built it in order to entertain the Governor-General in English style and that he only came once. Today, for a nominal fee, one can wander round, though an occasional room may be momentarily forbidden. Through the door, one can see the Raja's rather dour descendant drinking coffee or playing a melancholy game of billards.

There is another building, in Agra, that evokes in me something of the same forlorn pleasure. It is called the Dayal Bagh and was started in 1903, as a memorial to Shiv Dayal Singh, the founder of a 'path' or way by which people may aspire to self-realization and an understanding of God.

Shiv Dayal Singh's followers planned to create a shrine for use by people of all religious faiths, but there have been delays of all kinds – legal, financial, even spiritual. Nearly ninety years later, it is far from complete. There are many levels and towers and courts and pinnacles and, in front, masons and other craftsmen chip and carve all year. But there is no sign yet of the proposed huge central dome. Indeed, there is at least another thirty years of work if the plan is to be followed.

When it is finished, it will be larger than the Taj Mahal. India is the only country in the world where such a work could be going forward. The sadness is that it was started at a time when taste was uncertain. The carvings of flowers and animals are minutely worked, but the designs, frozen in 1903, are informed by an unfortunate sentimentality. The happy thing is that a whim can be indulged for so long. I was moved by it, for it told me almost as much about India as the Taj Mahal.

I travelled in India usually by car. It was alarming because the standard of driving has never been high. Against that, the cars were so old that they could not go fast enough to be really dangerous. The distances were enormous, but just when I began to think that a drive was boring, round the next corner was a scene of astonishing beauty – women washing a brilliant kaleidoscope of clothes at a bend in a river; or a funny sign – 'Hakim Mustapha Ali, specialist in piles and gass troubles. Blood, urine, sputum and stools tested here'; or best of all, a tea stall, where they put the tea leaves, the sugar, the milk and the water all together in a pot and then boiled them. Strained as a rule through an old sock which hung, covered in flies, from the top of the stall, it tasted delicious.

Indians are the most helpful people. They may make things as complicated as possible, but are virtually never deliberately obstructive. I remember only one obstinate driver. We were driving to Jaipur and stopped at Fatehpur Sikri on the way. I longed to see this town, built by Akbar but soon deserted for lack of water.

The driver was in a hurry. He showed me where the mosque was, and when I had seen that said: 'Now we go.' I protested that I hadn't seen the famous palace and all the rest. 'There is nothing else. I know this place.' I bought a book of postcards and asked him where all the places shown on them might be. He sulked. I grabbed my lunch box, found the wonderful buildings and sat gazing out over the plain, happy to be alone.

An old man came to sit beside me. 'You see that little farm down there? That's where I live. But I love it here and I like to tell strangers about Fatehpur Sikri. No, not for money, but because it is so beautiful.'

He told me about the deserted city and about his patch of land, where he hoed a bare living. 'And do you know,' he asked, 'who saved this place for us, for India, when it would have fallen down? It was your Lord Curzon.' A simple peasant who, eighty years later, knew about the Viceroy.

Late that evening, the car broke down. The rain fell thick and grey. The driver, who had said we might be attacked by bandits, went back to a village for help. Two hours passed. The rain stopped and the boy, whom the driver had brought to run errands, somehow got the engine going. We drove back to the village. The driver was not looking for help. He had found a bed for the night and was asleep, leaving us to the bandits.

The exact flavour of India is intangible. There are the beauties – the palaces of Rajasthan, the temples of the south; the absurdities – a notice in the hotel in Madurai, 'Do not jump or quarrel in the lift'; the tragedies of poverty and violence.

As I had been in Saudi Arabia, so also in India I was fascinated by the everyday quality of religion. The Indians are not driven by the Western need for everything to be explained or accounted for. Every day I was told of miracle cures, of photograph frames of one guru filling with sacred ash, the statuette of another pouring forth honey every morning.

I wanted and still want to go back and back to India. It was years later, when I was living for a spell in Jaipur, that I understood what that old Calcutta hand had meant. It was the morning of the festival of Holi, when everyone throws colours at everyone else. As I came out of the house, I met the gardener, who had every day for three months touched my feet with respect. He emptied a bucket of indelible Prussian-blue water over me. It was done with no malice. It was the balance of things, the state of mind for that day.

CHAPTER TWENTY

AN IDEAL VILLAGE

I took Sue's friend Hugh Geddes with me when I went to look at some cattle we had put on the fields at Leycett, the other side of Madeley. Leycett was the mining village whose whirring wheel and high spoil heap I used to see across the lake from our old house. As a boy, I had been down the mine, crawling for the last yards to the workface, both excited and horrified by the life of the miners.

Now the wheel was still and the mine-shafts capped; thin grass and stunted trees tried to establish themselves on the sterile slopes of the slag heap. The Coal Board had closed the mine in 1968 and torn down all the buildings, including the pithead baths, built in the 1920s and admired by Nikolaus Pevsner, as well as the three streets of houses built by my great-great-uncle. Only his school still stood, determinedly kept open by the displaced villagers, who had great faith in it.

The cattle we had come to see hung their heads, their coats staring; they had liver fluke, a parasite that can lurk in the land. There were nearly three hundred acres at Leycett, much of it derelict from the mining, which had gone on there since the fourteenth century. It was perplexing to know what to do with this land.

Hugh was an architect. 'Why not rebuild the village?' For the next four years, with Colin and with Hugh's partners, David Levitt and David Bernstein, we tried to do just that.

There was a peppery, rebellious quality to Hugh's nature that appealed to me. His face and his head, with thinning, rusty hair cut short, were too big for his body and he moved with a long stride and heavy step that added to the impression that he was determined to have his own way. But once he decided that you had understood him

255

and his ways, he revealed an attractive, almost conspiratorial humour that made him an especially warm companion.

We spent many hours and days that lengthened into months working out exactly the kind of village we wanted to create. So much of modern town planning appeared to Hugh to be a disaster. We visited many of the New Towns together and Hugh showed me how unnatural they felt, their populations so often composed of one class and one age of person – young factory-working couples with children. The white-collar workers and executives did not live in the New Towns, but bought up bijou cottages outside and spoke only to each other. There were no old people to give a natural stability to the community and, as yet, no youth to bring life into the place.

Our idea was to try to reproduce the haphazard mixture of a village that has grown up over the centuries. We planned to build 450 houses, of which half would be built by housing associations for people on the local authority housing lists. The other half, varying in price from reasonably cheap to positively expensive, were to be for private buyers. We planned also some old people's housing and some accommodation for students at Keele University, three miles away, and the teachers' training college at Madeley.

The housing would not be in separate sections, but jumbled together, so that rich and poor would live side by side as they do in any naturally-developed village. Similarly, the shops would not be all together in one place, but dotted about, again as in an ordinary village, as we believed that the life of the community was enhanced by chance meetings on the street when people were walking from one place to another.

To give the village a purpose, we felt it should have an industry of some sort, although we expected many of its inhabitants to work in the Pottery towns seven miles away. It was Colin who suggested that we make an equestrian centre, partly because it was a very rural and English interest and partly because nearly all horsey activities took place in the South, and we thought the North needed some share in this national pleasure.

Quite apart from the social content of the village, we were very conscious of environmental questions. Our wonderfully eccentric planning consultant, Leslie Ginsburg, had written a paper entitled *S.L.O.A.P.*, which stood for Space Left Over After Planning. The burden of his argument was that planning regulations imposed so many restrictions on the ground plan of any development that much land was wasted. As a great many of the limitations were imposed for reasons of safety from the motor-car, we decided to have no cars in the village.

Our intention, in any case, was to cram the buildings onto as small an area as possible, something like twenty-five acres, to use another twenty-five for the equestrian centre and to preserve the remaining 250 as a park dedicated to the village, with a lake running the length of the village on one side and a high wall on the other. We hoped, given the lie of the land, to achieve something of the feeling of an Italian hill-village – not such a silly idea when one thought of Mow Cop, a village ten miles to the north, founded, according to a delightful theory of Alan Garner's, by the soldiers of a disbanded legion of the Emperor Hadrian.

There were so many aspects to be sorted out before we could even think of applying for planning permission. We spent much time with very grand consultants of all kinds. Hugh was so persuasive and convincing that huge organizations which I would have expected to sneer at us threw themselves into the enterprise with enthusiasm, reducing their fees to quite uneconomic levels.

Ove Arup, the engineers, tested the land for us. Their first report was funny in its way, but depressing. The site had more geological faults than any they had ever seen on a piece of land that size. Moreover, it was so riddled with old shafts and tunnels that it was like a Dutch cheese below the surface. When I asked this gloomy expert what he would do with the land he said: 'Plant rhododendrons on it and never go on it again.' We were cast down for a while, but we learned from them how even these hazards could be safely overcome.

The equestrian centre led us into all sorts of by-ways. Our idea was to have every kind of attraction ranging from the best show-jumping down to sixpenny rides for children. We planned a horse zoo, with horses of every known breed, and a carriage museum.

All this would, of course, bring traffic problems to the region, but here again we were counselled by Britain's leading traffic expert, Sir Colin Buchanan, whose organization charged us a risible amount for all their work.

The oil crisis of the Seventies was looming and the horses led us to the idea of lighting the streets with methane gas, generated by horse manure. We thought also of heating the houses by taking advantage of some deep old mine-shafts to operate heat-exchangers.

Sometimes the fancies went too far. There happened to be an

American traffic theorist at Keele University, Dr Fishman, who became excited by the project and urged me to forbid even the ownership of cars. He wanted us to have a pool of cars, owned by the village, from which the inhabitants, who were either to contribute a flat rate or to pay a modest hiring fee, could take out whatever car they needed for a particular occasion. Two or three housewives might take a Ford Consul to go shopping, a young man might borrow an MG to take his girl out for the evening and there would be a large limousine available if a whole family were going on holiday. Dr Fishman was taken aback when I pointed out that in the Potteries there was an annual Wakes Week when everybody went on holiday at the same time, so that to be safe we would need at least two hundred limousines.

When we felt that we had solved every puzzle and found answers to every possible objection, Hugh and I went to Stafford to talk to the County Planning Officer, Mr John Barratt. He was one of those people who would have made a good salesman, something of a mythomane, but brimful of ebullient confidence. He told us that we had virtually no chance of doing what we wanted. Leycett was in the Green Belt and he saw no need for the village. We said that derelict land topped with a slag heap did not add to the beauty of a Green Belt region. We left with the impression that more important than any regard for the Green Belt was a project of Eric Morley and Mecca Dance Halls to build a kind of Disneyland near Wolverhampton, called Merrie England, that had Mr Barratt's support and with which we might be thought to be in competition.

Hugh was never much put off by setbacks of this kind, being quite certain that his cause was the better one. We decided to carry on and to persuade the councillors, in whose power the decision really lay, of our good intentions. We put in our planning application at the end of January 1973.

The interest that the scheme generated was stimulating. I thought about little else and, of course, enjoyed learning about things to which I had never before given a moment's thought. I found it extraordinary to be treated by those who supported the plan as if we were eighteenth-century benefactors and with loathing by those opposed to it. 'These brothers think they can wrangle anything through. They toss in £100,000 and hope to walk away with two million,' one councillor asserted.

In fact, if we had wanted to do that, we would probably have built a golf course, which is what all the estate agents advised us to do. Fortunately, nearly everyone was on our side. The publicity we got both locally and nationally was encouraging.

Ian Nairn, the distinguished architectural correspondent of the *Sunday Times*, wrote an article entitled 'The Village of the Century' in which he said:

> I have in the past been to a meeting to announce a new village – a decent idea, too – where I wouldn't trust the operators to sell me a secondhand tyre lever. Leycett is not like that; if the architects can match the spirit and sensitivity of the client, it could be the village of the century, lining up with Port Grimaud in visual appeal and with the very best parts of the New Towns in social intent.

The process ground on and our hopes rose. By the end of the year we had the approval of the Rural District Council and a provisional agreement from the County Council. Mr Barratt had come round to being a supporter. Merrie England had not gone ahead and he had transferred his enthusiasm to our plans, even making a broadcast on local radio praising our scheme.

There was another hurdle to come. Because the new village was a major departure from the structure plan for the region, it had to be referred to the Department of the Environment for ministerial approval. We also had to advertise the plan in the newspapers, inviting any objections, and we had to hold a public meeting.

This meeting, in the secondary school in Madeley, was a splendid success. There were one or two crotchety objectors but the vote, which must have been a record in cases of a large development, was more than eighty per cent in our favour.

The advertisement, however, produced an objection from the Coal Board. They said that they wanted to do opencast mining on the site. This, at first, seemed a disaster, but as there were several years' work ahead before we could start to build, we realized that this might be made to work to our advantage. The Coal Board would be obliged to put the land in order when they were finished, they could restore it to fit in with our plans, doing our landscape work for nothing.

We negotiated. That was fun; and yet again I had to study a new field of expertise. There was a large and wily Welshman called Mr Amos who could run rings round me in any discussion, but who was quite sympathetic to our aims and anyhow relieved at the friendly way we treated with him, compared with his own countrymen, who, he said, were so suspicious that they would stand freezing at their gate in pouring rain for an hour to argue rather than let him on their land, let alone into the house to talk. His assistant Mr Johnson was equally amiable. After six months we had a firm agreement.

In those six months a real disaster had come about. Peter Walker had brought in his reforms of local government, discarding counties, altering boundaries, changing names and scrapping rural district councils to push country people under the control of urban councils, whose members had little understanding of their different needs.

The Newcastle-under-Lyme Borough Council, which now covered Leycett, behaved with impeccable honour. Defying their new planning officer who, whilst not motivated by malice and envy, managed to give that impression, they reaffirmed the approval of their predecessors.

No such decent motives inspired the new County Council. Our ally, Mr Barratt, had been swept away with the reorganization. His replacement did not share his views. The Minister had not pronounced one way or another, but had left it to the County to decide. They refused permission.

The councils of all the surrounding parishes protested, but the County Council was implacable. We could have appealed, but one of the grounds on which they had rejected our scheme was that it might attract people away from areas where they planned to build. This seemed to me a feeble objection, admitting that our plans were better than theirs, but it meant that in appealing we would have to show why Leycett was a better place to build than each one of their potential sites. It would be an expensive process with two lawyers employed every day for possibly six weeks. Furthermore we were told that only fifteen per cent of appeals succeed. Not having £100,000 'to toss in', we gave up.

A few months after our refusal, the Chairman of the County Council, Mr Newman, went to prison for taking bribes in planning cases. I was struck by how small the sums involved had been to sway the judgement of this public figure. We would have had £2,000 to toss in, but happily temptation never dawned.

In one mood it was the greatest disappointment of my life, but, in the way that we all wonder whether we have really grown up yet, I am not sure that I had ever really believed in it. It was such an entrancing daydream – to build a village, something that really might endure, at any rate in some form, for centuries. Could I ever do such a thing? One day, maybe, when I grew up.

The aspect that I found the saddest was the dashing of so many hopes. The people of Leycett had a moving tenacity of spirit, a powerful sense of place. They had clung to their school, but even that had gone by now. They still had their cricket club. They came from their new homes to group together to play for a village that didn't exist and now never would. They had written to me in their scores asking me to keep a house for them where they belonged. I had made promises that I could never keep.

I had to turn to other work. The photographer Anthony Blake had built up a series of remarkable pictures of France's leading chefs, their kitchens and the food they produced. His publishers wanted someone to write a text to go with the photographs, and to collect snippets of information about the knacks and tricks of the profession and a few recipes to make it into a practical as well as a stylish book.

In reality, I was not in the least qualified to do this. I was never a cook and my French was rusty; all I had ever claimed to be was an eater. The one thing journalism teaches one is how to grasp the essentials of a subject quickly and how to convince people one is interviewing that one is well versed in their subject, so I took on the job.

At first, it was appalling. We had chosen to cover the twelve provincial restaurants which had three stars in the Michelin Guide. I had eaten in one or two of them before on agreeably dizzy occasions, but the experience of going from one to another in rapid succession was bewildering. The food was so astonishingly good and in such a different league from what I was used to writing about that I could not imagine how I would ever be able to create an individual portrait of each chef, the more so as this was in the middle of the imagined revolution of *nouvelle cuisine* and Paul Bocuse's *bande*.

Twice I went round France, staying two or three days in each place until I had come to understand the differences between all of them and to realize that each chef had his own inimitable characteristics. Ultimately, I concluded that it was easier to identify the few things that they did have in common besides their skill, which were industry, generosity and, in some cases, a lively interest in women.

The success of this book led on to my compiling a dictionary of the food of all countries, intended to help travellers who, when abroad, could read a menu but could not understand the waiter. Under each country I listed the dishes most likely to appear on any menu and translated them, so that it was easy for a reader to find something he might like to eat without having to know a word of the language. It was a pocket book and was published in some seven or eight countries and has sold, one way and another, more than a quarter of a million copies. I have never bothered to total it up, but I would be surprised if, under my contract, I have made as much as £15,000 from the profitable little book, a circumstance that colours my view of publishers.

There was much that went well in our lives, but the failure of Leycett and the fact that the farm did not prosper as it might have done weighed heavily against the fairly easy but somewhat uneventful course of things. Sue was still young and she may well have felt that life was in danger of passing her by. More importantly, I became more and more dependent on my drivers and their inevitable invasion of our privacy.

I worked for some time on one of the committees amassing evidence for the report of the Snowdon Working Party, 'Integrating the Disabled'. As a result, I became more and more aware of the burden that caring for a disabled person imposes on the family. There was a Catch-22 element to the situation: the more help that I got, the less private our lives became; the less outside help that I used, the more Sue herself had to help me.

We planned a holiday in Ireland, taking the children. My elder son, Sebastian, would look after me, which would avoid the need for a driver. On the first day, we got as far as Scotland in time for lunch at Caerlaverock Castle. Full of enthusiasm, I held the picnic basket as we wheeled downhill across the grass, looking for a good place to spread the lunch. We hit a bump. The chair stopped dead and I slid helpless on to the ground. My legs under me made a noise like Rice Krispies as they snapped.

I was some time in hospital, and then weeks at home, more demanding of attention than ever. Temperaments differ widely as to what they can withstand. There are many things that Sue can put up with that would defeat others, but for this kind of difficulty her nature was ill-suited. We each withdrew from the other.

CHAPTER TWENTY-ONE

SAHARAN JOURNEY

Colin and I were dining with Wilfred Thesiger at a restaurant near the House of Commons. Cyril Smith was at the next table, alone, if a man of that size can ever be said to be alone. As we ate our lamb cutlets, Wilfred said in a loud voice: 'It's a bit different from our last dinner together – a rich goat stew out in the open with the Samburu.' Cyril Smith looked alarmed.

We had camped by Wilfred's house in Kenya on our way to Lake Turkana. Remembering the pleasure of that journey, I felt restless and, as Wilfred talked on about his travels in North Africa, I knew that it was time for me to go somewhere. When he spoke of Morocco and Algeria and the Sudan, I became excited and, as we drove back after dinner along the Embankment, I decided that I would make a journey throughout the whole Sahara.

When I look at the book that I wrote about the journey, it stirs up strange emotions. I had set off with very little idea of what it would be like, having the conventional impression that the Sahara was a vast and lonely place that hardly anyone had ever crossed – in my ignorance both overestimating the dangers and underestimating the difficulties.

Most of the books that I read, with the exception of an account by Richard Trench of a perilous trip of incredible courage from Morocco to Timbuktoo, dated from the Twenties and Thirties. One of my favourites, not for its literary merit but for the grandiose and priggish attitudes, was *Mysterious Sahara* by Count Byron de Prorok, published in 1930. His journeys had mostly been made in 1926, the year I was born. His maps had great areas with question marks on them, indicating places that were still unexplored. Influenced by this kind of reading, I had not realized that there would, on the major routes of the modern Sahara, be a steady stream of tourists quite apart from a considerable trade of the kind that has gone on for centuries.

I had also not realized that the amount one learns on a journey decreases proportionately with the number travelling companions. A group of five, which is what we usually were, is a capsule, interesting enough in its way as a study in human behaviour, but rarely allowing much intimate contact with the inhabitants of places one travels through. Nonetheless because the journey lasted well over a year, and because we so often got held up in places by long delays of all kinds, I did get a broader understanding of Saharan life than I might otherwise have done.

A great deal of the experience, on the other hand, was entirely personal. When we were in those parts of the desert that were untouched by tourism or commerce, when we were, as I had been in the Empty Quarter, stripped of all ordinary concerns, reduced to the barest minimum of need, I felt that lifting sensation of near mystical freedom, perhaps even more powerfully than I had in the more uniform wastes of Saudi Arabia.

The amazing diversity of the Sahara, with its mountains rising to eleven thousand feet, its depressions sunk below sea level, its black, burnt, tumbled rocks and red sands, white sands, grey, grey gravels, swirling dunes, flat sheets of granite, and pinnacles of sandstone, all thrown together as if yesterday, with no rhythm or pattern, made me feel that I was witness to the Creation. Yet, seen with a different eye, it was all timeless. The sands were ground by the eternal winds, wearing down the mountains, sculpting the sandstone, smoothing the granite.

I lay in Mauritania, in the night, not far from where Antoine de Saint-Exupéry, the French author and aviator, landed his plane in unknown territory and there felt a soaring of the spirit – a sensation borne in, I suspect, on all lovers of the desert by a comprehension, usually unattainable, of the magnitude of space, coupled with that consciousness of the creation of the world.

By day, when calmer thoughts prevailed, I was moved by the tenacity of life. I revelled in the solitary trees that clung on when others had all gone and the solitary wheatear that might be sitting in them, and gave a lot of thought to the desert ticks that, lacking a host, can survive for ten years without nourishment or water. There was hope even in a nuclear age.

If I gained strength from, as it were, the private aspects of this desert journey, sifting the important from the unimportant, I certainly learned a good deal about my shortcomings in other directions.

The explorer Robin Hanbury-Tenison had a lot of advice for me about organizing expeditions. He had, after all, been given the OBE for his masterly mounting of a scientific expedition to a rain-forest in Borneo involving hundreds of scientists of different disciplines.

He suggested that I should make people pay for the privilege of being allowed to come with me. If people pay, he maintained, they work much harder to make the expedition a success. I am sure he is right, but I could not imagine charging people for something of which I was the sole beneficiary.

I advertised for a mechanic and drivers and a young man to push. I had already got a photographer – at least I had had one, a superb-looking girl called Carinthia West, whom the newspapers described as a girlfriend of Mick Jagger, always adding that she had the longest legs in Britain. Soon before we were to leave she broke one of them. However, she suggested Tim Beddow to replace her.

The advertisement produced scores of applicants and streams of unlikely candidates came for interviews. I was always drawn to the odder ones, who knew about Roman irrigation or Islamic heresies, and, being a poor judge of character, would probably have ended up with a crew of introverted charlatans. Sue, however, deflected me from the riskiest of my selections.

There was one about whom no one could have had any doubts. Ernie Cook was one of those Englishmen who personify our warlike, as opposed to military, character. He joined the Royal Marines because he liked fighting and, finding not enough of it for his taste, transferred to the Sultan of Oman's army. He had practical knowledge of the desert and it was plain to me that with him we would have no fear of anyone.

Ernie was a man of infinite resource. With his help, I bought two ancient Mercedes Unimogs and he supervised their doing up and the buying of equipment. Without him, the expedition would never have set off.

The others I chose more for their charm – Peter Macdonald convinced me of his mechanical ability, and Jocelyn de Moubray, who wrote from Eton, talked about literature and racing, which encouraged me to think that he would make a versatile companion, and it turned out that his mother had been at Cambridge with me. About a week before we left, a girl called Olivia Wentworth-Rump begged me to take her with us and I did.

As we travelled through Tunisia and Algeria, it was soon apparent that I was not designed to lead any kind of team, let alone an expedition that could end in our dying in this inimical desert.

Part of the difficulty was that I had no specific plan, but preferred to drift and see what happened, rather than try to create events or to go to see those things or places that I knew were there from reading of them in other people's books. Worse was a feeble desire to please everyone, so that in the end no one was satisfied.

I do not know what happened to all that schooling that was supposed to prepare me for leadership and the ruling of an Empire. I had none of that certainty that amazes me in soldiers and politicians, so that a mild unease hung over the party. Fortunately, the journey was sufficiently fascinating and demanding for this not to matter much at first, but after two months Olivia went home and a month later Sue, in answer to a desperate request, found Anthony Cazalet, a mechanical wizard, to replace Peter Macdonald, whose skills had not been quite what I had hoped. After a while Ernie too left. He had taught us much, but he was a man of action while we were gradually becoming a team of lotus-eaters. He flew from Niamey and I never heard from him again, even when the book about the journey came out.

Tim wafted through all situations with the air of someone who was only half-substantial, Jocelyn retreated from discord or embarrassment into T. S. Eliot and a cloud of cigar smoke, while Anthony's principal objective was to do as little as possible, in the greatest possible comfort. We moved gently on until the trucks betrayed our optimism. We flew home for a rest while they had new engines fitted in Niger.

A few days after getting home, I had a car crash. My breast bone and a rib or two broke and Sue, flying over me to land up by my feet, bent my head so hard that she crushed a vertebra between my shoulders.

After a spell in hospital. I went back to Netherset even more helpless than usual. It was more than the last straw; the burden for Sue had become worse than intolerable. Although she looked after me most scrupulously, our life together was over. We agreed with Colin to sell the farm and, as soon as I could, I flew back to Niger. This time, Rose Cecil joined us. Rose was a cousin of Sue's and a great friend of Anthony Cazalet. She was intrepid, funny and the most uncomplicated friend it is possible to have. With Tim and Jocelyn, we five were to journey on for many months.

The first part of the journey was inspiring from my point of view. We travelled through Mali to Timbuktoo and on then to Mauritania, the least touched country in North Africa. In those great sweeps of glorious dunes, along the banks of the Niger river, through the land of the ancient Sahel empires of Ghana, Mali and Songhay, on the empty way to the oases of Walata and Tichit, I could forget that I had thought my life was settled and even find in Saint-Exupéry's wind and sand and stars an excitement at the thought of forging a new one.

Much happened. Rose fell ill and, furious, she flew home. It was perhaps as well for, soon after she left, just about when the pains of my chest and spine were gone, we drove into a minefield and were blown up. No one was much hurt, but I flew through the air and landed a good ten feet from the wrecked truck, acquiring new pains to replace the old.

It took us time to recover from this. We had to buy new cars in Senegal, as the other truck was written off in an accident, and we had such a complicated arrangement with the Customs in Dakar that the Chief Inspector still sends me a Christmas card every year.

By the time we got to Kano in Nigeria, Rose had decided she was well enough to rejoin us and, at last, we felt complete again. We covered five more countries, suffering every kind of misery, danger and horror, but with these four people I experienced that other wonder that desert writers speak of.

Captain Angus Buchanan, one of my favourites from the Twenties, lovable for his simple decency, wrote about 'that free-and-easy, comprehending comradeship, that belongs to the wise when long on the Open Road'.

I myself wrote that to travel for so many months with the same people is to create a bond which has no parallel in everyday life. It is a bond that lasts, for, ten years later, I feel in many ways closer to those four people than to anyone except my family.

Jock and Betty's new house in Nairobi was a very different affair from the first one they had. It was a solid, red-sandstone building that would not have been out of place at the edge of a Yorkshire town, the home of a millowner. It sat in 120 acres of virgin forest at the edge of Nairobi Game Park. Warthogs rootled among the flowerbeds and guinea fowl scurried about the lawns.

Inside, the house did not have many rooms, but they were grand with panelling and polished wood floors; and a broad dividing staircase rose from the huge hall. Jock and Betty found it comic, but comfortable.

There was a good reason for buying so over-splendid a house. As their Safari business developed and their lecture tours multiplied and their books sold, they became interested in wild-life conservation and especially in one species of giraffe. Most of the remaining giraffes of this kind were living in an area of land that was going to be given over to smallholders. Jock and Betty set about trying to save as many as possible. They raised several orphans on their land, never confining them, but allowing them to grow up, breed and wander away when they wanted.

It was enchanting to stay at Giraffe Manor, as they renamed it, as one might well be woken up by a giraffe poking its head through the bedroom window in search of biscuits. As their campaign for the giraffes grew, they flew to the Gulf to see a sheikh, who had shown a lot of interest in the idea of acquiring more land for their project. They came back empty-handed. He had virtually promised them a quarter of a million dollars but, just as they were leaving, the sheikh said: 'By the way, you've never told me what this kind of giraffe is called.'

'It's the Rothschild giraffe,' said Jock.

'What? If you think I'm giving money to save a giraffe called Rothschild, you must be mad.'

It was to this house that I went to start to write my book about the Sahara. I had no wish to live in England any more. Madeley had been as near to ideal as it is possible for any fixed place to be. I never wanted to live in a city again and, without those familiar fields to roll over in my buggy, I would not be happy in the English countryside. Kenya was, I thought, a possibility.

Over the years, I had come to know it well. The landscape held always that enlivening freedom of the wild, and I had learned enough from Jock so that I could roam round it without the need of guides.

After the upheaval of an attempted coup, I moved to the coast at Malindi. I dislike that thing of boy soldiers pointing a rifle at you and you debate whether or not to mention to them that the safety catch is off. Perhaps they don't know the difference between the safety catch and the trigger. I stayed at first in Jock and Betty's house on the beach and then took a house of my own. Here was another kind of beauty from the plains and highlands, and, in addition, the intriguing vestiges of the Arab domination of the East African coast. Not far out at sea, one could see the Arab dhows, with their lateen sails, scudding, as they have for centuries, south to Mombasa and to Zanzibar, until the trade winds change so conveniently to carry them north again to Arabia.

My house was raised a little above the shore. When the sun rose, the Muslim fisherboys, standing naked as they poled their boats through the reef, made postcard silhouettes of which I never tired, and a little later brought their catch for me to buy for lunch. They brought, too, bundles of marijuana which they sold by the 'arm'. By the port, next to the mosque, stood two phallic symbols, one circumcised, the other, according to my Kikuyu maid, who had strong opinions on this subject, 'uncut'.

Living in perfect amity with the descendants of the Arab traders, the Giriama tribe formed most of the rest of the local population – simple agricultural people, their women bare-breasted but with their bottoms padded with countless layers of cotton, so that they made a shelf on which you could have set a tea-tray. The sea meant nothing to them and few of them could even swim. Their principal concern was to avoid evil spirits. At a Giriama funeral the body is powdered over with white. Nothing looks so dead as a black man powdered white – and the mourners tell him so. 'You are dead, old man, very, very, dead. You will never sing again, never dance again, because you are dead. You will never make love any more, not walk any more, not talk any more. No one will ever see you again, not ever again, not even once again. You are dead, so dead, so dead.'

There was much about Malindi that was delightful, but it was changing. There had always been numbers of old colonial figures, retired and waiting for the end. They were friendly and rather sad for the most part; they had staked all and lost. There were the awful hordes of German tourists, who came on sex safaris to sleep with the whores or to debauch the Arab boys. And increasingly, there were Italians, who built more and more noisy hotels, and were said to be finding outlets for ill-gotten Mafia money.

I would never have stayed in Malindi, but I could certainly have found somewhere in Kenya that was free from these horrors and free from the spreading violence of Nairobi. Two things deterred me. The first was the nearly complete division between black and white. The two societies, although not necessarily opposed to each other, simply do not mix. In white houses I have occasionally met an Asian, but only very exceptionally an African. Wilfred Thesiger, in his remote Samburu town, lives only with African tribemen, but I was not looking for, nor indeed ready for, his austere kind of life.

I rather liked the young white Kenyans. They had an energy and a resourcefulness that I see less and less in Europe. At New Year, they all gathered at the beach at Watamu, south of Malindi, perhaps two or three thousand of them, from all over the country. They had a curious blend of abandon and formality. At midnight they greeted each other not with a kiss, but with a handshake. Yet they all got stoned and slept wherever and with whoever they happened to fall. They were essentially Kenyan, but no black people came to the party. I could not live in a country where this happened.

The other reason was a tragedy. While I was in the desert, Jock had developed a brain tumour. He had been pounded with radiation, operated on and been given six months to live. His beautiful hair was now grey and sparse, his fine-cut features were puffed and his tanned face a mottled red. His thinking was muddled and he was given to crazy fancies, such as believing that he was immensely rich, but he was not really deranged. A warmth still shone from his kind eyes, but the doctors had taken away his dignity.

For some reason, we had more than once talked of what we felt about some disaster of this kind. Jock, almost more than anyone I know, was passionately convinced that he could not stand such a thing. Again and again, he had made Betty promise that, if ever the slightest indignity befell him, she would put an end to it.

Through the months that I was in Kenya, Betty and I mulled over the question endlessly, knowing really that there was nothing we could do. It would have been easy in theory. All that had to be done was to stop giving him some of his pills or to give him too many. Or there could have been an accident in the sea when he was taken swimming. It was what he wanted. But it is impossible for most of us to kill someone, however much we love them. The worse he became, the more painful was the knowledge of the feelings of the person he no longer was.

He was to live another two years, but when I finished my book I left Kenya. I could not live there without Jock, who had taught me to love it.

I went to France, and new beginnings.

CHAPTER TWENTY-TWO

AFTERWORD

The shape of a life is hard to define. Should it be drawn like a graph with ups and downs; like a cake divided into slices; or as an ambling river?

I have always wondered how much of me is the same person that I was twenty or forty years ago, or is one renewed, as one's skin is said to be, once every seven years? A kind of steady-state creation, versus the big bang of birth. Do you remember that sly child? Am I still him – if he existed that is? Certainly his pains and his cunning are there to be discovered by memory's efforts, but are they just scars like the slash on my knee from a bicycle fall, the skin supposedly renewed eight times.

It seems so endless the change. I have changed, I feel, even since I started to write this book. It appears to me that every facet is a contest.

First, the balance between heredity and environment, or perhaps between their combined forces and one's own particular nature. How could I have accepted for so long so much of the prejudice I was brought up with? But equally, why did I reject it? Would I, born in Germany, have been an enthusiastic member of the Hitler youth movement? How much, in South Africa, I admired those whites who defied their families and friends to denounce apartheid. Would I have had that enlightened courage?

Then chance versus choice. Would I ever have become a writer had I not happened to have lunch with John Junor? I incline to Napoleon's, or was it Caesar's view, probably both of them, that good generals are lucky. It is that they put themselves into such positions that, if there is any luck going, they will be able to take advantage of it.

Happiness versus unhappiness; hope versus fear. For me, those are questions of choice. In face of much hideous evidence to the contrary, I have to believe that the world is gradually becoming a better place – I choose to have hope.

Genocide, torture and brutality of every kind have existed throughout history, but slavery has nearly gone and we now have ideas of human rights, of the duty to provide aid for other peoples, not enough but a start. We no longer go on outings to Bedlam to laugh at lunatics; capital punishment grows rarer. Anyone who is disabled knows how attitudes have changed. The world is better.

It is the word 'better' that matters. Only human beings can know that one thing is better than another. And it is all one needs to know. Everything else follows from that.

The shape of life is still unclear. Since going to France, I have travelled more and more in all the continents, I have watched my children grow up, as well they might, to be better than me. My three wives continue on excellent terms with each other as well as myself. Anything may yet happen.

All I can otherwise say for certain is that my life had a beginning and will have an end. I am glad I was born when I was for many reasons – not least that had I been conceived today I would have been screened and aborted as having muscular dystrophy. I prefer to have lived. As to the end, I expect I shall be lucky again. Arthur Koestler once said to a friend who was going on about the perils of smoking, cholesterol, salt and all the rest: 'You know, living is a dangerous business.'

Dying, it seems to me, is a very safe business.

INDEX

INDEX

INDEX

INDEX

INDEX

INDEX